Keeping the Old Flag Flying

The World War 1 Memoir of Kenneth Basil Foyster

Canadian soldier, prisoner and internee

Mike Richardson.

Cover Photograph of 7ᵗʰ Canadian Battalion cap badge by L.L. Will.

Keeping The Old Flag Flying
Copyright © Mike Richardson 2018. All Rights Reserved.
The rights of Mike Richardson to be identified as the author of this work have been asserted in accordance with the Copyright, Designs and Patents Act 1988.
All rights reserved. No part may be reproduced, adapted, stored in a retrieval system or transmitted by any means, electronic, mechanical, photocopying, or otherwise without the prior written permission of the author or publisher.
Spiderwize
Remus House
Coltsfoot Drive
Woodston
Peterborough
PE2 9BF
www.spiderwize.com
A CIP catalogue record for this book is available from the British Library.
The views expressed in this work are solely those of the author and do not necessarily reflect the views of the publisher, and the publisher hereby disclaims any responsibility for them.

ISBN: 978-1-912694-39-6
eBook ISBN: 978-1-912694-40-2

Keeping The Old Flag Flying

Mike Richardson

SPIDERWIZE
Peterborough UK
2018

CONTENTS

Preface 1

Acknowledgements 3

Notes 5

Chapter 1
Origins 6

Chapter 2
Becoming a Soldier 12

Chapter 3
Training for War 44

Chapter 4
To the Front 67

Chapter 5
The Second Battle of Ypres 122

Chapter 6
Kriegsgefangener 149

Chapter 7
Switzerland 239

Chapter 8
Home 302

Chapter 9
After the War 317

List of Sources: 323

Preface

Kenneth Basil Foyster was one of nine siblings and a Church of England (C of E) rector's son, born in Victorian England in relative comfort and privilege. He emigrated to Canada in the early 1900s and enjoyed a somewhat mixed existence until 1914, when for subsistence reasons he enlisted into the Canadian Militia. Thereafter, he found himself mobilised, and like millions of citizens of the global British Empire, fighting in The Great War of 1914 to 1918. Kenneth served in the 1st Canadian Division, which reinforced the Allied forces on the Western Front in 1915. He fought at Ypres, was wounded, captured, imprisoned then interned, undergoing years of confinement until the war's end.

Sometime after the end of that tragic conflict, Kenneth wrote a memoir. Some 100 years on, it is high time that this remarkable account be more widely known. Thus, I have reproduced his text, and put it as best I can in political and military context, and in the framework of his forebears, peers and descendants. This biography is the result.

The narrative focuses on Kenneth's own words. His wartime record is clear and comprehensive, indicating an eye for detail, a good memory and a broad knowledge of international events, though after the war he may have read about the activities of the Canadian Expeditionary Force before he prepared his own version. He had also kept a diary.

Kenneth's memoir describes his personal journey, but the story of the 1st Canadian Division in 1914 and 1915 is its background. The division was forged from the disparate, largely militia regiments of the Canadian Army in 1914, hastily trained in Canada and England, deployed to the Western Front and all but annihilated during the Second Battle of Ypres in 1915, winning for themselves an exceptional fighting reputation. Indeed, Field Marshal Sir John French, Commander-in-Chief of the British Expeditionary Force (BEF), declared that the Canadians had 'saved the day' for the Allies.

It is possible to glean some idea of Kenneth's character from the family records and from what he describes. He seems to have been a capable, practical, independent individual, partly due to the necessity to rise above the privations that unemployment necessitated. His sister Hilda affectionately called him 'Slum' - 'Dear Old Slum', which may describe his personal administration. He appears to have been a good friend to the fellow soldiers he describes, but comes across as fairly self-contained. The memoir also suggests that he was rather frank and perhaps irascible. That said, his cousin Betty Tillard wrote to him during the war, whilst he was suffering some hardships of which we will hear, 'You were always so cheery, and I expect that is what has kept you going.'

Kenneth's account is naturally somewhat subjective and often painfully direct, particularly when he detects failure. His descriptions of the character and conduct of others, especially other nationalities, will seem intolerant to today's audience. But the reader should recall that his memoir was written nearly a century ago and perhaps everyone was more forthright then. Kenneth was also liberal in his praise of those who he thought deserved it, and to moderate his words and opinions would detract from his valuable reflection of the *zeitgeist* of the early 20th century. I have chosen to include almost all of them.

Finally, I have adjusted Kenneth's spelling, leaving in his North American usage, and tinkered a little with his punctuation, but have perfected neither.

Mike Richardson

2018

Acknowledgements

Kenneth's splendid memoir forms the bulk of this account. This book does not set out to be a history of the Great War, but to fix the context in which the memoir now sits, I have relied on and quoted from the erudite works of others. I am most grateful for the permissions I have received to do this. Foremost has been George H. Cassar's definitive account of the activities of the 1st Canadian Division at the Second Battle of Ypres, which describes the division's story from its formation in 1914 to its heroic manoeuvres in the Ypres salient in early 1915.[1]

I have also read Desmond Morton's valuable book about Canadian prisoners of war in Germany in World War 1.[2] In addition, I have consulted Colonel G. W. L. Nicholson's history of the Canadian Expeditionary Force[3] and Major T. V. Scudamore's brief history of the 7th Battalion, published in 1930.[4] An officer's perspective of the prisoner of war experience, and of being an internee at Mürren, is contained in John Harvey Douglas's book 'Captured'.[5] For background, I read Lyn Macdonald's '1915 The Death of Innocence'.[6]

---

1 Cassar, George H., *'Hell in Flanders Fields - Canadians at the Second Battle of Ypres',* Toronto, Dundern Press, 2010.
2 Morton, Desmond., *'Silent Battle - Canadian Prisoners of War in Germany 1914-1919',* Toronto, Lester Publishing Ltd., 1992.
3 Nicholson, G.W.L., *'Outside the Corps'*, Canadian Expeditionary Force, 1914-1919, Montreal: MQUP, 2017. Print.
4 Scudamore, Maj T. V., *'A Short History of the 7th Battalion C.E.F.',* Vancouver, Anderson and Odlum Ltd., 1930. This book has no pagination.
5 Douglas, John Harvey, *'Captured'*, George H. Doran Co., New York, 1918.
6 Macdonald, Lyn, *'1915 - The Death of Innocence'*, London, Penguin, 1993.

A fundamental source has been the Foyster records, as chronicled in notebooks, letters and documents by members of his extensive family. The Foysters were prolific letter writers and, though now 100 years ago or more, their missives sound as fresh today as they did then.

I have also received much assistance from my friends in the regiment that perpetuates Kenneth's 7th Battalion; The British Columbia Regiment (Duke of Connaught's Own), based in Vancouver. The Regiment generously invited me to join their veterans on parade during an impressive ceremony at the Canadian Memorial in Flanders in April 2015, as the Canadian Armed Forces recognised the centenary of the Battle of St. Julien in the presence of His Majesty The King of the Belgians.

Otherwise, I have used a host of written, on-line and personal accounts, particularly the records of The Imperial War Museum, The Commonwealth War Graves Commission, the International Committee of the Red Cross and documents held by The National Archives UK, many published on-line by Ancestry UK. I have made much use of the website 'The Long, Long Trail: The British Army in the Great War 1914-1918', an invaluable resource for those researching the First World War. In addition, I have received much advice and assistance from my vastly knowledgeable e-friends in 'The Great War Forum'. I would also like to thank the numerous individuals and organisations, in the United Kingdom, Canada, Germany and Switzerland, who have given me their generous support.

I hope that I have given due and appropriate acknowledgement to all in the notes and in the list of sources. I have tried to identify the owners of the copyright material I have used and to seek appropriate permission. Should anyone believe that I have used material without suitable consent or credit, they are invited to contact me so that this may be corrected in future editions. The photographs I have used remain the property of their owners.

Finally, whilst I have attempted throughout to be accurate, there may well be errors of fact or interpretation that are entirely mine.

Notes

Kenneth mentions many officers and soldiers in his account but gives little more than their surnames. To enhance the tale, I have attempted to identify these people, often from slender evidence, and have put the results either into the text or the footnotes. Some detections I am sure of, the others I have labelled with 'probably' or 'possibly' to indicate the level of confidence I have in my conclusions. A number may be inaccurate.

Throughout the book, I have often abbreviated infantry regiments and battalions. For example, the 1st Battalion of The Leicestershire Regiment is described as 1st Leicestershires.

Many of the officers and soldiers who died in service during the Great War were initially interred close to where they died. At the end of the war, some bodies were exhumed and concentrated at more central locations. As an example, and relevant to this book, Empire servicemen who had died all over Germany were brought together into four permanent cemeteries, including Niederzwehren, near Kassel. Deceased British service internees in Switzerland were concentrated in Vevey (St. Martin's) Cemetery on the northern shore of Lake Geneva, where 88 World War 1 casualties lie, including some of Kenneth Foyster's friends.

Chapter 1
Origins

Kenneth Basil Foyster was born on 12th October 1880. His distant ancestors came from Kenninghall in Norfolk, but one of their number, Samuel Foyster, moved to London in the 1700s to work. His son, also named Samuel, benefited from a handsome property inheritance, which in due course passed to Samuel's son, John Goodge Foyster, who was Kenneth's grandfather. After university, John was ordained, and in 1831, he purchased the patronage of All Saints' and St. Clement's churches in the attractive seaside town of Hastings in Sussex, famous for its proximity to the 1066 invasion landing sites of William the Conqueror. The two aforesaid churches 'for some reason of Georgian and protestant slackness had been united in 1770'[7], and John Goodge Foyster was rector of this accumulation.

In 1849, the two Hastings churches were re-divided and John Goodge's younger brother Henry Samuel Foyster then moved there and became Rector of All Saints', John retaining St. Clement's. John died, unmarried, in 1855. Thereafter, Henry Samuel's eldest son, Henry Brereton Foyster, became Rector of St. Clement's and on the death of their father in 1862, Henry Brereton's younger brother George Alfred became Rector of All Saints'. By now, the Hastings Foysters were established and well-to-do, and the Hastings parishes had become a family concern.

These two brothers both brought up substantial families in

---

7   Hastings Observer, 23rd August 1919, Page 5.

Chapter 1 Origins

their respective rectories. Henry Brereton and his wife Anna had eight children and George, who had married Adelaide Tillard, had nine. The eldest was Adelaide, known as Ada, who was born in 1868. There followed Arthur in 1869, Gerald in 1871, Hugh in 1874, Lionel in 1878, Kenneth in 1880, the twins Hilda and Harold in 1883, and the youngest son Philip in 1888, 20 years after the birth of his elder sister.

Kenneth and his siblings had comfortable, happy childhoods in their large rectory, though their mother was reputed to be a strict disciplinarian, and the All Saints' offspring were 'thick' with their St. Clement's cousins. There was, of course a disparity of age, the older progeny being grown-up whilst the younger were still children. Kenneth recalled happy times, with games and activities, and the epicurean benefits of a well-stocked fruit garden. But children being children, rivalries developed and occasionally fights broke out. The parents split the worst offenders up when possible and this extended to choice of school. The majority of the two families' sons went to board at the famous old English public school of Marlborough College, but seemingly to prevent contention, a couple were dispatched to the equally notable Haileybury.[8] The daughters, as was customary in those distant times, were educated locally and at home.

Kenneth duly arrived at Marlborough in 1894, but unlike his brothers and cousins who took advantage of the educational privileges bestowed on them and passed on to fruitful careers, his sojourn there was somewhat less eminent. He did however, suffer a bad bicycling accident, crashing into a coal cart, rendering himself unconscious and suffering a gashed head and smashed finger. He recovered at home and missed a school term. Seemingly not having the ambition to go to university, Kenneth left the College in July 1898 at the age of 17.

---

8   In England, a public school is in fact a private one with sizeable fees. In those days, most pupils boarded during term time, returning home for the holidays.

While Kenneth was enduring school, his elder brother Gerald had joined the Indian Civil Service. Having set out on a promising career as an Assistant District Commissioner in the Punjab, he sadly contracted typhoid, dying in Mooltan in 1897.

Rather than university, Kenneth attended the small Downton College of Agriculture in Wiltshire. In 1900, he graduated with five prizes and a certificate in 'practical proficiency in agriculture, chemistry, veterinary science, botany and knowledge of livestock.'[9] Kenneth left Downton for a farm in King's Lynn, Norfolk but this job came quickly to an end for unknown reasons and he returned home to Hastings. Thereafter, it seems that he fancied a change of air, and in the summer of 1901, he travelled to Canada *en route* to a 'business university at St. John, New Brunswick', but nothing further is known of this enterprise. Instead, Kenneth ended up doing temporary jobs in New Brunswick and Manitoba. Kenneth did not establish himself in any particular sphere and he came home as 'there was no work to do'.

In 1903, Kenneth went to work for a mining company in Durham and to learn to be a coal mining engineer. It is assumed that he succeeded, as he proceeded to collieries in Carmarthenshire in Wales gaining his 1st class certificate as a mining engineer in 1908. But once again, Kenneth steered a new course, this time travelling to Saarbrücken in Germany in 1910 as an English correspondent at a German firm that built large gas engines for the mining industry. Why Kenneth took this unusual step and what his journalistic responsibilities at the company were are unknown, but from perusing family correspondence, it appears that his sojourn was not a happy one. On his return in 1911, he went to try his luck once more in Canada.

As Kenneth perambulated in this fashion, his father George had retired and with his wife and daughter Hilda, moved to Aspley Guise, an attractive village in Bedfordshire. George died there in 1911 aged 75, and unhappily, having started what promised to be

---

9   The Times, 13th August 1900, Page 10.

Chapter 1 Origins

a glittering career in the War Office, Kenneth's younger brother Harold died a week later having contracted typhoid in 1908, thereafter languishing in a sanatorium.

Meanwhile, elder sister Ada had married a priest named Edmund Wethered and was busy raising four children in Oughtrington in Cheshire, where her husband was the rector. The oldest brother Arthur had become an electrical engineer, working in Edinburgh and producing a daughter with his wife Gertrude. They returned to England to live in the village of Pinner in Middlesex in 1914, Arthur also joining the Royal Naval Volunteer Reserve.

Kenneth's brother Hugh attended the Colonial College at Hollesley Bay, Suffolk and then emigrated to New Zealand, where he became a sheep farmer in Hawera on the southwest coast of North Island, marrying a local girl, Amy Good. The next in line was Lionel, who was the only sibling to take the cloth. He first worked as a curate for his brother-in-law, but as Kenneth put it, 'having got it into his head that he would be a missionary', Lionel moved to Canada in 1910 and was appointed as rector in the remote, coastal settlement of Bay du Vin in New Brunswick. It is worth reflecting on the effect that the British Empire had on such aspirational families in those days. Vast areas of the globe were British, and exciting careers were to be had in these places without really leaving 'home'.

Younger sister Hilda remained in Aspley Guise but joined the Voluntary Aid Detachment, a scheme in which the British Red Cross was given the role of providing supplementary aid to the Territorial Forces Medical Service in the event of war. She became Commandant of the Aspley Guise detachment. In 1909, on leaving Cambridge University, the youngest brother Philip went to The Royal Military Academy, Woolwich and was commissioned into the Special Reserve of the Royal Engineers. He then took up employment as a civil engineer in Cheshire.

Having returned to Canada, it is assumed that Kenneth was seeking some kind of mining work as he arrived in Sydney, Nova

Scotia where coal was extracted. He was to spend two years there, years which he described as 'bad times' and it is assumed that steady work was yet again unforthcoming. Nevertheless, he was able to visit his brother Lionel in his austere New Brunswick parish, spending the Christmases of 1911 and 1912 there.

Kenneth seems to have traversed the Atlantic a couple of times during the period 1912 to 1914 but having failed to find suitable employment in New Brunswick, he moved westwards across Canada to Victoria on Vancouver Island in British Columbia where he arrived in April 1914. In those days, the island was a large coal mining centre.

Chapter 1 Origins

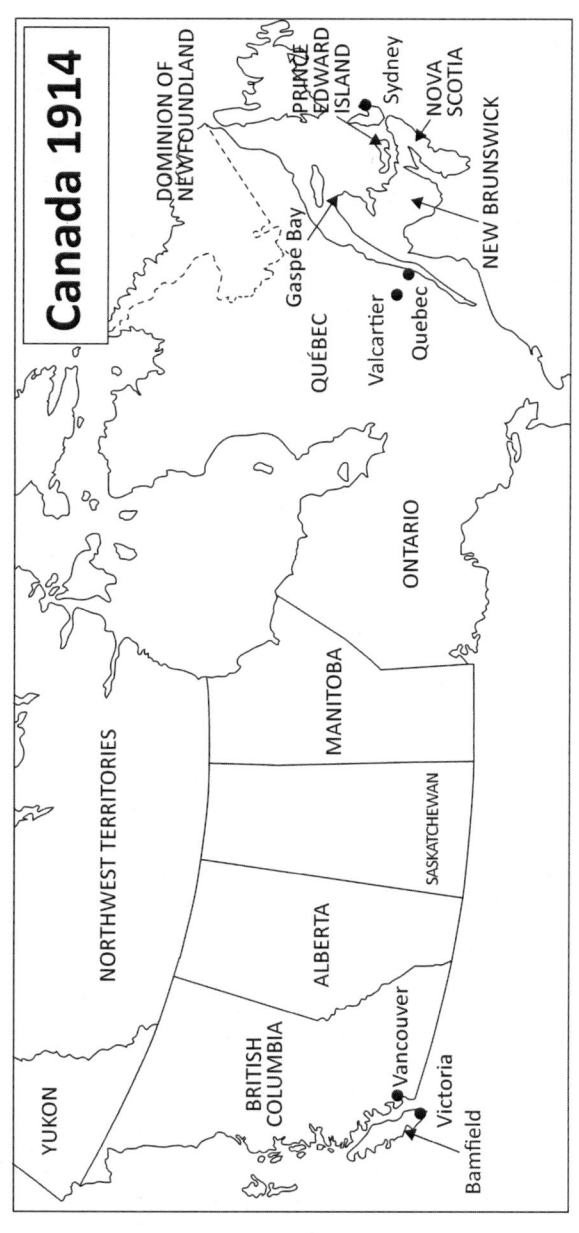

Chapter 2
Becoming a Soldier

Kenneth commences his detailed account of his World War 1 experiences with a rather pithy but insightful declaration:

> 'The War found me, as it found the Empire, in difficulties and solved those difficulties for us. The Empire was on the verge of civil war in Ireland, and the war produced, for the time being at all events, such unanimity among all sects and classes as had never been known before. I was out of a job and the war found me one.'

This assertion calls for some elaboration. In the early 1900s, Ireland was under British rule but there was considerable internal dissent. British Prime Minister H. H. Asquith's weak Liberal Government needed the support of other parties to survive and it received some conditional assistance from John Redmond's Irish Parliamentary Party, which promoted Irish home rule, a subject with which Asquith had some sympathy. However, in return for Redmond's cooperation, in 1912 Asquith was compelled to introduce to Parliament the Third Home Rule Bill. This Bill 'offered only limited self-government and asserted the supreme authority of the UK Parliament over all persons, matters, and things in Ireland.'[10] but it was hugely divisive and fiercely opposed by the British Conservative Party that preferred that the island be partitioned into a largely Protestant north, Ulster, and a Roman

---

10 '*Living Heritage - Parliament and Ireland, The Third Home Rule Bill*', published online at: www.parliament.uk.

Chapter 2 Becoming a Soldier

Catholic (RC) south. In Ireland ill-feeling was high, rioting broke out in Belfast and both sides of the divide created paramilitary forces to defend their principles.

Clearly, this conflict was of great concern within Britain and, it seems, further afield. Kenneth considered it a threat to the cohesion of the vast British Empire which in the early 1900s, comprised about one quarter of the world and its population. In the event, when Britain went to war with Germany in 1914, the Third Home Rule Bill was of necessity postponed, but this left unsolved issues and great tension throughout Ireland. 'Civil war in Ireland - not war on the continent of Europe - is what London feared 100 years ago. Would the British Army mutiny if ordered to force the Protestants of Ulster into Home Rule? Was the British Empire about to crumble from within? This was the question at the start of 1914.'[11]

As for Kenneth's comment on unanimity, it may be that he believed that the Great War, to which the whole Empire contributed men and materiel, brought a measure of pan-Empire harmony. But it also created in the dominions and colonies a greater degree of self-worth and a desire to have more say in shaping their national destiny. If he is making a more social comment, there is no doubt that the war changed relationships in Britain fundamentally. Mass employment of women, as the men enlisted and left for the front, and the military comradeship that sprang up between the differing classes of society are just two aspects that made for a more egalitarian world, a process that the Second World War augmented.

Kenneth gives the background to his own part in these momentous events:

> 'In 1911, I returned to Canada, and after some two years at Sydney, Nova Scotia, I was overtaken by the bad times

---

11 Fisk, Robert, '*In 1914, Britain feared civil war in Ireland more than it feared war in Europe*', The Independent, 19th January 2014.

then existing and decided to go west. So, after a visit home I made for British Columbia and reached Victoria on April 10th 1914. From that time on, I tried everywhere and in every way to get a job, always without success.'

Presumably the 33-year-old Kenneth, whose employment aspirations had met with only fleeting success thus far, was attempting to exploit his engineering qualification in the Vancouver Island coal mines, which were extensive in those days. But fate was to lend a hand as, whilst he sought work, living in lodgings, there was unrest in the very industry he hoped to re-join.

In September 1912, the newly-formed United Mine Workers had had several disagreements with Canadian Collieries, which owned the Dunbar Mine on Vancouver Island. The issues included gas safety and union recognition. When a miner named Oscar Mottishaw was fired for alleged trouble-making, the union became involved and the miners staged a 'holiday' in protest. The company promptly locked them out and replaced them with Chinese, British and United States miners. By the spring of 1913, some 3,500 workers at mines across the island were off work and rioting had broken out.

Some companies made settlements, but peace was only restored when the provincial government sent in the local militia. At that time, this force consisted of two regiments: the 5th (British Columbia) Regiment of Garrison Artillery and, raised in 1912 to meet perceived coastal defence needs, the 88th Regiment (Victoria Fusiliers). International events would soon demand that these regiments take on a rather more strategic role. Nevertheless, the stage was set for Kenneth to play his part, as he now describes:

'On July 25th, it was suggested to me that I should join one of the regiments and get sent to Nanaimo [on Vancouver Island] for the winter, where a garrison was kept owing to some recent strike riots. On thinking this over, I was very much taken with the idea and set about it that afternoon.'

Chapter 2 Becoming a Soldier

Kenneth's first military aspirations were somewhat subjective. Service would put a roof over his head and a meal before him. It was better that the hand-to-mouth existence to which he had been reduced. He continues:

> 'The next day Sunday July 26th, I saw a telegram posted up that Austria had declared War on Serbia and I knew that 'Armageddon', as the Montreal Star used to call it, had come at last and that we were in for something much more exciting than strike duty.'

Kenneth had made a decision that would shape the next few years of his life. He now tells us how his military service commenced and gives a little philosophical background:

> 'On Wednesday July 29th, all preliminaries having been gone through, I enlisted in the 88th Victoria Fusiliers.[12] Next day I attended a recruits' drill at the Drill Hall and at the close was told to come again that day [next] week.
>
> I believe that all or nearly all who enlist pass through three stages. The first stage consists of unbounded enthusiasm. The second reaction during this stage in peace time [is that] one is ready to kick oneself for having joined at all, in war one feels one is doing a painful duty. The third stage is halfway between. One grouses more or less according to temperament, but when all is over will join up again whenever a war comes along. One has in fact become a soldier.
>
> The last stage is well illustrated by the South African Veterans in Canada.[13] I have heard many of them say they

---

12 His enlistment was reported in the Daily Colonist on 2nd August 1914, Page 5.
13 Canada was urged to support Great Britain in The South African War that commenced in 1899, but due to the opposition by some Canadians to fighting a distant war, the government did not commit itself. Instead, the Prime Minister sent a battalion of volunteers. More than 7,000 Canadians took part in the conflict. By the war's end in 1902, four of them had earned the Victoria Cross,

have done their bit and would not go to war again, yet they were the first to join when this war broke out, and when only single men were taken, they made such a row that married men were included and a separation allowance arranged.

I think we all went through the stages in due order. I know I did and I had the first one very badly indeed. So, when I was told to come again in a week I was full of indignation. Here we were on the verge of a world war and they wasted a whole week. I was ready to drill all day and every day. I sought out the Captain of my [militia] company[14] the next day, he was a real estate agent, and told him my grievance. He soothed me down as best he could and assured me that one as keen as I would soon learn that there was no chance of my being left behind. I went away only half satisfied and got through the next few days as best I could.

On Monday August 3rd, a notice was posted up summoning us to a battalion parade in the evening. Things in the war area were looking blacker and blacker and I was filled with the deepest anxiety that the Liberal Government at home would shirk their duty and cling to peace. I was airing my views to the American lady at the boarding house and saying that I would rather see the Empire beaten than disgraced, when she said to me, 'You are a soldier and can say what you like, if you had been a civilian I should say you do not care as you won't have to fight'. I took this as a huge compliment to a three-days-old recruit.

I duly turned up at the parade in the khaki uniform I had been given last time. There was no drill, but they dished us out with rifles, bayonets, kitbags, haversacks, water bottles etc. and an assortment, a regular heap of small straps,

---

but about 270 lost their lives and more than 250 were wounded. Derived from 'The Canadian War Museum' at: www.warmuseum.ca.
14   A sub-division of the 88th Fusiliers.

Chapter 2 Becoming a Soldier

buckles and hooks which later resolved themselves into the Oliver Equipment.'

The Canadian-made Oliver Pattern Equipment was ineffective and unpopular as Kenneth describes in uncompromising detail later on. But he continues:

'When this was done it was 10 p.m. We expected to be dismissed but nothing happened and at last a rumour went round that we were to be kept all night. This proved to be true and at about midnight we marched by companies to the Regimental Institute and billeted there.

Our company was put up in the billiard room which besides the billiard tables, on which we were not allowed to lie, had no furniture whatever. Our greatcoats were neatly rolled, and we did not want to undo them, so we laid on the bare floor and slept or not as best we might. I got no sleep at all as the night was broken first to sign a pay roll – I never got the money by the way – and secondly by my having to go on guard at the entrance for a time. I should explain that at that time our 'company' was 10 strong. The whole militia of Canada was rather a joke and a plaything before the war.

At 5 a.m. we were dismissed and told to reassemble if we heard all the hooters in the city blowing hard. I went home to breakfast and bed leaving strict injunctions to call me if the hooters went. I got up at dinner time and spent the afternoon alternately reading and going to the Institute to see the notices. There were many notices that day, first an order for recruits' drill in the evening, then for a battalion parade and then recruits' drill. I went to the recruits' drill and was drawing some kit at the stores after, when the Sergeant came up to me and said, 'You are in E Company aren't you?' I said, 'Yes'. He said, 'Parade in full marching order tomorrow morning at 11'.

On my way home, I was twice stopped and asked if any of our men had gone yet and I began to feel important. On going to my room, a man called to me from his and told me to my joy that England had declared war. It was such a relief, I had been so afraid we shouldn't and that in years to come we should get what we should have deserved.'

With hindsight, Kenneth's attitude seems implausible, but it was far from unusual. In an age of intense national competition, the Kaiser's Germany was broadly viewed by the citizens of Great Britain, and seemingly many people in the dominions and colonies, as a threat to European stability and to the status of the all-powerful British Empire. In addition, the British public had great sympathy for 'poor little Belgium', which The Kaiser invaded on 4th August causing Britain to declare war. This was greeted with enthusiasm and volunteers flocked to join the Army. Few people foresaw the lethal devastation that tactical stagnation and technological development was to visit on early 20th century battlefields. Kenneth goes on with his account:

'In the morning [August 5th], I packed all my things, gave my key to the landlady to keep and repaired to the Institute. There I found two companies; E and F. There were two sergeants fixing up the Oliver Equipment for them and we waited our turn. I was a strap short and had some difficulty in getting it and so was not able to get away when they let us go for an hour for dinner. In one of the intervals of waiting I went across the road with two or three other men for a drink, and the reception we got from the crowd outside made us, as one of them remarked, feel heroes already. There was quite a crowd outside and the colours, recently presented to the 88th by the Daughters of the Empire, were on view close by.[15]

---

15 The colours usually consist of a standard, or flag, that once constituted a rallying point for a regiment on the battlefield. Nowadays, they are largely ceremonial, but still embody the identity and spirit of the regiment. They are

Chapter 2 Becoming a Soldier

At last, at 1.30 p.m. all was ready, and we fell in outside. Recruiting had been very brisk in the last few days and half of us were absolutely raw recruits who had absolutely no drill whatsoever. I was quite an old stager, so they arranged us so that those who knew how to form fours were even numbers. Every single man did his level best with the result that we sloped arms (how we never knew) formed fours, turned and started so well that a sergeant who was watching in the crowd and dreading a fiasco told me later he was ready to throw his hat in the air. We marched off down Government Street headed by the fife and drums band and looked so smart that a time-expired regular who had been hesitating which regiment to join, there were three in Victoria, went straight away and enlisted in the 88th and joined us at Esquimault [an area of South West Victoria] that night.

We marched right away to Work Point Barracks at Esquimault. On arrival there, we put our kit in one of the rooms and had some supper; bread and cheese. We had no sooner started than we were called away for something and when we got back it was gone.'

Despite the missing supper, this must have been a stirring day for the newly-enlisted volunteers. The Victoria Daily Colonist reported, 'A picturesque incident yesterday afternoon was the informal showing of their new regimental colors to the men of the 88th Fusiliers by the Daughters of the Empire as the troops passed their headquarters on Langley Street on their way to Esquimalt. They were received with the utmost enthusiasm and admiration.'[16]

Kenneth's company was tasked to travel by boat to defend the tiny outstation of Bamfield on the west side of Vancouver Island.

---
revered.
16   The Daily Colonist, Victoria, Vancouver Island, BC, 6th August 1914, Page 5.

As Kenneth relates, this mysterious mission was actually for a highly strategic reason:

> 'Someone told me to keep my eyes open for a nice job, I heard the Captain (of our company) give some orders to a Corporal and when he had done I tackled the Corporal. He said he had been told to get a 'good man'. I said, 'Here you are then you won't get better', so he took me. We had to convey the kit to the boat. It had come in a cart and we rode in the cart with it. The Driver and the Corporal stopped for a drink on route, contrary to all regulations, while I looked after the kit, and they brought me out a bottle of beer. They arrived at Dry Dock, then occupied by the Artillery, we unloaded the cart and put our kit and a huge pile of stores on board the *S.S. Quadra* [a lighthouse tender] and down the hold. We worked hard and got done early, to the corporal's huge delight, and then waited for the others, talking to the sentries and the men on board the *Quadra*.
>
> The others arrived at about 9 p.m., first the new recruits straight from Victoria and then the rest from Work Point. The *Quadra* was a horrid little tug. The only covered-in part of her deck was a passage way 10 feet x 3 beside the engine room. We had to sleep in the hold. The floor was covered with sail cloth and it stunk of paint and onions in areas, one end being paint and the other onions. I was in the paint end.
>
> We started soon after and we tackled the steward for food. I had had none to speak of since breakfast. The Canadian Militia used to starve its men during the first 24 hours of mobilisation. The steward declared he had none and that he had to pay for what was eaten on the ship. We told him what a nice fellow he was and how we adored him and at last he brought us some beef sandwiches.
>
> The west coast of Vancouver Island is noted for its

Chapter 2 Becoming a Soldier

rough seas and it was not at all calm that night. I was not in the least sick despite the paint, but many were and as they could not stand the hold they had to go up on deck where it had started to rain. My troubles next day [August 6th] were not those of sickness but those of hunger and there was no breakfast. At last I found the sergeants were getting breakfast, so I made particular love to one sergeant who, thinking I was in his company which I wasn't, gave me a rasher of bacon and a cup of tea. I ate the bacon, it was fried, with my fingers and was thankful.

It was a long, weary, cold, wet morning. In the course of it we landed some 20 men and a lieutenant at 'the Pitchins' [probably Pachena Point, some 15 kilometres south of Bamfield] to guard the lighthouse. They had to go in small boats in a heavy sea and land as best they could on a rock between the waves. Some were horribly seasick, and we had to get up their kits as they refused to face the hold again. The remainder of us; captain, lieutenant and 30 men, reached Bamfield at 1 p.m.

Bamfield is the Canadian end of one of the two trans-Pacific cables. The other one starts from the [United] States and so was neutral. [The Canadian one] is situated on the west coast of Vancouver Island in a small inlet fairly well protected by islands. It consisted of the cable station with a wharf below and an incline leading down to it. On the other side of the inlet was a life boat station and higher up the creek was a store. It was right in the heart of the woods in absolutely unopened country. There was a rough road that led to 'Pitchina' and I believe to civilisation, but the only communication was by boat.'

The British Empire's trans-continental All-Red Line was an astonishing construction. Inaugurated in the early 1900s and consisting of a matrix of undersea cables that joined the countries of the British Empire and encircled the globe, it allowed timely telegraph communication across the Empire and was to become particularly of use in war. From the remote Bamfield station, the cable went to Fanning Island in the mid-Pacific, and thence to Fiji, New Zealand, Australia, India, South Africa and, via the West Indies, to England. No wonder the cable station required protection.[17] Kenneth continues:

> 'As soon as we landed, some Canadian regulars who had been there before us, went on board and left. They had left us absolutely nothing in the way of food and not even a cookhouse. We got our stores up the incline and our ammunition which consisted of 30 rounds per man only and having found an old store we set it up and all got to work peeling potatoes etc. and cooking a dinner. We got dinner at last at 2.30 p.m. and had a good one, it was the first real meal I had had since the day before. Then we began to settle in.
>
> We were lodged in a large room on the ground floor of the cable station and slept on the floor with two blankets apiece. We pitched a tent outside for the guard, a guard was set as soon as we got there, made a shed for the cookhouse and made ourselves as comfortable as we could. It rained hard the next day, but except for that it was fine all the time I was there.
>
> It was soon found that drill of any sort was impossible as there was no room for it, so our life settled into guards and fatigues. There were two sentries posted all the time, one up by the cable station and one down on a path by the water's edge. As the latter was quite out of sight and sound at night, the reliefs for that post slept in the cable house down by the water where they could be got at in case of alarm. We

---

17 In November 1914, the German Dresden-class cruiser *SMS Emden* raided the cable's terminal on Direction Island in the Cocos Islands, but was destroyed by the Australian cruiser *HMAS Sydney*.

Chapter 2 Becoming a Soldier

went on guard once in four days and our days were thus divided into fours. The first day guard, the second off guard, and on leave, during this day we used to go boating and bathing in the creek etc. The remaining two days we were on fatigues. This consisted in clearing the bush around the station and erecting a barbed-wire enclosure with gates and watch towers. We took it very easy only doing two hours in the morning and the same in the afternoon.

We were as I said all in the first enthusiastic phase and we wanted very much to learn our drill. So, when it turned wet on the 7th the day after our arrival we got the Colour Sergeant [a senior sergeant] to give us some manual training in the barrack room. He kept on till he was sick of it and refused to do any more. After that, he used to drill, as best he could, those who had volunteered for the Front, on the wharf.

The Canadian Militia could only be called on for service in Canada, so that one had to volunteer for anything outside that. They took the names of those who wanted to go to the Front again and again, I think there were 19 out of the 30.

Life at Bamfield was not so bad at that time of the year. Our chief trouble was the food. Our stores consisted of bully beef, beans and some other vegetables and we got rather sick of it. Also, the bread was not good. We had brought flour and as our cook was, or said he was, a baker we thought ourselves lucky, but the bread he baked was the worst I ever tasted. On one occasion, it was uneatable and he remarked that he was sorry but he had forgotten to put something in. However, we would not be pacified but took it to the Captain. He made a great row about it and told the cook that if it happened again he was to throw it away as he would rather have the flour wasted than the men fed on muck like that. It was rather better after this.

On August 15th, we had a concert and invited the crews of the *Iris* and the *Lebro,* which were there, to attend. I was Master of the Ceremonies and had hoped to get the [company] Captain to take the chair, but he was away, and the Lieutenant refused. So, one of the sergeants and the Quartermaster of the *Iris* took it between them.

The people in the cable station had not behaved very well to us, considering we were there to protect them. Protection was really needed, though what our small force could have done with old worn out rifles and only 30 rounds I don't know. At that time, there were hardly any British men-of-war in the Pacific. There was the small China Squadron 10 days' sail away which had all it could do where it was, and a few old boats which had been watching the Mexican trouble on the Pacific side and the *Canadian Rainbow* [*HMCS Rainbow*, an Apollo-class protected cruiser] with only about a third of a crew. On the other hand, the Germans had had some rather useful boats in Mexican waters and they were then out somewhere. Some of them were afterwards rounded up in the Falkland Islands.'

The 'Mexican trouble' was a serious episode. In early 1914, nine American sailors were arrested by the Mexican Government for entering off-limit areas in Tampico. Hearing also that the German Government was delivering arms to Mexico, the United States invaded and captured Veracruz. As for the 'useful boats', as war was declared, Vice-Admiral Maximilian Graf von Spee's East Asia Squadron of fast armoured cruisers was loose in the Pacific and the threat to Vancouver Island's cable station and coal stocks, vital for warship fuel, seemed quite real. In the event, after a victory against the British West Indies Squadron at The Battle of Coronel in October, von Spee's force attempted to raid the Falklands. They were engaged by another British squadron and all five of the German cruisers were lost. This effectively

Chapter 2 Becoming a Soldier

ended German high-seas marauding and, presumably, the threat to Bamfield. Kenneth expands on the Canadian naval capability:

> 'At the outbreak of war, the *Rainbow* was filled up with Naval Volunteers. This was a force that had started some time before in Victoria and consisted of ordinary citizens. The Dominion Government refused for some time to recognise them, which prevented Vancouver following suit. However, the Victoria men stuck to it and when recognition came a few months before the War started they had had a bit of drill. They were to have gone for a cruise in the Behring Seas that autumn, but the War sent them on other business.
>
> In addition to the *Rainbow* the British Columbia Government had bought two new submarines from Chile. These were of a different pattern to ours and no one quite understood them, and the poor landlubbing volunteers must have had a bad time on them.[18] One man on sentry go [duty] on the deck of one of them walked too far in the night and fell overboard! Altogether until Japan joined in the war and sent a squadron across, things were rather serious for us on the coast.'

The submarines that Kenneth describes had been built in Seattle for Chile, but Chilean payments having fallen in arrears, the boats were offered for sale to Canada. The Premier of British Columbia, Richard McBride, paid for them using his own government's funds. The United States Navy sent ships to prevent the transfer, but the two vessels evaded them and were turned over at sea to untrained naval reservists and civilian volunteers from Esquimalt. Neither submarine saw battle service during the First World War. Kenneth continues:

> 'Despite all this the cable people as a whole did all they could to inconvenience and annoy us. They were always

---

18 Landlubber; an ancient, pejorative, nautical term for someone unfamiliar with the sea or seamanship.

complaining first at our using hot water and we were told to wash our plates in cold, then at our borrowing the boats and that was stopped, then they made fun of the sentries and said they could get in and out unchallenged. This finally roused the Captain and he shortened the beats at night and gave us orders that everyone was to be stopped.

I was on sentry go on the 16th between 11 p.m. and 1 a.m. and had quite a field day as I stopped 10 men including the Captain himself. One man, the engineer of the electric lighthouse by the wharf, came running up to tell the Chinese servants to turn on the wharf lights as a boat was coming in. He had left his engines running and was in a hurry and refused to stop when challenged and I chased after him with the guard and some others at my heels. He nearly got it that night as we were all angry at the way we had been treated.

I ought to say that one of the exceptions to this was the chief censor, an old retired colonel. He was especially nice to us and used to post up for our benefit the war news that came through. It was here that I saw the myth of the big naval battle in the North Sea that went all over the world.'

The naval Battle of Heligoland Bight took place in August 1914, but it is unclear what myth Kenneth is referring to. Nevertheless, whilst he was defending the British Empire in this way, Germany was invading Belgium and France, and Great Britain was at war. If Britain went to war, so did the Empire. Accordingly, Canada's Prime Minister, Sir Robert Borden, asked London what assistance could be given and was told that Canada should raise a division. Canada was ill-equipped in both trained men and materiel to achieve this, but in early August the Canadian Minister of Militia, Sam Hughes, announced the formation of a Canadian Expeditionary Force (CEF) to be mobilized at Camp Valcartier, a few miles northwest of Quebec. The CEF became the 1st Canadian Division. Canada was utterly unprepared for war in

Chapter 2 Becoming a Soldier

1914, owning only about 3,000 permanent troops, a few outdated machine-guns and artillery pieces, and an inadequate militia. The rapid formation of the 1st Canadian Division therefore was a sea-change in attitude and capability.

The Honourable Sir Samuel Hughes KCB PC was an interesting and divisive character as we will discover. He had served in the Canadian contingent in the 2nd Boer War and a plaque to his memory situated in front of the Lindsay Armouries in The City of Kawartha Lakes states, 'Soldier, journalist, imperialist and Member of Parliament for Lindsay, Ontario from 1892 to 1921, Sam Hughes helped to create a distinctively Canadian Army. As Minister of Militia and Defence (1911-1916) he raised the Canadian Expeditionary Force which fought in World War 1 and was knighted for his services. Disagreements with his colleagues and subordinates forced his retirement from the Cabinet in 1916.'

Kenneth had volunteered to join the CEF and now he would start to receive the training needed for war. He describes how this was achieved:

> 'On August 17th, the *Estavan* [a lighthouse tender] arrived with reliefs and we who had volunteered for the front line left on her that evening for Esquimault. We picked up the party from Pitchina and started down the coast. The *Estavan* was a huge improvement on the *Quadra* and a good many men got bunks. I didn't but as I found the cushion of a lounge to sleep on I did alright in the corridor.
>
> We reached Esquimault at 9.30 a.m. next day. We found the 88th camped in the Dry Dock and after our names etc. had been taken by an officer, we got leave and went off into Victoria. At that time, we 'soldiers' were the heroes of the hour and nothing was too good for us. There were free rides for all in uniform on the street cars though that was stopped a few days after. We expected to leave in a day or so and went round saying goodbye. I went to my boarding

house, where I was received with open arms and had dinner and a bath, and then went round looking up friends and got back at Last Post. We had a great bother getting a tent and blankets that night but were fixed up next day.

Our time at Esquimault was very pleasant except that the time of our departure kept on being put off, until we were almost ashamed to show ourselves in Victoria. We did no guards or fatigues, we that is of the Overseas Contingent, we finished parades at 4 p.m. and had standing leave from then to Last Post. During the day, we drilled hard.

On August 21st, most of us were inoculated against typhoid. The stuff ran out before it came to my turn. It was done in the stomach and next day the wretched men who had been done were doubled up with it. We had been inspected and passed by the doctor soon after arrival and since then anyone who fainted, and lots did as the weather was hot, got struck off the list. One poor chap who had been inoculated, and who I and another man were helping back to his tent, was in an agony lest he should be seen, but those who had been inoculated were allowed to faint, so he was all right.

I had been to my boarding house many times and on the 22nd I went to say goodbye. On my departure the landlady, a motherly old thing, came out after me and embraced me fondly. I thought it rather nice of her.

On August 25th, I heard that we were all supposed to get 24 hours leave before going and applied for mine and got it. I went up to Saanich that night and turned up at Ross's place unannounced at 9 p.m. They were sitting on the veranda and did not know me at first.'

Saanich is a suburb of Victoria and 'Ross' was Edward Rosslyn Tillard, a cousin of Kenneth's, who had also emigrated to British

Chapter 2 Becoming a Soldier

Columbia and married one Betty Sadleir in 1910. Ross owned a number of glasshouses in which it seems he cultivated flowers, but he served as an officer in The Suffolk Regiment during the Great War. Apparently, his mother Iona was staying at the time and Betty's sister Edith was living with them. It may well be that Edith was present at this farewell meeting, and we will encounter her again in 1919. Kenneth resumes:

> 'At last we were told officially that we were to leave on the 28th and the 50th Highlanders were to go with us.[19] A small contingent of the 5th Garrison Artillery left on the 26th.[20]
>
> I spent the afternoon and evening of the 27th saying goodbye to friends. That evening after lights out the subalterns [second lieutenants and lieutenants] formed a procession and marched round the dry dock singing and beating tin cans. Most of them are dead now.
>
> On Friday August 28th, we paraded at 8 a.m. and marched to Victoria, two companies strong. We had one suit of khaki, equipment, overcoat and one blanket. All the rest we left behind. Recruiting had been going on so hard that the new arrivals could not be fitted out and we left our stuff for them. With us went some 30 or 40 men in civilians who had recently joined and had got nothing at all.'

On 28th August, The Victoria Daily Colonist printed group photographs and names of those of the 50th Highlanders and 88th Fusiliers who had volunteered for the front. The portraits are small and grainy but Kenneth, standing straight and true on the left of a long line of contemporaries, is adorned with what appears to be a fine moustache.[21] He resumes the tale:

---

19 The 50th Regiment (Gordon Highlanders of Canada) was based in Victoria.
20 The 5th (British Columbia) Regiment of Garrison Artillery was also based in Victoria.
21 The Daily Colonist, Victoria, Vancouver Island, BC, 28th August 1914.

'We marched down headed by both our fife and drum and brass bands, and escorted by the rest of the Regiment and the Naval Volunteers. As we got into Victoria the crowd got thicker and thicker. People stood and shook hands with every file as we passed. One man, the tears pouring down his face, was shouting, 'Give them a cheer boys'. It was quite funny.

Opposite the Empress Hotel the crowd was right across the road and round the corner opposite the Parliament buildings, we had to force our way through. In a pause due to forming two deep, I heard my name called and saw Ross and Aunt Iona. A little further on I met them again. How Ross dragged his mother along through that crush I can't imagine. At the end of the gangway leading to the landing stage the police stopped all except those in uniform. Among others they stopped our men in civilians, luckily an officer saw them and got them through.

We went onto the landing stage and went on board the *Princess Sophia* [a coastal passenger liner]. The 50th arrived soon after, and the crowd followed them onto the landing stage. There were three bands there and as soon as one stopped another started and all the time we and the crowd were cheering hard. Then Richard McBride, the Premier of BC [British Columbia], climbed onto the shed roof and tried to make a speech. He stopped the band that was playing at the time, whereupon another started. After a lot of shouting that stopped, only for the third to start, and when he had stopped that everyone began to cheer harder than ever. Victoria. Silence being obtained at last he made his speech, and soon after we started.

As the *Princess Sophia* left the landing stage every factory and every boat in the harbour sounded its hooter and as we went along every boat that passed, including an old

Chapter 2 Becoming a Soldier

pole driver, blew its whistle and the siren on the *Sophia* was kept busy answering the salutes.

We arrived at Vancouver at 6 p.m. and got into the train and started. We had one end of the train and the 50th the other. All the officers were together. The 50th were under the command of their Colonel, Colonel Currie, who was afterwards Brigadier of the 2nd Brigade, the one we were in. We were under Major Byng-Hall, of whom more later.'

Colonel Arthur Currie, later General Sir Arthur William Currie GCMG KCB, was an insurance and real-estate broker, but he had served in the 5th (British Columbia) Regiment of Garrison Artillery, which he commanded, and had taken command of the 50th Regiment in January 1914. He was a large and relatively untrained soldier and '... he had a flair for military command. An intelligent, thoughtful person, free of the prevailing military ideas conceived and employed, he brought to his task a fresh eye and an open mind. As later events would show, he rapidly adapted his tactics to the exigencies of trench warfare and gained the reputation, deservedly so, as one of the finest commanders of the British Army.'[22]

Born in India in the same year as Kenneth, Percy Byng-Hall had been a regular soldier, first in the Derbyshire Regiment then the 34th Sikh Pioneers, in which he was awarded a DSO[23] in an excursion from the Punjab to China in 1900. He settled in Victoria where he was also an insurance and real-estate entrepreneur and in 1914, he was serving as a major in the 88th Regiment.[24] Kenneth continues to describe the journey:

'Everywhere along the line in BC we were welcomed. At Mission they brought magazines and fruit, at Revelstoke

---

22 Cassar op. cit., Page 61.
23 Distinguished Service Order; awarded to officers for individual instances of meritorious or distinguished service in war.
24 Derived from: Bosher, J. F., *'Imperial Vancouver Island - Who Was Who 1850-1950'*, Bloomington, XLibris Corporation, 2010.

they brought crates of apples and other fruit and distributed it. On that first evening one of the 50th fell off the train and was killed, we weren't allowed to leave the train except when ordered after that.

Next day the train stopped at a lake in the Rockies and in less than 10 minutes every man was in the water. It was one of the best bathes I have ever had. The water was extra warm and we much enjoyed it. One man got into difficulties but was rescued by one of our two ex-officers, who finding they were to be left behind, had reverted to the ranks and become privates.

That day we first heard a rumour that persisted all the time we were in the train, that a fever had broken out at Valcartier and that we were to go direct to England.

Once out of BC we did not have much attention paid to us, one exception was a small town in Saskatchewan which we reached late on the night of the 30th. Here they turned out to greet us with an exorable band. They were, they said, trying to give a send-off to all the troops that passed their town, though the noise they made was too horrible, we knew they were doing their best and hid our feelings.

We used to stop every day and get some exercise either drill or a short march. We reached Winnipeg on the 31st. Those who were in uniform marched in full marching order to the bath, where we had a shower, bath wash and a bathe. Meanwhile the civvies [civilians] had been cleaning out the train.

On September 2nd, we reached Smith Falls near Ottawa. There was a band to meet us, a good one this time, and finding they wished it we marched round the town to the band. In the intervals of their playing the 50th pipers insisted on performing. We had suffered more than enough from those pipers. At every station they marched up and down outside. There was no love lost between the 88th and 50th and we did not like the pipes. I believe only Highlanders do.'

The creation of the Canadian camp at Valcartier in August 1914 was nothing short of a triumph. This small, remote station, strategically located some 16 miles northwest of Quebec, was transformed into a huge, functional camp ready to receive, mobilise and train some 25,000 men in less than three weeks. The forest was cleared to produce miles of rifle ranges, tented accommodation, offices, stores, roads, water and electricity, telephone lines, a railway and even a cinema.

Dressed in his colonel's uniform, and riding his horse, Defence Minister Sam Hughes took personal charge. 'A man of great resource and energy, but obstinate, impulsive, overwhelmingly vain, and heavy-handed, Hughes made his own rules as he went along ...'[25] At Valcartier he was everywhere, personally driving the development of the site. However, by short-circuiting the military chain of command, his overall mobilisation plan was unnecessarily complicated and subject to delay.

To this new centre the vast, disparate, miscellaneous provisions of war started to arrive, and then the men, as Kenneth now explains:

> 'On September 3rd, we arrived at last at Valcartier and woke to find ourselves at the station. It and the line to it too were all new since the war. Before that time Valcartier was a small village in the backwoods. Valcartier Camp was some seven miles long by three-quarters of a mile wide built of tents in never ending rows. There were as a rule nine to a tent. Somewhere about the centre were the headquarters, two YMCA [Young Men's Christian Association] tents, and

---

25   Cassar op. cit., Page 17.

a street of canteens run by civilians, some of the battalions started their own canteens later.'

It seems that Kenneth's battalion was one of these. According to Major Thomas Scudamore, who served as a company commander with the 7th, the canteen made over $1,000 net in under five weeks and the battalion used this money to buy band instruments on its arrival in England.[26] Kenneth continues his depiction:

> 'Down the middle ran a road with broad ditches to take the waste, on each side of this were the water taps at which one could wash oneself and ones' clothes. Across the river was a pontoon bridge and on the other side the horse lines.
>
> Near the camp was the rifle range three and a half miles long with 2,000 targets. These were numbered in groups of 100 each and each group marked by a letter in the alphabet. They consisted of a trench some four feet deep and a huge bank in front with masked entrances at intervals. The different ranges were marked by plough furrows. The targets themselves were not very elaborate being merely sheets of cardboard fastened to an arm that could be hauled up and down with a cord.
>
> We were about the last to arrive at the camp, and when we got there the water and electric light along the roads were laid on and all was finished. Considering what I believe to be the case, that all this had been made since the war, it was not at all bad.'

Training at Valcartier was, due to the time constraints and other tasks to be performed, rudimentary. It consisted of musketry, foot drill, fitness training and route marches, which were constantly disturbed by seemingly endless clothing and equipment issues, and medical inspections as Kenneth explains:

---

26 Derived from: Scudamore op. cit.

Chapter 2 Becoming a Soldier

'When we got to Valcartier, they worked us hard and we were drilling all day and drawing kit. We drew everything and sent our old stuff back to Victoria with the exception of our trousers which we were allowed to keep as an extra pair. It was wonderful what we drew. We were supposed to be Canada's best and she was on her mettle to supply us with everything anyone else had.

On September 5th, we were inspected by the doctor. We had a very rigid inspection at Victoria and only four or five of the 88th were turned down. It was otherwise with some other contingents. One had to be perfect to pass, not only in perfect health but with a good set of one's own teeth. We were, as I have said, supposed to be Canada's best. After the inspection, we were all inoculated. This time it was done in the arm. Inoculation always makes one seedy for a time, and when next day we heard there was a review by the Duke of Connaught we all went sick. We were excused the review and were not sorry as it pelted with rain. He inspected us next day.[27]

It had been raining hard and on the night of the 7th our tent got flooded. Half of it was dry and we crowded into that half. There were a nice lot of chaps in that tent and the NCO[28] in charge was Corporal Muir, whose dead body I came across, though I didn't know it was him, in the trenches, of which more later.

On the 8th and 13th they took us down the river to a quiet place for bathing parade. The water was bitterly cold and all one could do was to plunge in, swim a bit and get out again.'

In September, the Canadian volunteer infantry was organised

---

27   Prince Arthur, Duke of Connaught and Strathearn was the seventh child of Queen Victoria and had been, since 1911, Governor General of Canada. He took a close interest in the development of the new division.
28   Non-Commissioned Officer; normally a corporal or sergeant.

into four brigades. Each brigade contained four battalions of 1,000 men. The men from the west of Canada formed the 5th, 6th, 7th and 8th Battalions of the 2nd Brigade, as Kenneth observes:

> 'The various contingents from all the Militia Regiments had been arranged into 17 battalions of Infantry besides the other arms of which I know little or nothing. We were the 7th Battalion and of the 2nd Brigade with Colonel Currie as Brigadier and Lieutenant Colonel Hart McHarg as Colonel [Commanding Officer]. Our battalion was made up entirely of BC men. The Victoria Companies were E and F. Mine was F under Captain Harvey. In the Overseas Contingent at Victoria I had been in No. 2 Company, No. 3 Section and No. 6 Squad which, as my number was 236, was rather a coincidence.'

Lieutenant Colonel William Hart-McHarg was a 45-year-old Irish lawyer from Vancouver, who had served in the ranks during the South African War and was an excellent marksman. His Second-in-Command was Major Victor Odlum and the Adjutant was Captain Stanley Gardner, who came from London.[29] Captain Robert Harvey, originally from Liverpool, had been the Warden of University School, Victoria. Of interest, Archibald Wrightson, the son of Professor Wrightson of the Downton College of Agriculture which Kenneth had attended in 1898, joined the 7th Battalion after the CEF had left Valcartier. He served initially as a private but was awarded the MC for conspicuous gallantry while serving as a lieutenant in November 1915.[30] Kenneth continues:

> 'On September 11th, we had a parade which we heard was to weed out those who were not to go. There were 30,000

---

29 Lieutenant Colonel Stanley Douglas Gardner CMG MC died of wounds in September 1918, whilst commanding the Canadian 38th Battalion.
30 The Military Cross; granted in recognition of an act or acts of exemplary gallantry during active operations against the enemy on land, and awarded to commissioned officers of the substantive rank of captain or below and for warrant officers.

Chapter 2 Becoming a Soldier

men in camp and it had been intended to send only 20,000. Name after name was read out and the men fell out looking gloomy, while us who remained trembled. It was a horrible ordeal. There seemed no rhyme or reason in the selection. Men who were fit, well behaved and good shots were called out with those who were not. Our section suffered very badly, I think there were only six left, I was one. But all they were doing was to rearrange the companies and sections and only those got sent back whom the doctor had refused and who knew it already. After that we moved into other tents and I did not get quite such a nice lot of fellows as I had before. Our company was made up with the 11th Irish [11th Regiment Irish Fusiliers of Canada] from Vancouver.[31]

There was a review by Sam Hughes Minister of Militia on the 12th and by the Duke on the 14th. At these we marched past each half-battalion in two long lines, a very hard manoeuvre for raw troops and our battalion were much complimented on the way we did it.

On the 17th, we were inoculated again and next day as we were feeling sick and sorry they fell us in with the rifles we had drawn on the 14th to take them to the stores to get them changed. This meant a three-mile march there and back and we didn't feel like it. We were all looking as rotten as we could, and the Colour Sergeant came down the line and asked a man here and there, myself included, if our rifles were all right, we said, 'Yes', and were told to fall out. The others were gone a long time. Later I met the Colour Sergeant and thanked him for letting me off he said, 'You looked so ill I didn't think you could do it'. My illness I may say was quite put on and must have been a good piece

---

31   The 11th Irish Fusiliers were eventually amalgamated into the successors of the 7th Battalion, the British Columbia Regiment, in 2002.

of acting. About that time, I was in the second or reaction stage of my career as a soldier.

On the 23rd, we were sworn in again. On enlisting we had taken the ordinary militia oaths and signed on for three years. Now we were sworn on as regulars to serve anywhere and signed for one year or the duration of the war and six months after.'

Kenneth's attestation paper describes him as an engineer. He is reported as six feet tall with a 36-inch girth when fully expanded. He has a fair complexion, blue eyes, brown hair and a scar on his left arm, perhaps from that school-days cycling accident.

All the training and administrative preparation had but one object; to be able to project a fighting division into the war. The next step would be for the CEF to cross the Atlantic for England and Kenneth describes how they set out:

'All this time we had been drawing kit. Hardly a day passed but we drew something or other, they dribbled in and in and by now we had got it all. The nights were getting very cold now though the days were warm, the season was drawing to its close and the time rapidly coming when the camp would be uninhabitable.

At last the time for leaving came. The first brigade left on the 24th, marching all the way to Quebec. We left on the 27th. We carried all our kit to the station and went by train from there to Quebec and went on board the *Virginian*. There was only our battalion and some details of the Medical Corps (I think) on the boat. She was a first-class Allan Liner of about 15,000 tons and a fast boat at that. When last she reached Canada, she was told to lie up in the river and no one among the crew knew what it was for until a few days before we went on board. My berth was in the steerage aft and right down on the lowest deck and I shared a cabin with a corporal.

Next day, having got our cargo which included some of the million bags of flour Canada had presented and which were marked 'Canada's gift', we anchored in the river opposite Wolfe's Cove and the Heights of Abraham and from there we had a splendid view of the whole battlefield which gave Canada to the Empire.[32] On September 30th, we started with the other boats down the river and disappeared from the public ken, our whereabouts from then on being known only to the Admiralty. Next day, we found ourselves in Gaspé Bay, a small harbour below the mouth of the St. Laurence, and there the convoy gathered.

Our life on board ship was punctuated by parades, three a day, which consisted in 'physical jerks' as we called Swedish drill, learning signalling semaphore and various things of that sort. We had bath parades at intervals, one man remarked, 'The Army is a grand thing to be in, you don't need to worry at all, they even tell you when you want a bath!'

At 4. 30 p.m. October 3rd, the fleet began to leave Gaspé Bay and when outside lined up in three parallel lines ahead. There were 32 transports, big liners all of them, escorted by 10 cruisers. A cruiser was at the head of each line and one was astern of the convoy and the others were round the flanks. I was told later that a whole cruiser squadron met us

---

32   In June 1759, a British force commanded by Major General James Wolfe headed down the St. Lawrence River and attacked the French garrison at Quebec. The British reached the rear of the city via a steep path up the cliffs to the Heights of Abraham, an undefended plateau. The French came out to meet them and were defeated, Wolfe losing his life during the battle. Wolfe's victory eventually led to the conquest of Canada by Britain.

at Cape Race. We were the fifth ship on the starboard line. Each boat carried in its stern a barrel with a length of rope attached so that it could drag it behind in a fog and let the ship behind know where it was. It was a wonderful sight that convoy, I don't believe so many liners have ever been together before.'

This exceptional fleet was escorted by the British 12th Cruiser Squadron, commanded by Rear Admiral Rosslyn Wemyss RN, and contained some 30,617 'fighting men' of Canada and 537 more from Newfoundland.[33] Kenneth goes on:

'On October 5th, we were joined by the *Florizel* [a Bowring Brothers passenger liner] with the Newfoundland contingent. On the same day, a man fell overboard on the *Royal Edward* [a Northern Steamship Company passenger liner]. The *Royal Edward* turned and stopped, and the ships astern gathered round. The flagship which was at the head of our line came rushing down covered with signal flags and the ships fell into line again with a frightened hurry that was most amusing. I was on deck and saw it all, the man was picked up by the *Grampian*, and the flagship having dealt out reprimands returned to her place.

These liner captains had been used all their time to being absolute head at sea. The Admiral began at the very start to pump discipline into them. On each boat were Canadian signallers and these were kept busy day and night handing down the line messages from the flagship, the wireless was not used for obvious reasons. One signaller told me he had just sent on a message of 101 words pitching into the ships astern, 'What do you mean by straggling? Why can't you keep up? Don't you realise the danger of this?' etc.

---

33   Derived from: Crawford T. S., *'Wiltshire and the Great War: Training the Empire's Soldiers'*, Marlborough, Crowood Press Ltd., 2012, Page 59. At that time, Newfoundland was not part of the Canadian Federation.

Chapter 2 Becoming a Soldier

On October 11th, strict orders were issued that no ship was to show any lights except a small one in the stern for the ship behind to steer by. This led to more trouble, a porthole uncovered for a moment or a match struck on deck and the [ship's] Captain would hear of it from the flagship. Our skipper was in a regular panic, he daren't call his soul his own and the others were the same. They huddled together, one boat overriding the one in front in what in ordinary times would be considered most dangerous proximity. But the sea was calm, dead calm, all the time.

No one knew in the least where we were going. The Captain knew where he was and that he was heading for the middle of the Bay of Biscay but beyond that he knew nothing. The wildest rumours were afloat, Valcartier had been bad enough in the matter of rumours but the boat was worse, all sorts of impossible yarns were circulated.

Thus, time went on and we got rather tired of it. We had parades lectures etc. daily. We were given our field service bandages on the 7th and duly sewed them into our jackets. We had concerts and boxing matches on the hatches below decks at night and it was then that our marching songs were composed. There were two, the first I think was pretty general throughout the contingent and went to the tune of 'I'm on my way to Mandalay':

We're on our way to Germany,
Beneath the Kaiser's roof we going to stay.
We'll drink his beer and give a cheer,
For Canada, far away.
We're sentimental for our country gentle,
We're British subjects that's why,
We're on our way to Germany,

Keeping The Old Flag Flying

We'll drink the whole place dry.

Not very classy and rather ill-omened as it turned out. Some objected to the 'British subjects' as we had Americans with us, but as was pointed out they were subjects so long as their enlisting oaths lasted. The other was in better style and more popular and was for our battalion only. It went to the tune of 'There's a girl in the heart of Maryland':

We're the boys from the West of Canada,
From the Province they call BC.
And we're out to do our best,
Along with all the rest,
All for the cause of Liberty.
Oh Motherland, dear Motherland,
Since we're one of your family,
We're the boys from the West of Canada,
From the Province they call BC.'

Chapter 2 Becoming a Soldier

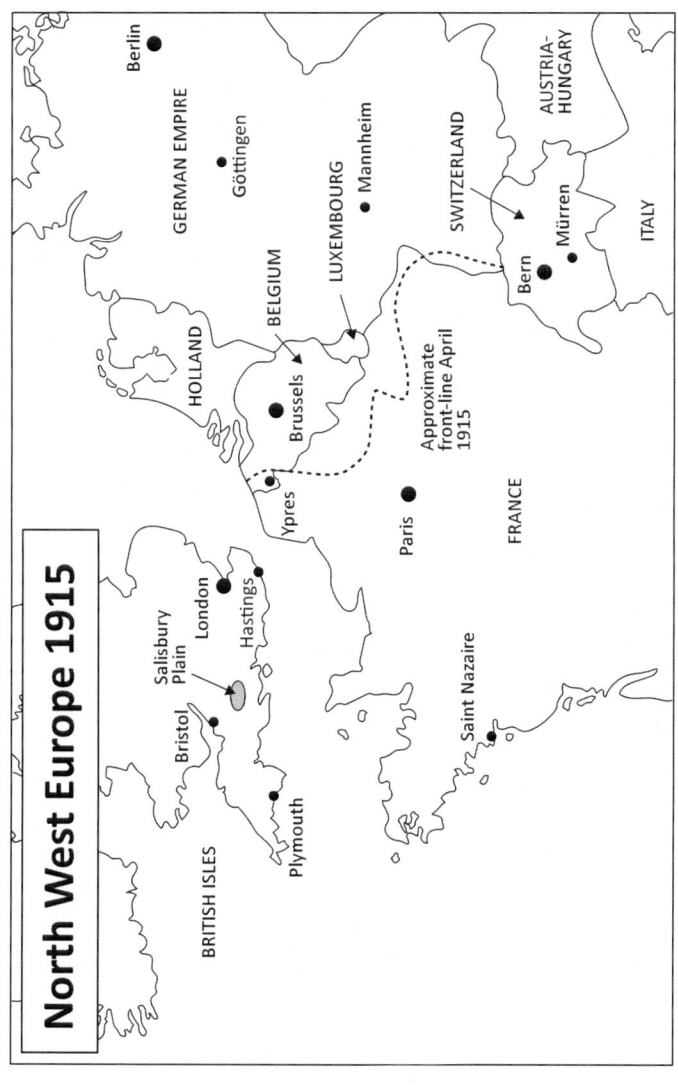

Chapter 3
Training for War

As Kenneth and his comrades composed songs and swapped rumours below decks, strategic decisions were again being made. The impressive Canadian convoy had been heading for Southampton, but due to possible German naval activity, at the last minute its destination was changed. Kenneth takes up the tale:

'At last soon after dinner on October 14th, the ships got the order full steam ahead and the convoy broke up and raced to Plymouth Sound. We were one of the first but not the first in. We had been expected at Southampton and I hear they had got a great reception ready for us there, but there were submarines or something in the channel.

The people at Plymouth wondered as they saw liner after liner come in, then word went round that it was the Canadians and the Hoe was filled with a cheering crowd. Tug boats took us in hand and dragged us up the Hamoaze [the part of the river opposite the dockyard] to Devonport being wildly cheered on the way from the training ships and we were the first ship alongside and another was fastened alongside us and the others were all over the place. The *Lion* and the *Tiger* [large battle-cruisers of a class dubbed The Splendid Cats] were there then. One, the *Lion* I think, was just ahead of us getting her ammunition on board and the other was in dock being fitted.'

Chapter 3 Training for War

The Canadians' unexpected arrival at such a scale congested the Plymouth dockyard, delaying the disembarkation of some of the troops until the 24th October. Kenneth describes the outcome:

'There we lay three days and after 30 days on board, we were longing to get ashore. Our grub ran out, they soon got some more, but as the boat had been provisioned for an ordinary eight-day run we had been kept a bit short and on the 15th there was a semi-mutiny and some of the officers who had been ashore got hooted [jeered]. Major Byng-Hall, who was Junior Major of the battalion, gave us a lecture about it. He was an ex-army officer and had got the DSO in the Boxer Rising in 1900 and understood men. In my opinion he was the best officer we had. Some of the men managed to get off the boats and got out of the dockyard by falling in at the rear of other parties and then disappearing up a side street and they generally came back blind drunk without having spent a penny but without a single button or badge left.

In this place, it would be well to say something about the drunkenness. Our battalion was especially good and well-behaved but some of the others got us an awful name on the Plains [on Salisbury Plain, the division's next destination]. The whole fault I put down to Sam Hughes the Minister of Militia. He was a temperance fanatic and had always stood out against allowing wet canteens in camp. Many of the men had been used to drinking and when they joined up, were deprived of it. If it had been sold on the ships, it might have worked off all right, but it wasn't.

When these men got let loose in England, with its to us ridiculously cheap prices and its strong beer, far stronger than anything in Canada, they were almost bound to make fools of themselves. It is only fair to say that the regiments that behaved worst, and with whom we were most angry, had the chance and took it to make the best name for themselves in our final smash up. I have seen it stated that though we came to them with rather a bad reputation, the generals at the front soon used to say they wished they had some more divisions like the Canadians.

We had come to England a fully equipped division not only with artillery, cavalry, transport etc. and medical staff, but with reserves as well, for we were four brigades strong and a division has only three. At Devonport, we took on our only English part, our general, Lieutenant General Alderson, a man who won the trust, respect, and affection of, I think, every man in the Contingent.'

Suffolk-born, British Army officer Lieutenant General Sir Edwin Alfred Hervey Alderson KCB was a hard-working officer who cared for his soldiers. He had been chosen for this appointment due to his wide active service experience, initially in The Queen's Own (Royal West Kent Regiment) then as a brigade and divisional commander 'in Egypt, the Sudan, and South Africa, where Canadian units (Royal Canadian Dragoons and 2nd Canadian Rifles) had formed part of his command - a decisive factor in his present appointment. Short, dark, with a bushy moustache, he was respected for his dedication and kind, gentle character. He was not a great field general, but sound enough as a soldier. ... he knew how to train troops and deserves credit for helping to mould the raw and unruly Canadians into a superb fighting force.'[34] Kenneth continues:

'During the voyage, we had been given our numbers. The contingent was numbered right through, more being allotted to each battalion than it really required so as to allow of any additions. My number was 16887. They have kept on numbering the Canadians on the same lines and some of the later men had numbers like railway cars.'

---

34 Cassar op. cit., Page 40.

Chapter 3 Training for War

It had been decided that the Canadians would complete their training for war on Salisbury Plain in Wiltshire before deploying to the trenches on the Western Front. The Plain is a large military training area that is still used by the British Armed Forces. Ninety-two special trains were laid on to take the Canadians there and they were accommodated in a variety of hutted and tented camps.[35] Kenneth describes their journey:

'On October 17th at 1.30 a.m., we landed and marched to one of the Plymouth stations. As it was the middle of the night we did not get a reception like those did who landed by day. We reached Lavington at 8 a.m. and marched to West Down South Camp on Salisbury Plain getting there about midday. The tents were all pitched and a large one was full of straw for our mattresses which was huge comfort after the bare ground at Valcartier. We had our dinner sometime after 1.00 p.m. and then rested all the afternoon.'

Lavington Station, no longer in service, was about six miles to the north of West Down Camp which lies near the village of Tilshead. A camp on the site of West Down South, consisting of buildings and huts, is still used by the British military today. The march was quite a demanding one as it led up the steep escarpment onto the Plain, but on their arrival at their various camps around the West Down area, the Canadians found large conglomerations of marquees and bell tents that had been erected for them by members of the British Territorial Force. Some of these had no duckboards and the occupants slept on palliasses; straw-filled cloth bags[36]. Nevertheless, the camp, on its carpet of greensward, looked inviting. Kenneth explains how he settled in:

'Next day, Sunday, most of our tent went to Lavington in the afternoon. We had difficulty in getting any food but

---

35 Derived from: Crawford T. S., *'Wiltshire and the Great War: Training the Empire's Soldiers'*, op. cit, Page 59.
36 Derived from: Crawford, T. S., *'The Canadian Army on Salisbury Plain'*, Halsgrove, Wellington 2012, Page 42.

found a little shop at last where we so ingratiated ourselves that the old lady would ever after give us more and charge us less than anyone else, and any of us who happened to be in Lavington always went there for food.'

Notwithstanding, it seems that the Canadians' rations were comparatively good. 'Each man was allowed a day's ration of 1lb of bread, 1lb of fresh vegetables and 1lb of meat or bacon per man ...'[37] Soon after their arrival, the Canadians commenced training, little expecting that the volatile British weather would soon come to dominate their activities, as Kenneth explains:

'The weather during the first few days on the Plain was nice and fine and, as we had no rifles, ours being packed for the voyage and not yet issued, we went on route marches. We saw lots of aeroplanes, at first, we gazed at them a lot but we soon got so used to them and we hardly bothered to look when one appeared.

On October 22nd, the rain began and with it all our troubles. It rained off and on all the rest of the time we were in England. At first the Plain got greasy, then it got muddy, then all the grass in the camps disappeared and was replaced by thick soup ankle deep. The area of soup grew and grew till it extended right up to the sides of the tents. We shall all remember Salisbury Plain for its mud, things got worse and worse and more and more miserable, the rain descended and the floods came, and the wind blew and many a tent fell. That is no exaggeration as in the New Year, Shrewton and Bulford villages were badly flooded.'

During the division's time on The Plain, training consisted mainly of 'physical conditioning, route marches, foot and arms drill, musketry instruction, and entrenching. Target practice was

---

37 Crawford T. S., *'Wiltshire and the Great War: Training the Empire's Soldiers'* op. cit., Page 61.

Chapter 3 Training for War

stressed in the training schedule.'[38] 'The object was to attain the speed and precision of British Regular soldiers who could fire 12 to 15 aimed shots a minute.'[39] 'Needless to say, the miserable weather played havoc with the training schedule. Cold conditions or mist hampered range practice; heavy storms of wind and rain interrupted tactical exercises. Men had to plough through ankle-deep mud all day, their clothing soaked by rain or caked with slime. Much of the time little or nothing was done.'[40] Kenneth adds his experiences, opinions and vignettes:

> 'We stuck it more or less contentedly and treated it all as a joke though it was rather a grim one. Some of the men got dysentery and there was an epidemic of cerebrospinal meningitis, one or two battalions being very bad with it.[41] Someone wrote to Lord Kitchener [Field Marshal Lord Kitchener, Secretary of State for War] and asked to have us moved. The answer was typical, 'If the Canadians can't stand the mud, I will take the Territorials out of their barracks and put them on the Plain and put the Canadians in their barracks'. Of course, we wouldn't stand for that. Major Byng-Hall addressed his half-battalion and said he wanted to stay with us but if we agreed to those terms he would have nothing more to do with us. Shortly after they asked us if we would like to shift camp to another part of the Plain. Our battalion said, 'No' most emphatically, and we stuck it out. I believe we were the only battalion that did not shift, and we were the first to be put into huts. Some never got into huts at all.

The first contingent consisted of 62 per cent 'old

---

38 Cassar op. cit., Page 43.
39 Ibid.
40 Ibid.
41 Sickness claimed the lives of 58 men during the Canadians' time on Salisbury Plain, mostly from pneumonia and meningitis, which was probably brought over from Valcartier. Derived from: Crawford T. S., *'Wiltshire and the Great War: Training the Empire's Soldiers'* op. cit., Page 62.

country men', that is natives of either England, Wales, Scotland or Ireland, and the percentage of old countrymen in our battalion was 93 percent. There was one of the few Canadian-born in our tent. I don't think he had been off Vancouver Island before and it was a great delight to us to introduce him to all things English. We all wanted to show him London, but when the leaves came he had to go alone. However, he travelled about on the tops of motor buses and seemed to have seen everything. He could not tell us where he had been, but whenever we mentioned a place he said, 'I saw that'.

On October 23rd, he and I, having both come off guard, went to Devizes. We went primarily for a bath as baths at West Down South were unobtainable, it being too cold to wash in the open. We were lucky in getting a lift both there and back and had a good time. The small boys of Devizes followed us about like a bodyguard and we gave them all the small Canadian coins we had not changed.

On the 24th, we were inspected by Lord Roberts.[42] By this time the camps were all mud and the inspection took place well outside all the camps. On the 25th there was an open-air church service taken by the Bishop of Salisbury for the whole division.

On the 28th, we got our rifles back. We had hoped that we were to get Lee Enfields, but we went to the front with the Ross and I don't think it was at all inferior.'[43]

It is worth pointing out that Kenneth's optimistic view of the

---

42 Field Marshal Frederick Sleigh Roberts, 1st Earl Roberts VC, was the last Commander-in-Chief of the Forces before the post was abolished in 1904, having distinguished himself during the successful Victorian campaigns of the Second Afghan War and the Boer War. A visit by such an illustrious soldier would be a significant honour.

43 The .303-inch calibre Short Magazine Lee-Enfield (SMLE) Mk III rifle was used by the British Army.

Chapter 3 Training for War

Ross was proved to be erroneous once battle was joined. The Canadian-manufactured .303-inch calibre Ross rifle had been purchased in bulk for the CEF but, although it was very accurate, it did not stand up to the rigors of warfare, as we will discover later. Meanwhile, Kenneth describes a Royal visit:

'On November 4th, we were reviewed by the King [King George V]. We had had a rehearsal on the 2nd. The Brigadier came to each battalion in turn and made them present arms. We watched the other battalions making rather a mess of it and one having to do it five or six times and the officers being told what to do with their swords, and we were determined to do better. We had already begun to fancy ourselves as a battalion, and when it came to our turn we did about as good a present as could be wished. We did it once, came to the order, stood at ease and the Brigadier went on to the next battalion.

The King was accompanied by the Queen [Queen Mary], Lord Kitchener, looking frightfully overworked, and Lord Roberts looking older and feebler than when he came before. There was no march past, the King passed down our lines and then we lined the road and cheered him as he motored away. We gave a special cheer to Lord Roberts, it was not so long after that he died.'[44]

Kenneth's memoir allows us now to catch up with his relations in England, as he relates:

'Leave was being granted to a percentage of each battalion weekly from Friday afternoon to Tuesday reveille. My turn came on November 6th. I went that night to Pinner, where I revelled in the first bath since Devizes. Next day I went on to Aspley Guise and spent a jolly time there leaving by the 3.30 train on Monday.'

44　Lord Roberts died of pneumonia 10 days later, on the 14th November, whilst inspecting Indian troops in France.

Keeping The Old Flag Flying

As we have discovered, Kenneth's brother Arthur, his wife Gertrude and their four-year-old daughter were living in Pinner. In December 1914, Arthur had taken up an appointment as an Assistant Inspector of Small Arms Ammunition for the Ministry of Munitions. Visiting Aspley Guise, Kenneth will have met his widowed mother Adelaide and sister Hilda. Kenneth's other siblings had left home, but no doubt there were also friends in attendance. In October, his younger brother Philip, who had remained in the Royal Engineers Special Reserve, had joined up for full-time army service.

Kenneth now relates how some of his colleagues had spent their time off:

> 'Some of the men had comic experiences while on leave. England was full then of Territorials and members of the New Army and they were most anxious to do their duty in the matter of saluting officers. We Canadians were a puzzle to them. In the first place we had brown boots, associated in their minds with officers only, then our coloured shoulder straps were something quite new and altogether they didn't know what to make of us and often saluted to be on the safe side.
>
> Also, some of us came in for salutes intended as a mark of respect to Canada. One man got two of these. He was walking down a street with his grown-up niece when he saw a captain and his company coming. He said, 'Here's where I ought to stand at attention till they are past us, I shan't'. When they got to him the captain gave the order, 'Company eyes, right', a salute given only to officers of field rank. My friend gave the officer salute in return (which is a different thing to the private's salute) and went on. Another day he wanted to see a fort in the Isle of Wight. He went up there but was stopped by the sentry who said no one could be admitted. He said, 'I am sorry, I have just come home with

Chapter 3 Training for War

the Canadian Contingent after 15 years and I should like to see the fort again'. The sentry sprang to attention and said, 'Pass Canada and all's well'.

On November 21st, we were officially known as the First British Columbia Regiment [In full, 7th Canadian Infantry Battalion (1st British Columbia)]. We had long been agitating for this. The other battalions thought it swank and when mother and Arthur came to see me and asked someone which was the First British Columbia line, he said he had never heard of them. When they said, '7th Battalion', he told them and added, 'You shouldn't call them by those fancy names'. But one by one they followed our example and I think they all had names before they left.'

Indeed, Lieutenant Colonel Hart McHarg had made quite a commotion about naming his battalion. He felt it was an excellent way to merge so many militiamen from four or so different regiments into a single team. After much fighting with brigade and division he finally got his way and, as Kenneth notes, all the other battalions soon followed suit. So did most other battalions raised by the CEF for the duration of the war. At the same time Hart McHarg also designed the cap badge, ensuring that it had 1st British Columbia on it. Kenneth resumes:

'Soon after this, I heard from a man I had known at Sydney that Day [not identified], a mutual friend, was in the 2nd Battalion at Bustard Camp. I went to see him on the evening of November 25th. I wish I had known he was in the contingent at Valcartier. On the Plain the camps were far apart, and I did not see him again.

All this time we had been going on with our training; all day and every day except Saturday afternoons and Sundays. On November 25th, we had a battalion route march to Lavington (some seven miles off) and had supper outside

53

the village and did some skirmishing on the way back in the dark. I and some others were doing sentry go in a belt of trees when we saw two men coming and challenged them. We found they were two artillery officers overcome with fury as we happened to be on their 'parade ground'. Meanwhile their signallers had got into touch with ours and angry messages were passing. The Colonel came up soon after and we passed them on to him. What harm we were doing to their precious parade ground, an open bit of Plain, I can't imagine.

On November 29th, Mother and Arthur motored over from Marlborough to see me. I had hoped to go to Marlborough with them for a bath, but it was too far so we went to the old lady's at Lavington and had tea there. On that day I saw Harrison [not identified], a man I had known in Victoria. He had enlisted in the 5th Garrison Artillery in June and hunted for me to enlist too but couldn't find me. I met him once while we were at Esquimault. I met him once again while we were on a route march in France.'

The rain and mud on the Plain continued to take their toll, but a reprieve was in the wings and Kenneth now tells us how his life was eased by a change of accommodation:

'On that same day, General Alderson came and saw our lines and said that they were not fit for pigs much less men and that we were to move at once. And so, on December 3rd, we moved into the huts at Lark Hill close to Stonehenge.'

Now known as Larkhill, this sprawling community, about three miles northwest of the town of Amesbury and on the southern side of the Plain, is today a British Army artillery garrison. Kenneth lauds his change of circumstances:

'Oh, the joys of those huts after the leaking crowded tents with the sea of mud all round them. The huts were

Chapter 3 Training for War

good and large, I don't know the dimensions, there were about 40 men in each. They had two tables, a shelf to put kit on, benches and best of all a stove. In the tents if one's clothes got wet by day they never dried, we had got floor boards, but they were slimy. Often when it rained the rain came through and some tents were blown down. Now we had lots of room, could eat like Christians at a table, could dry our clothes and warm ourselves and were dry at night. The place outside soon got muddy but we made chalk paths and did our best and anyway the huts were clean.

The huts were not quite done when we got in and we finished them ourselves. An order came out, just too late to stop us, that no one was to move in till they were finished and passed. We put up the shelves and made a small bunk for the sergeants, big enough for two per hut. They were installing electric light and finishing the horse sheds when we left. The poor horses had the worst of it, at the best they were picketed under trees and many a Canadian horse was buried on Salisbury Plain.

Life in the huts was nice and comfortable, we had plates, knives, forks, mugs, tins for dishes and for tea and pans for washing in. Also, the cooks got proper stores and were able to serve other and better food than the eternal Mulligan or Irish stew which was all we could get from the dirty muddy trench fires in the open. I had been anxious about my feet. An infantryman is no good with bad feet any more than a horse is. At Lark Hill, I diligently nursed them and kept a pair of socks going wearing them alternately day by day and drying them between. I put it down to this care that I never suffered with sore feet at the Front. Often, I was dead with fatigue after a march, but my feet were always, except on one short occasion, sound and good.

I took to shaving in the evenings, I had plenty of time

then and could get hot water. One day a man named Bevan asked for the loan of my safety razor after I had used it. I kept two blades which I used alternately and that was the worst. I lent it and he went into raptures over it, his own must have been bad. Next night he came again and it being the good one that time he came regularly afterwards.

[Bevan] was the first casualty in our platoon. He was filling sand bags on March 16th [1915] and got out of the shallow trench to do it better. In this way, his head showed over the parapet of the front trench some 30 feet ahead, and he was shot through the head and killed instantly. I went to his funeral that night. There were a number of officers there, some three or four of us men and the pioneers who made the grave. He was buried by our Chaplain (every battalion had one) in the little graveyard we had made behind the lines and when at Estaires we saw the wooden cross with his name on to be put on it. He was a very nice chap and we all felt it very much at the time, he being as I said our first. A day or two before he was shot he had, in an idle moment, made patterns with empty cartridge cases in the parapet at his firing position. He had put his own and some girls name and the word *Kismet* [destiny].[45]

On December 8th, we were all vaccinated and on the 9th our company had the job of cleaning up our lines at West Down South. The mud had already settled quite a lot during that short time.

One of the luxuries we enjoyed at Lark Hill was a bath house. It was just an ordinary hut fitted with eight huge coppers with fires underneath, four were for the regimental

---

45   16861 Private Gordon Bevan, aged 26, originally hailed from Teddington in Middlesex. *'List of Officers and Men Serving in The First Canadian Contingent of The British Expeditionary Force, 1914',* Pay and Record Office, Canadian Contingent, London.

Chapter 3 Training for War

wash and four for baths. Later they fitted it up with an inside porch and each side of that were alcoves with seats round where one had one's bath in huge tin pans. But when I first went for a bath on December 12th, we had our bath in the open hut and the draught from the frequent opening of the door was rather chilly. While I and some others were sitting in our baths in a state of nature, a sergeant came in shouting, 'Party attention', and [was] followed by Alderson and his staff. We were told to 'carry on'. Alderson seemed very pleased to find so many there.

On the 14th, we were given cots. These consisted of three flanks and two stools six inches high to support them. Many of the men did not use them but I used mine as it was better than the bare floor. We had had no straw mattresses since leaving West Down South. From this date till January 11th, we did no parades but only fatigues; making roads, railways etc.

All soldiers and sailors were given free railway transportation on their Christmas leave in 1914. Our leaves were arranged over a period of about three weeks. A percentage went every three days and one party overlapped the next. They arranged as far as possible that those with homes in England should get Xmas Day and those in Scotland New Year's Day. I got mine on December 23rd.

We left the camp at 12.30 and marched to Amesbury station. There was a long pause there and we finally got our passes and tickets at 2.15. Soon after a train came and some of us fought our way in and got to Salisbury. I wanted to catch the 6.10 at Euston to Daventry. I got into a train, found it was a slow one and was told to change at Basingstoke. We got out there and waited. A train came in and we fought our way into that and when it had started found it was the same one we had been in before.

It stopped and stopped, a most horrible journey. It was an hour between Vauxhall and Waterloo and I finally got to Euston at 8.30, too late even for the last train to Aspley. I put up at the Euston Hotel. I started at 7.10 a.m. next day. Spent the day with the Wethereds at Staverton and went on to Aspley Guise in the evening. I left on December 28th at 5 p.m. and caught a special at Waterloo getting to camp at 2.30 a.m.'

Staverton was the home of Kenneth's elder sister Ada, her husband Edmund and their four children, and Edmund was the local vicar. Kenneth continues:

'On New Year's Eve, there was no 'lights out' and at midnight a band paraded the huts with tin cans mouth organs etc. We had a holiday next day. On January 5th, I made my first attempts at seeing the dentist as I had toothache. After many failures, I saw him at last on the 12th. The pain had stopped then and he said they would do. I had it now and then at the Front and in Germany but did not get them properly attended to till I got to Switzerland.'

We will discover more about Kenneth's expedition through Western Europe that occasioned the above dental regime, as his story unfolds. He resumes:

'On January 6th, Major Byng-Hall gave the first of several lectures. He spent his time on leave pumping returned officers as to conditions at the front and gave us the benefit of it. The lectures were voluntary and quite informal and were held in the evenings, I went to them all. On January 7th, I was picket on a hut which had just been quarantined for cerebrospinal meningitis. I think there was only one case and he got over it. On January 9th, they gave us straw for mattresses and after that we slept in luxury.

The shooting accommodation on Salisbury Plain was

Chapter 3 Training for War

very inadequate at that time. They were making more ranges as fast as they could but there were so many troops in training one could not always get an innings. It was a pity as it was the rapid fire and straight shooting of the Regulars that saved the situation during the first months of the war. Incidentally I might say that this excellence in shooting was due to the fact that each man's rate of pay depended on what sort of shot he was. This shooting for pay was started I believe by Haldane and whatever else he may have done that should be remembered in his favour.'

Lord Haldane had been Minister of War from 1905 to 1912. His reform of the British Army, including the creation of the Territorial Army, is widely believed to have enabled the efficient mobilisation of the BEF and the Territorial Force in 1914. Kenneth now continues his description of the Canadians' training regime:

'Our first innings on the ranges was on November 13th when we were there all day and only fired 10 rounds per man. We had to go whenever we could and on Sunday December 17th we spent a long day there and got a lot done.

The Imperial Army was arranged on what is known as the Platoon System, a comparatively new arrangement or rather a reversion to an older one. The Canadians were on the old single Company System. In the Platoon System, each battalion consists of four companies each with two captains. Each company has four platoons each under a lieutenant and each platoon has four sections each under a sergeant or corporal. There are besides a company sergeant major and company quartermaster sergeant to each company, and a platoon sergeant to each platoon. Under the old system each battalion has six companies each under a captain, each company has four sections each under a sergeant and each section two squads under corporals. Each company has also a colour sergeant, who unites the duties of discipline pay and stores for the company.

We had started to learn the platoon drill on October 26th, but after a few days it was dropped again. Now on January 19th we took it up for good. Our F Company was united with H Company, the two being under H Company's Commander Captain Haines with our Captain Harvey Second-in-Command. I was in 11 Section, 15 Platoon, No. 4 Company. The companies and platoons were numbered through the battalion and the sections through the companies.

We were very pleased with our new comrades. H Company came mostly from New Westminster and were an exceptionally nice lot of chaps and Captain Haines was a very nice sensible man. On that first day, he left his men and came over and talked to us, and though of course he always knew his old men best we all liked what we knew of him.'

The Canadian battalions were some 1,000 strong, of whom about 30 were officers. The battalion was normally commanded by a lieutenant colonel, with a major as second-in-command. A captain or lieutenant filled the role of adjutant (in charge of administration) and a captain or lieutenant was the quartermaster; responsible for stores and transport. The battalion included a medical officer and a chaplain. Headquarters also included the regimental sergeant major, the most senior non-commissioned officer, plus several specialists. Each of the four companies contained about 220 men.

Captain Leslie Haines [and his men] derived from the 104th (New Westminster) Fusiliers.[46] He was a real estate developer, owned a liquor store in New Westminster on Columbia Street in Vancouver, and had been in South Africa in the ranks. Although he was on the youngish side, his hair had gone prematurely grey and he was considered to be quite a combat veteran. He was a

---

46   Records of The British Columbia Regiment.

Chapter 3 Training for War

very highly respected officer, sombre and serious rather than high-spirited, which boded well for the battalion's future endeavours.[47] Indeed, Captain Haines was promoted to major in September 1915 and served throughout the war, winning a DSO in 1916.[48] Kenneth resumes:

'All this time, men had been leaving us and getting commissions in Kitchener's New Army. I was asked indirectly if I would like a commission and said, 'No', I did not think I knew enough to be an officer, to make a good private was the most I hoped for. But a lot of men did get them and some of them were no good at all. Some however were our best men. We kept our officers, though some like Byng-Hall and Haines were ex-army officers, but we lost our F Company Colour Sergeant. He had been an officer in the Indian Native Army and was as good a man as any. While he was with us F Company was the smartest in the battalion.[49]

They used to warn one more man for guard than was wanted, taking one man from each company. The cleanest man 'got the stick' i.e. got let off.[50] Whenever there was a representative of F Company he always got the stick; the others only got a look in when we were unrepresented.

The man who followed him was not much use and the company had gone down. However, we had the H Company Colour Sergeant for Company Sergeant Major. He was

---

47 Ibid.
48 Haines's DSO was recorded in The Gazette (London Gazette), Supplement 29608, Page 5570, 2nd June 1916.
49 In fact, just over 100 men from the 7th Battalion accepted commissions; rather a lot, which indicates a pressing need for officers. Records of The British Columbia Regiment.
50 In the British Army 'The Stick' was a Swagger Stick, a short stick or riding crop, which was awarded to the smartest man on parade. He was often excused duties as a result.

a smart, very nice, quite young man and he kept things going.[51] No. 4 Company, officers and men thought very great shakes of ourselves and though I say it, who should not, I don't think we made at all a bad showing. I was and am very proud of my company as well as my battalion.

Our training had been rather strenuous since we started again, it was said that Kitchener asked Alderson if we were ready to go to the Front. Alderson said, 'No', we had done nothing but fatigues for weeks. 'K' replied, 'Then get them ready as soon as you can'.

On January 20th, we had an especially hard day. We started out at 5.45 a.m. and spent the morning manoeuvring and got back at 1 p.m. Started again at 3 p.m. marched to near West Down South and dug trenches in the dark. Then we sat in them and shivered for two and a half hours waiting to be attacked by the 8th Battalion. When at last they found us we marched home, not the short way over the Plain, impossible in the dark, but round by the roads. We got in at 3 a.m. I was dead tired and during the last few miles had been thinking about having to lay down my bed and expecting it to be the last straw. Imagine my joy when I found it all laid ready along with most others in our hut by a man, who for some reasons, had not gone with us. It was quite a hard day, some 20 miles marching and 20 hours at it. There was no reveille next day and we had a good lie in.

All this time we had had the Oliver Equipment, a horror invented by some Canadian doctor who ought to have known better. Military packs are all inefficient, but this was the worst. There were straps to hold a blanket behind one's shoulder blade and a greatcoat in the small of one's back. A cartridge pouch that dropped what it contained and

---

51   17074 Company Sergeant Major Thomas Hepburn from Chilliwack, British Columbia.

Chapter 3 Training for War

no provision for the pack proper at all. All the weight was where one can carry least and in doubling, the coat behind thumped ones back. Why the military authorities can't go and see and copy proper packs l can't imagine. In the backwoods of Canada and countries like Switzerland where loads are carried long distances on men's backs, much the same type of pack board has been evolved which hangs and distributes the weight as is best fitted for the human frame. Why can't soldiers have the same?

Bad though the best is, there can be no doubt that the regular [British] web equipment as used in this war is heavenly after the diabolical Oliver and when on January 27th it was issued to us, we were filled with delight. That night a man came to our hut and said would we like to see a procession. We said, 'Yes', and it entered. Headed by a mouth organ playing a dead march came two men with a bed plank on their shoulders and on it the Oliver Equipment, behind came another man with reversed arms. They solemnly went round our hut and then went on to the next.

We had been trying to get a regimental band and the proceeds of the regimental canteen at Valcartier were to go towards it. The other officers wanted a brass band, but the Colonel insisted on drums and fifes. So, the matter rested for some time and then the Colonel got his way and the band started. On January 30th, our company coming home from parade met the band out for practise and were the first to march home to it. After that it went on marches with us and we had it on church parade. We took it to France with us but after we landed we did not see it again.'

The time for training was nearly at an end and the Canadians started to anticipate their next move, to the Western Front. Kenneth tells us how the pace quickened:

'The time was now fast drawing near for our departure. The division as it left for the front consisted in infantry (I know nothing about the other arms), of three brigades. The 1st, 2nd, 3rd and 4th Battalions were in the 1st Brigade. The 5th, 7th, 8th and 10th in the 2nd Brigade and the 13th, 14th, 15th and 16th in the 3rd Brigade. The 6th had been turned into cavalry. The Fort Garry Horse and the others were left as reserves.[52] Though each battalion had a large base company, some of the men in it were not fit to go and we for one had to fill up from outside.

They drafted men from the 11th from Saskatchewan into our battalion. This I think was rather silly as they were the first non-British Columbia element in it and men from British Columbia had just come from Canada. They had asked for volunteers in the 88th as reinforcements to the 'Princess Pats'[53]. There had been such a rush that they drew lots and the lucky ones were said to have refused 40 dollars for their chances. When they got to England they found the Princess Pats had been reinforced from the contingent and that they were to go to the 16th, a kilted battalion. They were very disgusted, they wanted to come in with us and they did not want to wear the kilt. Now why could not the British Columbia men have reinforced us and let the others go to the 16th?'

The soldiers who went from the 88th to the 16th (Canadian Scottish) Battalion did not fare well. Almost all of them became casualties during a night attack on Kitchener's Wood during the 2nd Battle of Ypres in April 1915. Perhaps less than a dozen

---

52 The 34th Fort Garry Horse was a Canadian cavalry unit. At Valcartier, it was converted into the 6th Infantry Battalion and went to Salisbury Plain in that mode. However, it was then determined that the regiment would form a Canadian Cavalry Depot in the UK and thereafter, it departed for Canterbury to do so.
53 The Princess Patricia's Canadian Light Infantry.

remained with the battalion after the battle and most of those became casualties by the end of 1915.[54] Kenneth goes on:

> 'There were four kilted battalions. One, the 17th [The 17th Battalion (Nova Scotia Highlanders)], was left behind, the other three were all in the 3rd Brigade.[55] The Princess Patricia's Light Infantry were a special lot and did not belong properly to our contingent. They were mostly old soldiers and the Canadian Government wanted to send them on as a first instalment. They embarked at Montreal, while we were crossing Canada in the train, and had a great send off. But when they got to Quebec a cable arrived from Kitchener which ran, so the story goes, 'Don't be a fool wait for the escort'. So, they had to land again and come across with us. They went to the Front sometime in the autumn.'

As Kenneth has indicated, the Princess Patricia's Canadian Light Infantry was composed of former British regulars and Canadian veterans of the South Africa War. These experienced soldiers did not join the 1st Canadian Division, but landed in France with the British 27th Division in December 1914 and were involved in the 2nd Battle of Ypres thereafter.[56] Kenneth rounds off his sojourn on Salisbury Plain:

> 'On February 4th, we were inspected by the King. The inspection was held away out on the Plain and he came all the way by rail. At Amesbury, he changed to an old carriage with a small engine and came over the light railway that stretched some five miles across the Plain. At the saluting base was a small platform and we all marched past eight deep to the massed bands of the contingent. Afterwards we lined the railway and cheered him as he left.

---

54 Records of The British Columbia Regiment.
55 Along with some other Canadian units, the 17th Battalion was left behind in England to provide reinforcements for Canadian units in the field.
56 Derived from: Cassar op. cit., Page 27.

On February 5th, we were given 120 rounds each and next day it was made up to the full 150 rounds. All was now ready for departure.'

In light of Canada's lack of a coherent military force in mid-1914, and given the acute problems of time, space, organisation, equipment and weather, the mobilisation and training of the 1st Canadian Division in a few months in 1914 was an astonishing achievement. It had created a competent force of disciplined men. But they were, as yet, untried in battle.

So now it was off to war.

Chapter 4
To the Front

By the end of 1914, the Great War had reached the stalemate that characterised the next four years of military turmoil in Western Europe. It must be remembered that the Germans also had a substantial commitment on their Eastern Front, where they were fighting the armies of Russia, and this front, initially at least, took the preponderance of German resources.

Nevertheless, on 4th August 1914, some 1.5 million German soldiers under Helmuth von Moltke invaded Belgium and France in accordance with an operation known as The Schlieffen Plan. This had been developed in secret over a number of years and involved the manoeuvre of seven armies. Armies 1 to 5 advanced through neutral Belgium and then swung south into France, whilst Armies 6 and 7 attacked the French border.

The small BEF, consisting of the seven immediately available Regular Army divisions and led by Field Marshal Sir John French, was stationed around the town of Mons in Belgium. After engaging the advancing German infantry, the BEF conducted a lengthy, gruelling fighting withdrawal from Mons to positions east of Paris on the River Marne, the French Army likewise drew back. Having dislodged the defending French and British armies, the German forces swung southwest in an attempt to envelop Paris. They came within 40 miles of their objective, but the plan was not rigidly adhered to, due partly to the Germans' exhaustion and the inability of logistics to keep up with the momentum. On advancing to the east, rather than the west of Paris which was the plan, the Germans exposed their right flank.

The French Army, under its Commander-in-Chief General Joffre, seized the moment, emerged from the Paris area and, with the aid of the BEF, struck the exhausted Germans along the Marne River, forcing them to withdraw and then dig defensive positions behind the Aisne. The Allies prepared their defences opposite and both sides extended their positions to the English Channel; the 'Race to the Sea'. These initial positions became the immense lines of trenches which ran from Nieuwpoort on the Belgian coast to the Swiss border. They altered only by a few miles as each side made successive attacks during the next three years, until the Allied breakthrough of 1918 which led to the Armistice.

The opposing lines became substantial pieces of engineering, with deep trenches, fortified dugouts, concrete bunkers and the incorporation of extant French defensive forts. 'The trench system usually consisted of three parallel lines, the front, support and reserve, all protected by thick belts of barbed-wire. The lines were not straight but zigzagged at right angles to minimize the effect of shell blasts and enfilading fire and were entered from winding communication trenches. In between the opposing front line trenches lay 'No Man's Land', a strip of desolation filled with shell holes, tree stumps, corpses, and the general debris of constant fighting.'[57]

As Kenneth will explain later on, the actual state of trenches depended very much on the time and effort put into them and who had been occupying them. On moving anywhere away from the existing lines, units and formations hastily dug shallow earthworks to protect themselves from the inevitable counter-attack and barrages that would follow.

The trenches were frequently shelled by the increasingly heavier artillery available to both sides and, before an attack, immense barrages that might last a week pounded the occupants. In

---

57   Cassar op. cit., Page 55.

Chapter 4 To the Front

this uncompromising climate, and seeing no practical alternative, commanders attempted sizeable frontal assaults. Preceded by pulverising artillery bombardment, waves of infantry crossed No Man's Land in thick formations into the teeth of overwhelming machine gun fire. The bulk of these attacks ended in massive casualties. But they painfully built up an understanding of, then an ability to exploit this new form of warfare that had become dominated by weapons technology.

Between December 1914 and January 1915, the BEF had conducted some limited, largely unsuccessful assaults on the German positions. In February, there were no major actions as both sides manned their lines in the miserable, cold, wet mud that characterised the battlefields. The British sector was now in the northern part of the Allied front, between the Somme Valley in the south and stretching into Belgium, and British forces were sufficiently strong to be split into two armies. General Smith-Dorrien's 2nd Army's sector lay to the north and encompassed the ancient Belgian town of Ypres. The Allies held the city and the surrounding Ypres Salient, some seven miles wide, that protruded eastwards from the town for about five miles. The Germans eyed this somewhat vulnerable dispersion and it was known that they were planning to attack it.

Kenneth's now explains how the Canadian 1st Division travelled towards the beckoning maelstrom, specifically his 7th Battalion that now mustered 1,026 officers and men:

> 'We left Lark Hill at midnight on February 9th. The right-half battalion had left some hours sooner. We marched to Amesbury and entrained. We asked the station people where we were going, and they said they thought Southampton, but when it got light next morning we found ourselves at Avonmouth near Bristol.
>
> We went on board the *Cardiganshire* and soon after, we started. The *Cardiganshire* was an old cattle boat and we

were lodged below in the cattle stalls and it was far from comfortable. We were very crowded and there was hardly room to stretch one's legs at night. We were fed throughout the voyage on bully and 'hard tack' biscuits and were given tea at meal times, the tea being the only cooking that was done. Every day we drew rations. One of the hatches was left partly off and a man carrying a heavy case of biscuits stumbled and fell down the hold and broke his hip. They had an awful job getting him up, poor chap. After that the hatches were closed. It was great carelessness leaving it open and our Platoon Sergeant had complained of it before the accident happened.

On the voyage, they gave us our first issues of rum and on that subject, I want to say a few words. We heard that there had been an agitation at home and in Canada about the rum. I don't know if it was true, but I quite believe that the health of the Army in France largely depended on its rum. Quite apart from the stenches inseparable from trench warfare, it must have been awful in the hot weather, there was nothing that so enlivened us or to which we so looked forward as the rum. After a cold wet night on sentry go in the trench, the rum in the morning seemed to give us a fresh lease of life, it stopped the shivers as nothing else could and made us cheerful once more. And it was good rum, I doubt if one could get such good rum in civil life. It used to take my breath away, we drank it neat, but after that it made us feel good all over. At first each man was made to drink his tot on the boat, about two spoonfuls, then and there so that if he didn't want it he wouldn't draw it and give it to someone else. In the trenches, they got to know the teetotallers and divided it out between the majority of us who knew what was good.

We had 'parades' on the voyage, mostly inspections

Chapter 4 To the Front

and roll calls, there was no room for anything else, and on February 12th we reached the mouth of the Loire. We were just in time, it had been calm all the way even in the dreaded Bay [of Biscay] but no sooner were we safely in the Loire than a storm came up and some of the 3rd Brigade got it pretty bad.

I think the storm kept us from landing as the harbour was hard to enter, however that may be, it was not until the 14th that we entered the harbour of St. Nazaire and docked. We landed in the evening but soon after were sent on board again. They landed the stores and some horses there were on the boat and they dished us out with goatskin coats, scarves and mitts. We rather laughed at this, but we were very glad of them later.'[58]

Behind the scenes, calculated decisions were being made that were to influence the fortunes of Kenneth and his comrades. It was determined that the Canadian Division was to reinforce the 1st Army to the north of the British front line. Kenneth describes his passage eastwards:

'We landed finally at 3 a.m. on the 15th and marched to the station and entrained. We were put into box cars bearing the inscription '40 men or 8 horses'. There were 36 in our car and it was an awful squash. We started at 8 a.m. It was not so bad during the day, but night was an abomination. The first night we lay anyhow and most of us couldn't stretch our legs and some couldn't even lie down at all. Next night the Sergeant made every man lie with his head to the side with the result that all were equally squashed, but all could lie down full length.

Our first big stop on the first day was at Nantes and

---

58   An interesting comment as many men did not like the coats. They became foul-smelling when wet.

we were all on the lookout for grub. I came on some men interviewing two French women. They had made them understand bread, but butter beat them altogether and they appealed to me. I told the women, *'Du beurre'* and they were filled with delight. I told them how much to get including some for myself and when we at last got our money changed one of them started off. Just then they shouted, 'All aboard.' I hung around to the last minute and then went up the train to my car. Just as the train was starting the woman turned up breathless and shoved bread, butter and money into our hands. We lived well after that and we gave our biscuits to the kids along the line. We evidently were not the first to do so as they used to shout, 'Souvenir biscuits' at us.

At intervals during the day they gave us each day tea and sugar and we got 'hot' water at certain stations. The Frenchman's idea of hot water is something rather too cold to shave in and it was a horrible drink we had. Only once I think was it anywhere near boiling.'

Eventually, the 7th Battalion detrained in Northern France:

'On February 17th, we reached Strazeele [a village about five miles east of Hazebrouck and seven miles west of the Belgian frontier] and marched to billets in a farm, being rather crowded in a straw barn. Strazeele had been at one time in the hands of the Germans during the sag in the French Lines before the First Battle of Ypres [19th October to 22nd November 1914]. They told us they had been driven back by the English. They had not done anything desperate, not having had time, but the farmer's wife and daughter spent three days in their cellar. Now they were well back of the lines and one could only just hear the guns. They were very good to us and we bought coffee and eggs galore, the straw barn was too crowded and we had to wash in a muddy ditch, but it wasn't bad on the whole.

Chapter 4 To the Front

It was here that the first of us got lousy. One man was found to be crawling and as he was not over clean he was banished, the men declaring the lice were stamped 'BC'. Then one of the cleanest men of the lot found some on him so we gave ourselves up to the inevitable. There had been occasional cases at West Down South which had been dealt with at once, barring that we had been 'clean' up to this. We all knew we were bound to get them and all the billets in France were alive with them, I suppose I am not partial to vermin, fleas rarely bother me, anyhow it was a long time before I got any.

Major Byng-Hall was, as I have said, the Junior Major of the battalion. The duty of the Junior Major is to stop at home. This didn't suit 'Byng' at all, so when we left he resigned and took command of our company, Captain Haines being Second-in-Command, and Captain Harvey going as Second-in-Command of No. 3 Company. The Major was sent on to France in advance of us and met us at Strazeele, but we did not see much of him till we got to Ploegsteert. There were two other majors in command of companies, Major [Guy] Moberley[59] of No. 1 and Major [Percy] Rigby of No. 2.'

No. 4 Company's platoon commanders were Lieutenants Carleton Holmes, Henry Macdowall, Geoffrey Hornby and Orlando Brothers.[60] No. 3 Company was commanded by Captain Richard Cooper.[61] Kenneth describes his Company Commander:

---

59 Born in India, Guy Moberley was a 45-year-old contractor from Armstrong, BC.
60 Holmes, from Victoria, was killed on 24th April and Vancouverite Hornby on 24th May 1915. It seems that Brothers, originally from Leeds, survived the war. Henry Macdowall, also from Victoria and from a distinguished Scottish lineage, had been educated at University School, Victoria, British Columbia, where Captain Harvey had been the Warden, and became a lawyer. Macdowall was taken prisoner on 24th April 1915 during the battle of St. Julien, eventually being transferred from Germany to internment in neutral Holland and then repatriated. He re-entered the legal profession and became a solicitor.
61 Irishman Cooper survived the war. He became a Unionist politician,

'Major Byng-Hall had been in the Regular Army and had the DSO for the Boxer Rising in China [1900]. He had been a real Estate Agent in Victoria and like most real estate agents, stories were told of him. But we thought that whatever he was or had been in private life was not our concern at all, all that mattered to us was his ability as a soldier and of that there could be no doubt. His chief characteristic was his care for his men, he had always been noted for it. He was, we found, sinfully proud of his company and if we did not get not only [what] all the others got, but what he thought we ought to get, he was up in arms. At home, he had generally overruled the Colonel and Senior Major Odlum and had as a rule run the battalion, and so now he generally got what he wanted.'

Major Victor Odlum was 43 and an interesting character. A newspaper editor, being known for some extreme political views, he was an ex-Regular officer and had fought in South Africa with The Royal Canadian Regiment. One of his best friends described him as being, 'unable to open his own jaw once he decided to keep it closed', so seemingly he was a somewhat stubborn individual and his men either liked or hated him. He ended the Great War as a brigadier general. During the next war, he was first appointed as a divisional commander, but was found to be too rusty for the job and he became a diplomat. Both his brother and cousin also served in the 7th Battalion. Kenneth continues:

'On a march, he [Byng-Hall] marched himself every foot of the way, his horse trailed behind with someone with sore feet or his batman on its back. He used to say that though he carried no rifle he carried a pack and a heavy one (his batman told us he used to put all the heavy things in the Major's pack and the light into his own) and while he could march, his men could and when he couldn't, he would halt his company.

---

representing Vancouver South from 1917 to 1921.

Chapter 4 To the Front

He used to drop down the ranks on the march, getting into blank files and chatting with the men and then getting to the front again at the halts. He had always been the most get-at-able of all the officers. In the trenches, he would wander down the trench and sit down and talk, tell us what was going on, fetch us maps etc.

Once I remember I was sitting in the trench talking to another man. The Major came along and sat down. We were going out that night, and the Major said, 'I am going to spend the next three days kicking, I am going to kick about a lot of things and one of them is that I think the heroes in the trenches ought to get the papers'. Sure enough, soon after that we did get papers issued to us. He told us he had been kicking about something on the telephone, and the Adjutant said, 'Why is it No. 4 is always complaining, I don't get complaints from the other companies?' The Major promptly rang up Major Moberley and said, 'If you have any respect for me make a kick, I don't care what it is about, but kick. Gardner says I am the only one who makes complaints so make one at once.'

It was the same in billets, he would come wandering around with the eternal pipe in his mouth, and talk to the men, generally the Victoria men who he knew and remembered best. Just before our final smash, he told us he was convinced the Germans would try to invade England. He said he knew the Germans, he has been six years in Germany and had them under him in China, and he was convinced that when they saw it was all up they would do all they could to land a force in England to burn and harry. He did not think they would get there, but if they did, he said, he would be sorry for the Germans as he didn't believe we would leave one German man alive in Germany.'

After a reasonably agreeable stay in France, the 7th Battalion trudged eastwards and crossed the Belgian border:

'On February 20th, we were inspected by General French [Commander-in-Chief BEF], and on the 21st we marched to Ploegsteert in Belgium. Our officers at that time had not had experience of the French roads and they chose those marked first class. These in France are all that wretched *pavé*. A *pavé* road consists of granite setts [blocks] in the centre and mud at the sides of the road and is about the worst for marching on imaginable. Ever after that they chose second class roads which are macadamised. Besides this we were the last company and we had not got Byng with us, and so we suffered most. They made us close up at the halts so that sometimes we got [no rest] at all.

In marching, there is supposed to be a five-minute halt every half hour, at one of these halts we had just come to a stop, had jumped a stream and laid down on the grass, when the whistle went to fall in again and we had to go on another hour. After this every man halted where he was when the whistle blew. Altogether, it was by far the worst march we had. Captain Haines said he had done 30-mile marches in sand in Egypt, but this was worse than that. Men were falling out all the way. Some threw away their goatskin coats, then word came that any man doing that would be fined 25 dollars. So, they went back for them and found the transport had picked them up.

We were quite dead beat as we drew near to Ploegsteert, we met regulars and asked, 'How much farther?' and got the answer, 'Not far', but we had been told it was 'Only another mile' for the last hour. From what I have since heard from men who were in it, I believe that the 'only another mile' dodge was used with great effect in the retreat from Mons.

Chapter 4 To the Front

We got in at last at 5 p.m. and were billeted in a farm and slept in a straw barn. The people were not nearly so high class as those at Strazeele, but quite friendly and kind. The woman stood at the door giving us cups of coffee as we came in and got her reward in the amount of things we bought later. As soon as we had got rid of our equipment, our packs had gone on the transport, and had had five minutes lay down we quite revived and were able to go and get coffee and things at the house.'

Ploegsteert is about three miles north of Armentières and nine miles South of Ypres. Before taking part in active operations, the Canadians were required to be attached to units holding the line in front of Armentières so they could acquire the skills of trench warfare, as Kenneth explains:

'Ploegsteert, or 'Plugstreet' as officers and men all called it, was right close to the firing line and well within artillery fire, and Ploegsteert Church was shelled daily. We were just outside the village and there was another village about a mile on the other side of us.

We had been sent there to learn the game, as was the custom with all new troops. Later when the New Army came out they had officers who had been out before, but we were all new to this trench warfare and had to learn it from regulars who had invented it. On the morning after our arrival an officer of the Hampshires came and gave us a lecture and after him the Hampshire doctor lectured us on sanitation in the trenches.'

The 7th Battalion had good mentors. The experienced 1st Battalion of The Hampshire Regiment belonged to the 11th Brigade in the 4th Division and had fought in many of the fierce battles of 1914. The 7th Battalion War Diary[62] notes that at this

---

62   The National Archives UK, WO 95/3768 - 2 Canadian Infantry Brigade: 7 Canadian Infantry Battalion.

time the weather was dull, foggy and wet. Kenneth describes the drill:

> 'After that we went through the whole business. We did fatigues for the Hampshires, made hurdles of brush wood, corduroy paths [made of planks], barbed-wire stands etc. On the night of the 24th, our platoon went to the rear of the trenches to dig a communication trench. Of all the mud I have ever met, Ploegsteert clay was the worst. It was easy enough to get the spade full, but it stuck to the spade like glue and every ounce one got up had to be scraped off. This is no exaggeration but solid fact. Moreover, the mud was mixed in places with dead Germans in a 'potted meat' condition and the result was not a pleasant odour. At the back of the trenches was Ploegsteert Wood and in it the reserve trenches. A path of corduroy led through this, but one couldn't use it after dark. The road outside was swept by German machine guns and impassable by day but used at night. On this road two nights later one of our lieutenants was killed.[63] Bullets were whistling over us as we worked.
>
> Altogether I suppose it is safe to say that it was on this night that we received our baptism of fire. I had always thought of getting it in open order making an attack, I did not think it would be in digging gluey clay and dead Germans. 'What is it like when you're first under fire?' is a question often asked. One hears from some how frightened they were at first and how they got used to it later. Kipling says:
>
> 'When you're first under fire and wishful to duck,
> Don't look or take heed to the man who is struck,
> Be thankful you're living and trust to your luck.
> And march to your front like a soldier.'[64]

---

63 Lieutenant Herbert Beaumont Boggs of No. 3 Company, who died on 26th February 1915 aged 22. He was the son of Beaumont and Louise Mary Boggs, of the 'Pacific Club', Victoria and is buried in the Ploegsteert Cemetery. Commonwealth War Graves Commission (CWCG) at: www. cwgc.org.
64 Kipling, Rudyard, 'Young British Soldier' in *'Barrack-Room Ballads'*,

Chapter 4 To the Front

Well, I don't think very many of us felt wishful to duck, some did, but it seemed foolish as one doesn't hear a bullet till it is past, and as to taking heed to the man who is struck, we didn't because there wasn't one. I have always said that I personally got my baptism of fire at Sydney while working at the wash plant in the winter. The stock of iron stone of the steel works was just over the fence and when they blasted the frozen heaps, pieces used to come hurling over and strike the bank beside one. I soon got used to it and merely felt annoyed and I found that rifles and shrapnel fire was much about the same.

Our Platoon Commander, Lieutenant Macdowall was in charge of us that night and I think he then for the first time realised his responsibility. He seemed overjoyed when we all got back safe. 'Dowley' had been very unpleasant while crossing the Atlantic but had got tame and wasn't so bad in the end.

On the night of the 26th, our company went into the trenches for 24 hours, mixed officer for officer and man for man with the Hampshires. Everyone had a Hampshire of his own rank to look after him. The Hampshires kept a trench of their own. One company was always at rest billets at Sailly [Sailly-sur-la-Lys, a few miles to the rear] for three days, one in reserve trenches for three days and two went one at a time into the trenches for 24 hours for six days, the one not in the trenches being at the farm nearby. We met them at their farm and were divided up amongst them. We thought we had brought enough with us but we found the Tommies laden with sacks of things. I asked my Tommy what he had got, and he said, 'Grub, you are in for 24 hours you know'.[65]

Methuen, London, 1892.
65 The general appellation 'Tommy Atkins' to describe a soldier was used widely, and somewhat derisively, in the 19th century. Rudyard Kipling describes in 'Tommy', one of his Barrack-Room Ballads of 1892, how the uncaring way in

We marched in and relieved the other company and got our firing positions. It was a beautiful trench, they had worked hard to make it comfortable and it was far superior to that of the York and Lancs beside them.[66] The front and back were lined with sandbags and the floor boarded. Each pair of men had a rifle rack to hold the rifle and keep it dry and at intervals were boxes of bombs. At the back were the bivvys or places to sleep in, covered with corrugated iron and a few inches of earth. The firing positions were raised above the floor of the trench so that those walking past were completely under cover.

It was my first acquaintance with the Tommies, I shall have more to say of them later, and here we first experienced Tommy's kind heartedness. We had brought grub but not really enough, but they heaped things on us and we did excellently. They were they said very proud at having to teach the Canadians.

As our trench routine was largely fashioned on that of the Hampshires, I may as well give it here. Starting with the evening, everyone 'stood to' that is stood by his firing position during all the time of twilight. When it was quite dark the word came down, 'No. 1 up'. At that everyone left the front trench except those detailed for sentry go. These were in pairs No.1 and No.2 and took an hour up in turn throughout the night. The rest were engaged in fatigues, fetching rations, putting out wire etc., on listening post or reconnoitring patrol. Those who had been on day sentry got a bit of sleep. There were about two night sentries to

---

which the soldier was treated in peace time contrasted with the praise lavished on him when he fought for his country. The poem served to modify this attitude.
66   Kenneth is probably mistaken. The 7th Battalion War Diary (The National Archives UK, WO 95/3768) records that the two training regiments were the 'Hampshires' and the 'East Lancashires'. This makes more sense as the 1st East Lancashires were also in the 11th Brigade.

Chapter 4 To the Front

one by day. With us the night sentries did not fire at all. In front of the trench was the listening patrol consisting of two men who lay out there two hours at a stretch. They could communicate with the sentries by pulling a cord.

The reconnoitring patrols did not always go out. When they did they consisted of an NCO and two men and crawled out often to the enemy's barbed-wire to learn what they could. In the morning, everyone stood to during the twilight. Then the rum came round and in full daylight everyone went off to sleep except the day sentries again in pairs who sniped off and on all day. Of course, as the Hampshires changed every night, the men could do without sleep and such things as fetching rations were omitted.

One thing the Tommies remarked at in us was our familiarity with our NCOs, and the way our officers chatted with us. I don't think this was at all subversive discipline and I know it was conducive to better relations between ranks. We all knew each other, and from what I have heard and seen, I don't think they did in the Regulars.

I don't know why it was but during the whole of that 24 hours I hardly stopped shivering once. It certainly was very cold, but I had my goatskin coat on and at Fleurbaix I didn't feel nearly so chilly. When the rum came round in the morning, the Tommies got theirs first, but gave me a spoonful and I got my share of ours after. In the afternoon, I heard there had been another issue and that I, who was the outside man in the platoon, had been overlooked. The Platoon Sergeant said he had some over which he was keeping for a tot at night as he had toothache and would give me some then. A little before we left he came to me with a cup. I couldn't see how much was in it and gulped it down. As I did so he said 'Don't drink it all its for three men', but it was too late, it was gone. I was very sorry and promised him my share when we got to our billets but when we got there, there was no rum for us.

During the morning, our guns had been shelling a German redoubt and smashed it up. We had an aeroplane sailing above their trench observing. The Germans were plugging away at it all the time with their artillery, machine guns and rifles but it took no notice of them. It was a fine sight and one we often saw – one of our aeroplanes sailing calmly about and the cotton wool puffs of smoke from exploding shells round it some of them close and some hopelessly bad shots.

In the afternoon when our guns had finished the Germans replied by shelling us and we had a hot hour or two. But all the result was a few sandbags displaced and one or two men hurt. We heard for the first time the words, 'Stretcher bearers at the double' coming down the trench and saw them rush along in answer.

Messages were always passed from mouth to mouth down the trench and it was wonderful to think that word could go that way all the way from the sea to Switzerland.

At 7 p.m. our reliefs came and we left. When we got to the village we parted from the Hampshires, they were going to billets at Sailly and we returned to our billets.'

Once this period of training and initiation was complete, it was decided that the 1st Canadian Division was capable of taking over a section of the line in the Fleurbaix sector, about four miles southwest of Armentières. The division occupied three brigade sectors and maintained two battalions in the front line at any one time and these battalions occupied the line for four days at a stretch. The sector was relatively quiet, but still prone to sniper activity and there were the inevitable artillery salvos. Kenneth describes the journey:

Chapter 4 To the Front

'On March 1st, we marched to near Fleurbaix. It was a very different one to the last. We went at a leisurely pace. At one point, we had to wait for some time as the Germans were shelling a bridge we had to pass over. We were travelling parallel to the firing line. At about midday we went into a field and waited there for some hours, while other battalions of the brigade passed us. We passed them again further on and then halted and they passed us and so on for the rest of the march. We got to our billets in the end (I think they had a job to find them) in a barn without straw and rather draughty, but we were only there for the night.

Next day General Alderson addressed our battalion. The speech was in the papers as he said the same to the whole division. He told us we were the first division unmixed with Regulars to be trusted with a length of trenches. He said, 'My old regiment, the Royal West Kents, has been here since the beginning of the war and has never lost a trench. The Army says, 'The West Kents never budge'. I am proud of the great record of my old regiment and I think it is a good omen. I now belong to you and you belong to me, and before long the Army will say, 'The Canadians never budge'. These words recurred to me later as I will tell in its place.

That same night March 2nd, we went into the trenches in front of Fleurbaix, which we were to hold from then on.[67] We relieved the Bedfords.[68] As we filed in at one end, they left at the other. No-one was left to show us the trench but the machine gunners. We went on and on down the trench in the dark slipping on the grey boards, falling into mud holes, those with rubber boots on being unable to stand.

---

67   The trenches were at La Boutillerie, about a mile south of Fleurbaix.
68   2nd Bedfordshires in the 21st Brigade of the 7th Division. The Battalion War Diary (The National Archives UK, WO 95/1658/2) states, 'Relieved by 7th Regt. Canadians, 9 P.M., Marched to ESTAIRES, arrived 11 P.M.'

Then we drifted back again and then forward again, and it was some time before we got settled. Then our officers had to explore the trenches behind and all this muddle because the Bedfords didn't wait for us to take over properly. It was as well the Germans didn't attack just then.'

Contrary to Kenneth's comment, on 28th February the Bedford's War Diary records, 'Met officers of 7th & 5th Regiments Canadian Division, showed them round billets. 4 officers (1 per company) came into the trenches with Battn.'[69] Perspective is all. Kenneth now illustrates the widely differing standards of trench condition across the battlefront:

'The trench was a different and much inferior one to the Hampshires. There were two trenches close together. The front one was narrow, clay lined and with a few greasy boards at the bottom and deep holes at the side. Behind was another with the bivvys in. This rear trench ended just where we were, and all traffic had to come down a communication trench into the firing line. There was a continuation, but it was not deep enough. Once when we started to deepen it we found out why when we came on a regular grave yard of dead Germans. One never saw dead English lying around but of Germans there were plenty – we found some in old trenches in Ploegsteert Wood.

Further to our right there was a gap in the front trench between our platoon and the next, owing to the ground being covered by the trenches on each side. Behind this was the Major's headquarters. The German line was 350 yards ahead of us and behind them a hill. Whether this hill prevented them from shelling us I don't know, but they never did. When we shelled them, they shelled Fleurbaix village.

The ground all round there had been fought and re-fought

---
69   Ibid.

Chapter 4 To the Front

over in the First Battle of Ypres, and they said there were 40,000 dead; 25,000 Germans and 15,000 English, buried, half-buried and unburied in front of our brigade area. Our reconnoitring patrols often came across them. One machine gun sergeant was very fond of going and searching their pockets for souvenirs. He was a regular warrior, he drifted from war to war and was in Mexico when this broke out. I think he got killed later. Once they brought in a German rifle and after some trouble we opened the breech. It was quite an attraction and men used to come from other parts of the trench to have a shot with it.

On our left behind the next company was a ruined convent, with a large piece of ground surrounded by a high wall. The side walls were intact, and the rear wall only broken in places and was used by our artillery officers as an observation post, but the front wall was gone and the remains of it formed the parapet of the trench. No 3. Company was kept in reserve all the time we were there. They lived in bivvys behind the convent with the battalion headquarters, there also was our graveyard.

We made a list of improvements to the trench while we were in it. At first the bivvy accommodation was far too small and as we were three days in and three days out one had to sleep so each section in our platoon made its own bivvy and then things were better.

I have given the routine of trench life. We cooked our food on braziers in the back tent. We got so much bully beef that lots of it was wasted. They gave us fresh meat as well, but we did not get the Maconochies, or tinned meat and vegetables, that the Imperials [British] got, except right at the end.[70] I understood that the Imperial Government

---

70 A Maconochie was a tinned mixture, purporting to be beef stew, that consisted of sliced turnips, carrots, and potatoes in a thin gravy.

bought them all up and the Canadian Government couldn't get a look in. At night, the place was more or less lighted up with the star-shells and rockets the Germans sent up, they saved us all bother in that respect.

We were told that the Germans didn't fire if you sang to them. We found this was true and often if we had a large fatigue out or were expecting reliefs, the order came down to sing. I remember one wet cold night when we felt most unlike singing the Major came storming along, 'I ordered you to sing, why aren't you singing?' We tried but it was no use, so then he ordered an issue of rum and that set us going all right.

We used to go for our rations to a deserted farm about half a mile behind the convent, which was as near as the horse transports could come. But there were snipers hidden in deserted farms at a distance from the road and they used to snipe at us. So, after a bit they brought them to the convent in hand carts and we used to carry them from there. They hunted these snipers for a long time and got them at last. They were fully armed with Mausers and German cartridges, they were of course shot. What nationality they were I don't know but they were completely cut off from the German lines, and probably posed as farmers by day.

It was wet and rainy all the first time we were in the trenches and from this came my only attack of sore feet. I had been out after rations and they were dead sore when I got in, and very bad next night when we got to billets, but dry socks and a rest put them all right again.

We were relieved by the 5th [Battalion] on the night of March 5th. Each officer and NCO took the corresponding one round and showed him everything and then we marched out by sections. We were billeted in a straw barn of a farm

Chapter 4 To the Front

between the trenches and the village and very comfortable it was, nice and warm and lots of room. This farm was run by a man who had been court-marshalled twice as a spy, but it could not be proved. While they shelled everywhere else the Germans spared this farm. So our people crowded it with troops and put their artillery around it. There were lots of spies about. The Germans knew all that was going on. We tried to hide our coming, but soon found they knew all about it. The 5th called themselves, 'Western Cavalry' – they had wanted to be cavalry but as they couldn't they went as infantry. Once when they were in the trenches, the Germans put up a wooden horse with a '5' on it.

We spent the day of the 6th in a wash and brush up. One could not wash or shave in the trenches and one's putties got so caked with mud that they had to be cleaned before they could be put on again. One was generally mud from the knees downwards.

We had a bath while we were out at a brewery in Fleurbaix. They had large half-barrels and we had our baths in them. We were let out for an hour or so every day a platoon at a time and got what we wanted in the village.

There were still some of the villagers left in Fleurbaix and a few of the shops were open. These people got quite used to being shelled and retired to their cellars and came up again when it was over. One day I wanted to get some matches. I was stopped in the village by the military police who said shelling was going on. I said I wanted matches and they told me the people of the shop I was going to were in their cellars, but another was open. There, not 100 yards from where the shells were bursting, I found a shop doing a roaring trade.

We went back to the trenches on the night of March 8th.

The next night I was on ration fatigue. I was given a huge sack of meat and a man to help me. He had his equipment on and I hadn't, so I carried the sack and he helped me up with it when I put it down for a rest. Just back of our trench was a brook with a bridge across it. This bridge was made of two battens laid from bank to bank with planks across, but the planks ended at the edge of the banks and not at the end of the battens. Also, it seemed to be on a slope sideways and very greasy and the more care one took in stepping on to it the more one slipped. I always dreaded that bridge. This night with the weight on my back I stumbled in the dark over the end of a batten and rather than fall in myself I let the bag go into the stream. We hauled it out the other end. Sometime later I took a shovel and went to examine the bridge by daylight and found it inches deep in mud. When I had got this off it was all right.'

On 10th March 1915, the British 1st Army made a major assault on the German defences at Neuve Chapelle, some five miles south of Fleurbaix. Originally intended to be part of a combined Allied offensive to take advantage of the growing Allied military strength, the attack turned into an all-British affair. It was proposed to seize the village of Aubers and threaten the German defence of Lille.

The British 1st Army conducted the attack with four divisions of 40,000 men, including the Indian Corps, on a two-mile front. This assault was preceded by a heavy artillery bombardment, well-coordinated attacks created good initial progress and Neuve Chapelle was captured later that morning. Thereafter, the Germans counter-attacked and the British held on but were unable to advance further east to the Aubers Ridge which dominated the area. British losses were about 12,000 and the German Army lost a similar number. The battle was a limited success in that a few miles of territory had been captured and it showed that it was possible to break into prepared defensive positions. But it also

Chapter 4 To the Front

demonstrated that it was not easy thereafter to break through them. Nevertheless, important lessons were learned about the weight of artillery, the employment of reserves and communications. Kenneth describes the Canadian activity at this time:

> 'Our role on that day was to keep the trenches opposite to us full and prevent them sending reinforcements while our artillery bombarded the roads behind. The trenches opposite us were almost empty in the morning but filled soon after we began and stayed full.[71]

We started at stand to with each section in turn of a platoon firing five rounds deliberate, thus four sections per company were firing together. We did not see much to fire at so aimed at the top of their parapet. After some time, the Major came along and said, 'Make them keep their heads down, they have just got Major Rigby'. We made them keep their heads down as well as we could. I did not think they were firing at all but a man whom had been behind told me he could hear the bullets whistling overhead.

We kept it up for about two hours and then the day sentries, of which I was one, kept up heavy sniping all day. At stand to in the evening we gave them five rounds rapid. The result was that during the night at the least sound from our trench the Germans sent up a huge collation of rockets. They evidently expected us. In the evening, we saw a church on a distant hill on fire from our bombardment.

Our casualties were Major Rigby and one private killed. Major Rigby was another old army officer, a South African veteran, and had more medals than anyone else in the battalion. He had settled in the Kootenay district in

---

71 The 7th Battalion War Diary (The National Archives UK, WO 95/3768) for 10th March relates: 'Prepared to assault opposing trenches', which was one possible option during the battle. But clearly nothing came of it.

BC and came at the head of the Kootenay contingent. His men thought a lot of him. He was shot in the chest while directing the fire of his men and died soon after.'

Major Percy George Rigby commanded No. 2 Company. He was aged 43, the son of a major general, and born in London. He had previously been in the 1st Sherwood Foresters and had commanded the 4th King's African Rifles, serving in West and East Africa and during the South African Campaign, and was Mentioned in Despatches twice.[72] Rigby was actually killed by a sniper before the general firing started that day, but it probably took some time for the other companies to hear the news. He was highly respected by the men from Kamloops who numbered about 150 and were referred to as the Kootenay Contingent.

Many stories circulated about how Rigby was killed, but it appears that he was in the habit of swearing at the Germans as he did his rounds. He would colourfully and loudly belittle the Germans which gave his men quite a bit to laugh about. Unfortunately, on one of his rounds a German sniper lay in wait and as he raised himself over the parapet, he was shot in the chest, dying at the bottom of the trench a short time later.[73]

The only other 7th Battalion casualty that day was 29-year-old 17267 Private Anders Oberg whose parents lived in Sweden. Both these fallen are interred in the Rue-David Military Cemetery, Fleurbaix. It is believed that the 7th Battalion lost only five men in March.[74] Kenneth resumes:

> 'In the case of attack and on occasions like this and always at night, all firing was done from above the parapet. For sniping by day, we had loopholes protected by a steel

---

[72] Mentioned in Dispatches (MiD); the individual's name appeared in an official report written by a superior officer and sent to the high command. To earn this distinction, the officer or soldier would have shown 'gallant or meritorious action in the face of the enemy'. In World War 1, this was signified by a small bronze oak-leaf emblem to be worn on the ribbon of the Victory medal.
[73] Records of The British Columbia Regiment.
[74] CWGC op. cit.

Chapter 4 To the Front

plate. We had got three German loopholes spotted and could tell by the shots from which one they came. We found the Germans had got one of ours spotted so shifted it and they never found the new ones but potted at the old place always.

I fired 100 rounds that day being the first I had fired since leaving England. I began using the ammunition I was carrying but my rifle soon jammed, I cleaned it and used the new ammunition in the trench and had no more trouble. One fault of the web equipment is that the end of the cartridge is exposed to dust and dirt and the least dust will cause a jam. I was always cleaning my ammunition but even then, I could hardly trust it. Rifles will often jam from heat, which I suppose is not to be wondered at if you turn an un-cooled rifle into a machine gun as one does in rapid fire carried on to any length of time. We were not so expert in that as the old regulars who could fire always 15 often 20 or more rounds a minute and keep it up.'

As already mentioned during the account of his training experiences at Lark Hill, Kenneth's problems were also due to the design of the Ross rifle. The Canadian-manufactured, .303-inch calibre Ross was accurate and good for target shooting, but it was long, a disadvantage in the close confines of trench warfare, heavy, tended to jam in muddy conditions and during rapid fire, and did not work well with the British ammunition that was provided for it. It thus threatened the effectiveness and indeed the safety of the Canadian troops, and soldiers tended to discard it when they could get their hands on a British Lee Enfield. The 1st Canadian Division replaced the Ross with the British rifle in 1915. Kenneth describes the end of the engagement:

'On March 11th, we were relieved. We were to have gone to Sailly, but an order came for us to go to Fleurbaix village. We went off individually as our reliefs came and met outside our last billets and went on to Fleurbaix and were put up in a butcher's house over his shop. The house was deserted and the man we heard was a prisoner in Germany. It was cleaner in here, but I missed the nice soft straw.

The Major, thinking we were going to Sailly, had bespoken first baths for his company. So next morning before breakfast we had to go to Sailly for them, and we did not bless him. For once he had got us let in. We got no clean clothes either, which he thought we should. On our way through Sailly, unwashed, unshaved, covered with mud, we passed some newly arrived Territorials. 'Have you come from the trenches?' they asked. 'Yes', we said. They gazed at us in awe, I expect we looked war-worn veterans to them.

On the 13th, the Chaplain had Holy Communion in the afternoon to which I went. [75] Next day we returned to the trenches again. Bevan was killed on the 16th as already mentioned. I was working down the trench at the time and heard, 'Stretcher bearers at the double' and passed it on. A bit later I heard who it was.[76] We were relieved again on the 17th and went back to our first billets at the farm. Next day we had to hand in our goatskin coats and I was sorry to lose mine.

I think it was while they were in this time that the following incident happened to the 5th [Battalion]. It was a bright moonlight night and our men both 5th and 10th were out doing up the barbed-wire and could hear the Germans doing the same. The 10th said nothing and were left undisturbed but the 5th shouted insulting remarks across. Whereupon, the Germans retired to their trenches and turned on a machine gun. They didn't get anyone, but work was stopped for that

---

75 Possibly Honorary Captain The Reverend William Barton who was the 7th Battalion's Chaplain. Pay and Record Office op. cit.
76 Private Gordon Bevan is interred in the Rue-David Military Cemetery, Fleurbaix. CWGC op. cit.

Chapter 4 To the Front

night, and we were told that if we wanted to say nasty things to the Germans we must say them in a nice manner.

The Germans and we often left each other in peace to do work of that kind. We always knew what Germans were against us. Prussians blazed away all the time, Bavarians sniped when they saw something to snipe at and the Saxons did not fire at all. The Hampshires told us that once some Saxons opposite them put up a notice, 'You are Saxons, so are we, reserve ammunition for Prussians who are coming in tonight'. We used to signal misses when the sniping was on and so did the Germans [the firing-range practice of holding up a pointer against a bullet hole in a target after a shot so the firer could determine his accuracy].

On March 19th, we had baths and this time we got 'clean' underclothing which we had not had before. Some of what I got was clean, but the rest looked rather black and old. Theoretically we ought to have got them every time we had a bath but as two battalions came per day they were not able to manage it. They could wash the clothes but could not dry them in time, and up till then we had been unlucky.

Soon after this I began to feel and find lice. At first, I blamed the clothes, but I think this was due to the straw. I had lost my waterproof sheet coming from the trenches and just at this time the weather turned cold, so I dug a hollow in the straw to lie in and keep warm and I must have come on a nest of lice, the straw was full of them. I was very lucky so long without. Once I told a man I had none, and he was quite offended. He seemed to think I was casting aspersions on his cleanliness as he had just told me he was lousy.

We were due back in the trenches on March 20th, but orders to stay where we were, to our joy as it had turned out very cold. From that grew a crop of rumours of our going to make an attack. We always longed for that but never got it. On the night of the 21st we had an impromptu concert in the farm yard. Sometimes now, when I hear the songs 'Keep the home fires burning' or 'Mother Macree', I see the scene once again, the shadowy buildings in the dark all-round the square yard with the inevitable dirty pond in the middle and in one corner the group of figures and the candle light shining through the small opening of the barn door. How many there were who sang and listened that night who are now lying dead on the battlefield.

On one occasion while we were in this billet, either during this period or the last, I have not got it in my diary, we were all called out on some alarm from the trenches. It was in the middle of the night and they woke us up and told us to fall in. We did so and waited for a long time. Not an officer was to be seen, but at last they came in altogether from outside the farm – the artillery telephone I expect – and dismissed us.

We returned to the trenches on the 22nd. We found them very much altered and improved. The Canadian Engineers had taken charge of all trench work and did from this on. They had built up our parapet with sandbags and it looked like a fort and they were putting new and better barbed-wire entanglements up in front.

On the night of the 23rd, I was on listening patrol. We had had nice fine weather in billets, but now it was raining hard. It was rather a job getting through the barbed-wire in the dark and when that was accomplished one crossed a brook and lay down in a small hollow, which this night was full of water. The waterproof sheets merely sank to the bottom and the other man and I were soon wet through. In addition to this I had the communication cord which I had to keep in

Chapter 4 To the Front

my hand. The sentry in the trench had got too much of it and I could barely reach it while lying down out there.

We were first on and when we came off I told the Sergeant I thought it was worth a tot of rum. We had an hour or so to do later and when we got back off that, they told us to go to the Major for our rum. He asked if we were finished and on hearing we were, told the Captain to give us some. I could not see how much he gave us but took what I thought and handed it to the other man. He took what he wanted and told me to finish it and I found as much left as I had had before. I got a grand sleep after that. The man next me in the bivvy said it was adding insult to injury to wake him up by getting in and then to smell so strong of rum.

On the night of the 25th, I was on sentry go and for some reason or other I was dead sleepy that night, I was standing on a sandbag at the parapet and I couldn't keep awake. I suddenly found the man who relieved me pounding me and wanting to know if I was on sentry or not. It appeared that I had started snoring in a most horrible fashion. The other man and the Sergeant in charge of the trench, who was there, could not make out what the noise was. They saw me standing there and it was a little time before they found it was me. After that I did not even venture to lean against the parapet, and when my hour was up I had a good 40 minutes sleep and that put me right. The Sergeant thought it a huge joke against me. I had been told of this snoring before, apparently I do it when I am not comfortable. I don't think I do it in bed.'

Having been relieved by the 8th British Division on the 25th and 26th, the Canadians marched to new billets in the village of Estaires, some five miles behind the lines. Whilst there, they rested and undertook training in trench fighting and assault. It seemed as if the Canadians would participate in further operations in the Neuve Chapelle area, but as we will see, plans are prone to change. Kenneth explains what happened to his battalion next:

'On March 26th, we were relieved by the Black Watch, or those of them that were left after Neuve Chapelle.[77] Unlike the Bedfords, we waited until they had got in and had been shown the trench properly. Then we left individually and met in a field some distance back where our packs were taken by the transports and we marched by companies to Estaires. We got there at 11.30 p.m. We were billeted in a house which had been I think a home for old men. Each section got a room to itself. Our first need was water to drink, and some of us were guided to the village pump by a man who knew the way.

Next morning as we were lying in rather late, we got a rude awakening. A German aeroplane came over and dropped two bombs in a field near the town. The first woke us and the second shook out a cracked pane of glass over a man sleeping below, he sat up just in time to avoid it. Some chaps, who were up early and were washing at a pond in the garden, heard the bombs dropping and fled in all directions.

Breakfast was not served that morning, the stores not having arrived, so we went into the town and brought bread and butter and ham. I got bread and butter regularly while we were there. What bread we got at the front was small in quantity and not A.1. [the best quality]. It was all baked I believe, at Boulogne and handled some seven times in transit and the loaves looked as if they had been sat on. So, good fresh bread from a shop was very welcome.

I went on guard later that day and next day when I came off it took me all the morning to scrape the thick mud off my overcoat. Some men had cut theirs quite short. But I wanted

---

77 The 7th Battalion's War Diary (The National Archives UK, WO 95/3768) records this as the 1/5th Black Watch, which was in the 24th Brigade, 8th Division.

Chapter 4 To the Front

my knees covered when sitting down, so I pinned back the ends like a Frenchman as the corners were each about a lb. in weight. This time I did cut four inches off the bottom.

On March 29th, the Colonel inspected our company and was very complimentary over our appearance after five weeks in the trenches in France and Belgium, which sounded very swanky. Later the Major referred to the Colonel's remarks, ending, 'As for me I feel prouder of you every time I go out with you, dismiss'. He didn't often say much about it and got very red when he did.

On March 30th, Nos. 3 and 4 Companies went in the evening to dig trenches behind the lines [at Fauquissart, about four miles south of Estaires and Fleurbaix, and near to Neuve Chapelle]. We assembled in the market square and marched off through the long straggling town. As we went we sang at the top of our voices, 'Here we are again', 'Keep the home fires burning' and 'We're the boys from the West of Canada'. All the inhabitants and troops came to their doors to see us pass. We marched some four miles on the way near the trenches [and] when we got there, we started to dig and dug till 3 a.m.

The Bishop of London came to Estaires about this time. We gathered in front of the Hotel de Ville to hear him, but when he came he had been talking so much he had not much voice left and only gave us a short speech. After he had done we all yelled for Alderson who was there, and we got a speech from him too.'

The Bishop was Arthur Winnington-Ingram who visited on the 29th accompanied by the General Officer Commanding 1st Canadian Division, General Alderson. The Bishop was a controversial character. He was a very vocal supporter of the war effort, seeing it as 'a great crusade to defend the weak against the strong'. He toured several battlefronts, encouraged volunteers, including his own clergy, to enlist and 'freely used language about the German people which verged on xenophobia.'[78]

Again, unknown to Kenneth and his comrades, further strategic decisions were being made. General Joffre wanted to hand over the Ypres Salient to the British to allow offensive operations elsewhere and Field Marshall French agreed. The British 5th Corps, under Lieutenant Sir Herbert Plummer took on this task and only the very northern part of the Salient remained occupied by the French. Plummer would be allocated the Canadian Division to assist him in this new task.

The Canadians were assigned a sector of the Salient, roughly between the road that ran between the two villages of Poelcapelle and St. Julien in the West, where its boundary would be with the 45th Algerian Division, and in the east the hamlet of Gravenstafel about four miles northeast of Ypres and on the extremity of the Ypres Salient, where the Canadian sector abutted the 85th Brigade of the 28th British Division. St. Julien and Gravenstafel are connected by a low ridgeline and the Canadian Division would be holding a frontage of some two and a half miles. Both the 27th and 28th British Divisions had replaced the French on the southern side of the Salient. Meanwhile, activities in Steenvoorde continued:

> 'April 2nd was Good Friday, and they had a Good Friday Service in front of the Hotel de Ville. I don't know who it was who preached but one thing he mentioned struck me as very true. He said that the women had the hardest part to play in war, the mothers, wives and sweethearts. One had told him she could only wait and wait and wait. Apropos of this I will give the story of a man I knew. It is a particularly pathetic one.

---

78 Morris, Jeremy, *'Ingram, Arthur Foley Winnington (1858-1946)'*, Oxford Dictionary of National Biography, Oxford University Press 2004, online edition, January 2011.

Chapter 4 To the Front

His name was Sivell and he was in my section. He had had a hard time of it all his life and had at one time been in the mercantile marine. He had got a little place of his own in Vancouver Island, had got his vegetables etc. in and all fixed up snug for the winter. Then the war broke out and he chucked it all up, came to Victoria and enlisted. He was short-sighted, and the doctor turned him down, but one of the majors of the 88th who knew him got him in. He had a great bother in passing the doctor at Valcartier, as far as we could make out he went on his knees to them and they let him though at last.

When he came to England he met a girl he had known and been sort of engaged to for years. She insisted on being married before he left, and they were married just before Xmas. He told us that she was rich and his life in future would be an easy one. She told him she would have had nothing to do with him if he hadn't joined up. She used to send him all sorts of excellent parcels including periscopes etc.

Always after his marriage we noticed he was absent-minded and preoccupied. In July, another Canadian brought me a letter he had got from Mrs. Sivell, who had met his mother, asking for news of her husband who was missing since April 24th. None of us at Göttingen [where Kenneth later spent some time incarcerated in a German prisoner of war camp, as we shall learn] knew what had become of him so [the Canadian] wrote and told her so. He heard again later, all the news she had got was from an officer who had seen him badly wounded, but she said she hadn't given up hope. There could be no doubt that he was dead. How long I wonder did his poor wife go on hoping against hope?[79]

---

[79] 16936 Private Alfred Gilbert Sivell died on 24th April aged 38. His mother lived in West Norwood, London and his wife Elizabeth in Kensington, London. He has no known grave and is commemorated on the Ypres (Menin Gate)

Keeping The Old Flag Flying

Kenneth Foyster as a young man.
(Private collection. Photo by A. R. Perry, Hastings).

Kenneth Foyster in about 1914. (Private collection).

Chapter 4 To the Front

View of the Bamfield Cable Station from the west.
(The Bamfield Museum and Archive, Bamfield BC).

Keeping The Old Flag Flying

Officers of the 1st British Columbia Regiment, Canadian Expeditionary Force (7th Battalion). (City of Vancouver Archives LP363). Back row (L-R): Lt H.B. Boggs, Lt R.F.E. Buscombe, Lt J.C. Thorn, Lt W.L. Ford, Lt L.G. Hornby, Capt W.H. Edmund-Jenkins, Capt G.H. Gibson, Lt E.D. Bellew, Lt N.A. Jessop, Lt W. Ashton, Capt T. Locke, Lt H.A. Bromley, Lt H.C. Anderson, Lt G.G. Chisholm. Middle row: Capt R.C. Cooper, Capt T.V. Scudamore, Capt R.V. Harvey, Capt L.E. Haines, Capt S.D. Gardner, Maj P. Byng Hall, Lt Col W. Hart-McHarg, Maj G. Moberley, Maj P. Rigby, Capt the Rev. Wm. Barton, Capt F. Byliss, Capt J. MacMillan, Lt A.W. McNally. Front row: Lt H.B. Scharschmidt, Lt A. MacKintosh, Lt C.C. Holmes, Lt W.T. Barton, Lt R.D. Hodgson, Lt O.F. Brothers, Lt G.H. Leslie, Lt R.F. Steeves, Lt T.G. Forshaw, Lt R.P. Latta and Lt H.C.V. Macdowall.

Chapter 4 To the Front

Canadian Overseas Expeditionary Force 1st Battalion, 1st Brigade taken at Valcartier Camp, 1914. (Canadian War Museum CWM 19740416-003).

Victoria troops aboard the SS Princess Sophia,
leaving for Valcartier on 28th August 1914.
(Museum of the 5th (British Columbia) Regiment Royal Canadian Artillery).

Chapter 4 To the Front

General Sir Arthur William Currie, GCMG, KCB - Commander 2nd Canadian Brigade 1914 and 1915. (Canada. Department of National Defence/Library and Archives Canada/PA-001370, 1917).

Lieutenant General Sir Edwin Alfred Hervey Alderson, KCB who commanded the Canadian Expeditionary Force in 1914 and 1915. (Library of Congress, Prints & Photographs Division, Photochrom Collection LC-DIG-ggbain-17903).

Men of B Company, 7th Canadian Battalion at Lark Hill.
(City of Vancouver Archives CVA 802-1).

Chapter 4 To the Front

Members of the 1st Canadian Division on a route march in Amesbury, near Lark Hill, in 1914. They are wearing the Oliver equipment and carrying Ross rifles. (T. L. Fuller).

Keeping The Old Flag Flying

2nd (Canadian) Battalion in reserve at Brielan (Brielen), near St. Julien, Ypres.
Their shallow excavations resemble Kenneth's description of his own trenches
before the Battle of St. Julien.
(Canadian War Museum CWM 19940001-887-1).

Jack, Mr. Richard, The Second Battle of Ypres, 22nd April to 25th May 1915.
(Beaverbrook Collection of War Art, Canadian
War Museum CWM 19710261-0161)

Chapter 4 To the Front

The road on Gravelstafel Ridge along which the wounded Kenneth made his way on 25th April 1915. The modern Boetleer's Farm is in the distance.
(The Author).

Gottingen Camp: general view.
(Städtisches Museum Göttingen).

Keeping The Old Flag Flying

Gottingen Camp: general view with Bismark Tower on the far hill.
(Städtisches Museum Göttingen).

Gottingen Camp: canteen.
(Stadtarchiv Göttingen KGL Nr. 57 Photo 107 Kantine).

Chapter 4 To the Front

Gottingen Camp: vegetable cultivation beside the 'Promenade'.
(Städtisches Museum Göttingen).

Gottingen Camp: a learning class in one of the huts.
(Stadtarchiv Göttingen KGL Nr. 57 Photo 83: School in the camp).

On Easter Day [4th April], there was Holy Communion in the morning in the Hotel de Ville.

While we were at Estaires we had started a Company Band. A platoon sergeant named Wells had got it up. He got up all our concerts etc. and delighted in playing the fool on those occasions. The band consisted of a large biscuit tin for big drum, smaller tins for side drums, a fife, two mouth organs and a concertina. Sergeant Wells was hit in the arm by a machine gun on our big day, got taken prisoner, lost his arm, was exchanged and I hear afterwards toured Canada lecturing. He certainly could talk.'[80]

The next day, the 7th Battalion was on the move eastwards again:

'On Easter Monday April 5th, we marched to Steenvoorde [about seven miles north of Hazebrouck]. The band played part of the way. At first, they put it in the middle of the company and there it could not get the step and the result was horrible. So, our Sergeant complained to the Major and he shifted it to the front where it set its own step and all went well. At Steenvoorde it went with us on all our marches. Its place there was behind the leading platoon and as each platoon led in turns we all had the benefit of it. It got quite good and we were quite proud of it. We used to have concerts with the band in between the songs. Sergeant Wells mounted on a farm cart would give out, 'Number 72 Tipperary'. They had a repertoire of five or six tunes, but he always gave them a good swanky number.

That march to Steenvoorde was not at all a bad one.

Memorial. CWGC op. cit.
80 17079 Lance Sergeant Frederick 'Doc' Wells, who came from Montreal, became quite famous for starting the band. After the war, he wrote a column in the local paper on his experiences at St. Julien, went to Hollywood, became a baseball coach in Santa Clara, California, an actor and comedian. 'Doc' was the first man of the 7th Battalion to be taken on strength, having beaten everyone else to the Drill Hall that morning. Records of The British Columbia Regiment.

Chapter 4 To the Front

We rested some time at midday, passed through Strazeele once more, and arrived at 3 p.m. some hours before we were expected. We were put up in a farm and my platoon was billeted in a straw barn over the stables. It was a long narrow building entered by an ordinary ladder up or down which only one could go at a time.

We had a regular routine at Steenvoorde. Early morning exercise, generally a run, parades 9.30 a.m. 12 [noon], 2 p.m. and 4 p.m. The parades were sometimes routine marches, sometimes drill. While here they started giving us soup last thing at night. The Belgian frontier was about two miles beyond our billets.

While at Estaires and again here we had several football matches. At Estaires we were limited to a certain portion of the town. The football ground being outside this we used to fall in and march there and back. We did the same when we got our baths there. At Steenvoorde we played in some fields close to our billets.

On April 8th, Alderson inspected our battalion. He told us that we had been kept at Estaires in order to take part in the attack that had been cancelled and now we were going to the trenches again.

On 10th, we had a platoon competition. This arose over an argument between the officers. Each lieutenant declared his platoon was the best, so the Major said they should have a competition and he would get the Colonel to decide. So that afternoon each platoon was put through its drill before the Colonel and inspected by him. No. 16 had no officer, they had come to the front without one, so that the Transport Officer could be included. So, Captain Haines took it over for this occasion.

Our platoon lost a lot of marks by having our pack straps

over the shoulder straps of our jackets. We always wore them that way on the march as then one can easily throw the pack off, but the other looks better and we would have worn them under if we had thought of it as the others had. However, we made up for it in drill and the result was that all four were equal. So, the Colonel inspected our emergency rations – one tin bully beef and five biscuits which we were always supposed to carry, and we won that.

Next day April 11th, the brigade was inspected by General Smith-Dorrien. The inspection took place in a field just outside our billets. When it was over he spoke to the officers and sergeants, and his remarks were relayed to us by the Major. He said that all the time we had been at the front he had had Imperial officers spying on us, both while with the Hampshires under his command and while at Fleurbaix under Sir Douglas Haig. He had always hoped to get us back again. He said the reports he had received had spoken well of our conduct and steadiness, 'And that is not hot air', said the major, 'I know my company is steady. Often at night I have heard a burst of firing and come out of my bivvy only to find the sentries perfectly unconcerned, and if that is not steadiness then I don't know what is'. Smith-Dorrien went on to say that now he was going to do what he had done before and send the best troops available to the worst place. Where we were going the Germans were much more truculent than at Fleurbaix and the line harder to hold.

We had baths next day, they were the best we had yet struck – a regular bath house with shower baths and we much enjoyed them.'

The Canadian Division was now nearing the Ypres Salient and the site of its first substantial engagement with the enemy, as Kenneth now narrates:

Chapter 4 To the Front

'On April 14th, we left Steenvoorde for the trenches [an advance party had left on the 12th to inspect the new positions]. We went a battalion at a time on motor buses to Vlammertinghe. It was curious to see the long line of London motor buses going along with their windows boarded up and some of the old advertisements still showing. I was on top of one and we sang most of the way. We stayed some hours in a barn and then started to march. We passed through Ypres without a halt. We went through the square and saw the ruined Cathedral and Cloth Hall – then only bare walls. With our company went the band, Sergeant Wells in front waving a painted stick and the small boys of Ypres following him. Ypres was full of troops and there was a grin on all their faces as our band passed.

We had some six miles to go beyond Ypres and we took it easy so as to get there by dark. When we left the road, our half-company got out of touch with the rest and lost the way. So, we sat down and waited for someone to find us. While we were there our Sergeant Major had his water-bottle struck by a bullet, which spilt the spare rum he was carrying. We got to the trenches in the end at 11.30 and relieved the French.'[81]

In fact, the 7th Battalion had arrived at the area of the Gravenstafel Ridge. To the northeast and just beyond lay the German Army.

'At midnight, half the company and I with them went back for rations and ammunition. A Frenchman guided us back the two miles to get them, they had not arrived, so he took one of our men back to the trenches to show him the way. The transports arrived while they were gone so we

---

81 The 3rd Battalion of the French 26th Regiment in the 11th Division, according to the 7th Battalion's War Diary (The National Archives UK, WO 95/3768).

started down the first part which was straight and easy and met them. The Frenchman left us, and our chap began to guide us back. The way the Frenchman had come was very crooked and complicated, more so than it needed have been, and we began to think we were going wrong.

We crossed a brook none of us remembered (I found out later it ended a few yards to the right of us) and our guide on being asked again and again if he was sure he was right, began at last to doubt it and said he would go on and find out. So, we waited there a long time. At Fleurbaix one could see the direction of the trenches by the star shells, but here there were star shells all around the horizon as the Ypres Salient was like a horseshoe. At last we got tired of waiting and some of us set out on our own and got to one of the other company's lines. Here they directed us to our own and we got in at 4 a.m. and daylight, quite tired out.

It was not a very nice job there as there were gaps in the line and if one struck one of them you walked into the Germans. I did not go on rations again but another night the party got lost again in the pitch dark. The Ypres Salient was, as I have said, in the shape of a horseshoe and roughly six miles each way, the whole of it could be shelled by the Germans and here for some reason their aeroplanes had command of the air, ours had at Fleurbaix.

The trenches the French had left us were not up to much. They consisted of a bank in front only, nothing behind at all to protect one from bursting shells and no traverses – just a straight line. Where we were the trench was set back a bit for a length of some 200 yards and a slight rise in front hid the Germans from us. Under the front bank were the bivvys – rather good ones – that held four men each and one had to crawl into them and worm oneself into position. The French were most insanitary in their arrangements, really quite

Chapter 4 To the Front

filthy – among other things they had buried a man right in the trench at one place and he was not buried at all too deep.

I was dead tired that next morning and got into a bivvy to sleep, but some of our chaps were wandering about as we used to at Fleurbaix. The French had told us they had never been shelled. Anyhow we found a German observation post could look right down our trench and they soon gave us a sharp dose of shrapnel. In a very short time we had more casualties than all the time we were at Fleurbaix, though all wounded.

One man had a lucky escape, he was lying with his pack for a pillow and had just got up to seek shelter when a shell burst beside him. It riddled his pack and turned its contents into pulp, exploded half the ammunition he was carrying, bent his bayonet, tore the heel off one of his boots and only wounded him in the leg. Our Platoon Sergeant got one in the leg. It was not bad at first, but he walked to headquarters to report, grumbling all the way, but that night he had stiffened, and he had to be carried out.

After this there were strict orders that only section commanders were to be out by day and they had to bring food to the others. Those in my bivvy were glad enough to lie in and sleep though it seemed a shame in such glorious fine weather. Our Section Commander called us his bears and said we hibernated beautifully.

On the night of the 16th, I was on listening patrol, with by the way Sivell, we both heard and reported a lot of rumbling as of wheeled traffic behind the German lines, preparations I suppose for the attack a week later.'

The next day, the 17th, the British 5th Division launched a significant attack on the southern side of the Ypres Salient to capture Hill 60, a piece of elevated ground formed from excavations to make a railway line. Whilst of only limited elevation, the hill gave its occupier good all-round observation and was thus an attractive acquisition. Meanwhile, the Canadians continued their preparation:

> 'On the next night, I was on fatigue. The engineers were at work now every night building traverses with sandbags to prevent the Germans from infiltrating our trench as they did the first day. It was grisly work as the ground seemed to be paved with dead Germans. One night, our Lieutenant came away saying he could not stand the stench. Another night they dismantled a bivvy and under it found some Germans one with his arm sticking up. One of the engineers caught hold of it thinking it was one of us, and said, 'Here get up, I want to dig here'. I had to fill sandbags that night and having dug into Germans once or twice, I went to where grass was growing though it made the distance to be carried much further, but it was good clean digging.
>
> On the 19th, we were relieved by the 8th [Battalion] at 10 p.m. and went back to billets in a deserted farm in the Salient and were lodged in a cow byre.'

The position the 7th Battalion found themselves in on Monday 19th April was at Fortuin, about a mile and a half behind the front line. The battalion was now brigade reserve, and the front line of the Canadian Division's area of responsibility was held by the 2nd Brigade on the right and the 3rd on the left.

Kenneth found time to write to his family on 20th April and his letter was circulated around his siblings. He describes the inspection on 11th April, saying that the dispatch of the Canadians to a more intense area, 'is a great honour and we very much appreciate it.' He comments on the German shelling of Ypres, 'I don't blame them so much for shelling the Cathedral tower as it might have been used for observation, but they needn't

Chapter 4 To the Front

have smashed the rest as they did, nor need they have burnt the [probably Cloth Hall] standing beside it.'

Having described conditions at the front in more detail than his mother might have wished, Kenneth complains about a lack of rum. 'I don't know if this is part of the Temperance Scheme, if so it is taken hard that we should be deprived of our hard-earned rum because some brutes at home won't do their bit and foolish too as it kept off a lot of sickness.' In fact, it appears that the cessation of rum was caused by Maj Odlum; a teetotaller. He was promptly nicknamed Pea Soup Odlum as a result. Kenneth ends, 'Don't be anxious if it is eight or nine days before you hear again.' As fate would have it, his next communication would be somewhat later and in very different circumstances.

On 21st April, the line was held, from northwest to southeast, by the 13th, 15th, 8th and 5th Battalions. Kenneth describes the general scene:

'It was a grisly place that Salient. There was not a living thing but the troops and the wild birds. It must have been thickly populated before the war as on every hand one saw villages and farms, some whole, some completely ruined, and some half and half. Our artillery was quite close to our billet and they warned us of aeroplanes. Sentries were set with whistles which they blew when an aeroplane appeared and then everyone had to keep under cover. One day we saw some troops marching along a road when suddenly a number of shells burst amongst them. It was the most uncomfortable billets we had had.

On the night of the 21st, we went out at 7.45 p.m. and built some shelters in a field for reserves or something. We worked till 12 and then came home.

I now come to the worst part of my experiences – The Second Battle of Ypres. We had often – officers and men

Keeping The Old Flag Flying

alike – wondered when we should have chance to make our name and had longed for the time to come. We had always imagined ourselves doing it in an advance – some brilliant charge like the London Scottish.[82] We had never thought of doing it in a retreat. I imagine the former would have been easier and better. It is one thing to charge, take the trenches and then find half of your friends left behind, and quite another to stand and watch them fall beside you and then retreat and leave the wounded to the mercies of a merciless foe. I personally don't want to live through that time again.'

---

82 The 14th (1st London Scottish) Battalion, London Regiment conducted a famous charge during the Battle of Messines on 31st October 1914.

Chapter 4 To the Front

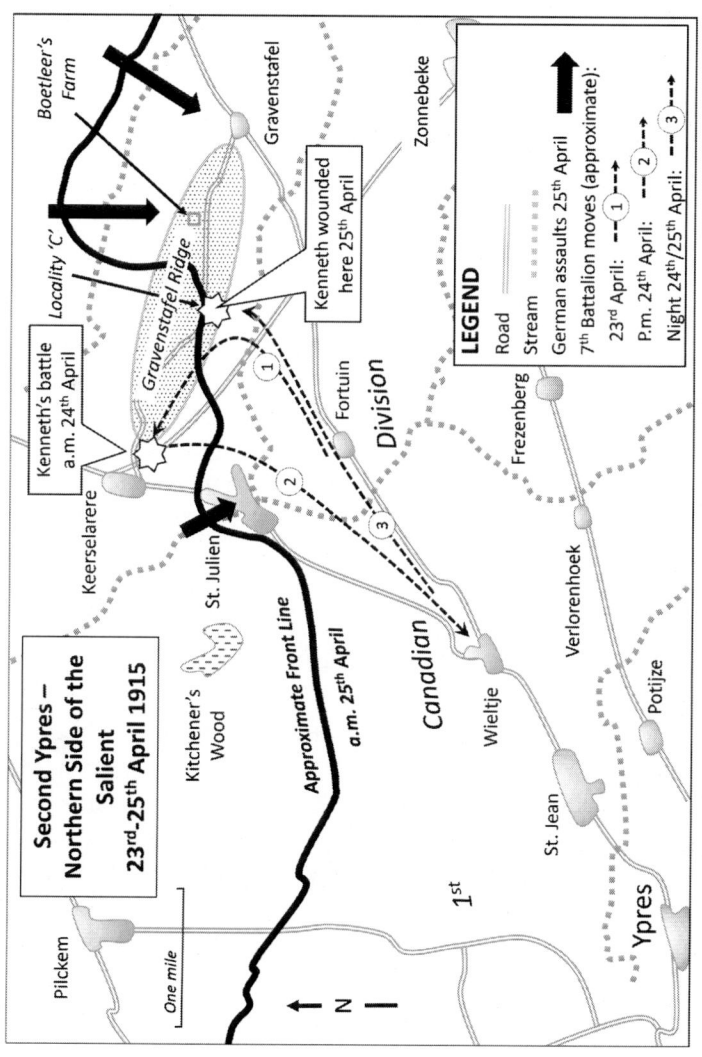

Chapter 5
The Second Battle of Ypres

On Thursday 22nd April, the German 4th Army launched its anticipated assault on the Ypres Salient in enormous strength. The German objective was to remove the bulge in their front line formed by the Salient, known to the German Army as the Ypres Sack.[83] As Kenneth has informed us, this campaign is known as the 2nd Battle of Ypres and it contained a number of specific engagements, the first of which, on 22nd and 23rd April, was The Battle of Gravenstafel Ridge.

The Germans had decided to attack the Salient on its northern side where both the Algerian and Canadian Divisions were new to the area and thus their positions were considered a weak point. At 5.00 p.m. on 22nd April, after a ferocious artillery barrage, the German Army introduced a horrifying weapon, releasing large clouds of poisonous chlorine gas from metal cylinders situated on the front line. There had been a number of indications of the German intention to use gas on the battlefield and some preparations were ordered. But the defending troops had few options to take and, in any case, as the concept of such a type of attack was impossible to envisage, few arrangements had been made.

Conducted by the wind that was blowing from the northeast,

---

[83] It should be noted that, at this time, the German High Command was concentrating its efforts on the Eastern Front against Russia. In the west, the object was to make less significant gains to divert attention from forthcoming operations in the east.

Chapter 5 The Second Battle of Ypres

the gas made its way towards the Allied lines in a low, greenish-yellow cloud, then enveloped the Algerian Division's positions and the French ones beyond them. Its impact was immediate and devastating. Chlorine causes a severe burning pain in the throat and eyes, intense chest pain and, as fluid builds up in the lungs, individuals fight for breath. Those inhaling significant amounts of the gas choke to death within minutes. Scores of the French and Algerian defenders fell, choking, sick and dying. Those who were still able fled in horror, struggling to get away from the choking fumes. As they did so, their reserves, seeing what had befallen their comrades, also turned and took flight. Behind the gas, where the air was now safe to breathe, 'wave after wave of German troops clambered out of their trenches and, with fixed bayonets, advanced cautiously across no man's land.'[84]

This mass exodus left a huge gap about four miles wide in the Allied line and advancing through it the German Army met no resistance. German units succeeded in penetrating some two miles to the west as far as the high ground of the Pilckem Ridge that lay a couple of miles to the west of the Canadian Division. The route to Ypres was exposed, as was the left flank of the Canadians, but fortunately the Germans failed to fully exploit their penetration. They halted and dug in. This stroke of luck gave the Canadians some vital time to bolster their defences. Initially, the 13th Battalion, on the Canadians' left, though feeling some effects of the gas attack, readjusted its positions to face the new threat on its left. Meanwhile, the 1st Division's reserve battalions, including the 7th, were brought into play. Fortunately, both Generals Alderson and Smith-Dorrien had seen the gas and its effects, and the Divisional Commander was quick to act. Kenneth explains how his battalion became involved in the defence:

> 'We were in our billets on April 22nd when the battle started. In the afternoon, we had been watching our artillery who were shelling hard and being shelled. We had our

---

84 Cassar op. cit., Page 103.

suppers at 5 p.m. and some time after that the order came to pack our kit. They told us we needn't include our blankets as we should probably be coming back, we were not due back to the trenches till the next night. I had just got a parcel with an extra lot of chocolate and cake. Half the cake I had eaten and the rest I left but put the chocolate in my coat pocket. We hung around then and after a bit saw some Algerians cross in front of the guns. Then some came into the farm and told us the Germans had been using poisonous gas and had broken the line.

Soon after that we got the order to fall in, we fell in under cover of the barn roof and again waited. Then we got the order to move off and we left – cooks and all – in the old artillery formation i.e. each section in a clump separated from the rest by some 200 yards.'

According to the records of British Columbia Regiment, the good management of Kenneth's company at this time was largely due to the efforts of the admirable Captain Haines. When the company was stood to, all the other platoon and company officers ran to watch the gas cloud smother the French. But Haines stayed at company headquarters and sorted out all the sergeants, who had showed up looking for their platoon commanders and orders as to what to do. By several accounts his demeanour made the sergeants realize they were about to get into some very serious business and as a result, the company was able to deploy in a short time.

Sergeant John McIlree was 15 Platoon Sergeant, Kenneth's platoon, and Sergeant Frederick Wells was with 16 Platoon. These two mustered their men on either side of the barn, alongside the Weiltje/St. Jean Road. McIlree recalled that his men were standing in ranks, while he was inspecting their rifles and kit, when a wall of smoke rolled over them that, he said, 'smelled a little like chloroform. The natural reaction was to breathe a little

Chapter 5 The Second Battle of Ypres

in, to smell it. But as soon you did your nose started to run and your eyes watered'.[85] He remembered the smell from his high school chemistry laboratory and told his men he thought it was chlorine. Unfortunately, one of the officers came back just as he said that. The officer tore a strip off him and suggested that he would get the men hysterical if he kept spreading such rumours. McIlree apparently took great offence at this officer shouting at him, but within a few minutes everyone was coughing, and they had to break ranks as the boys all tried to face into the wind to get some fresh air.

Then the first Algerians came streaming by. Soon the area in front of No. 4 Company's billet was a traffic jam. A battalion transport wagon was trying to get forward and got stuck right in front of 15 Platoon. The driver broke into hysterics and started shouting that the Germans had broken through, but one of Kenneth's corporals shouted at him to 'shut up you bastard!'[86] A short time later an Algerian sergeant jumped up on a mound of earth in front of the barn and started shouting at his comrades in French. Only one man out of 15 and 16 Platoons spoke French, so he interpreted, 'Look you fellows, these brave Canadians are going to fight. What's the idea? Come on, line up and go in with them'.[87] Soon a small band of stragglers gathered around the sergeant, but then a single shell burst about 100 meters away and the Algerians scattered. Kenneth takes up the tale:

> 'We were full of excitement as now at last we thought we were to make an attack. We crossed the road and lined up in a grass field and began to dig in. It was now getting dark. We had hardly started when they fell us in again and we went marching and halting, marching and halting till we got

---

85 Records of The British Columbia Regiment.
86 16844 Sergeant John McIlree, No 4. Company, CBC Interview, 1967. CBC Licensing.
87 17093 Private Fredrick Arnold, No. 4 Company, CBC Interview, 1967. CBC Licensing.

Keeping The Old Flag Flying

to battalion headquarters. There they put us in a field and we lay down there.

It was too cold to sleep, and I got up and walked about. We heard a cheer in the distance while digging in and had been told the line was closed again. I thought it was all over and I wanted to get back to our billets. Somewhere about midnight our rations and water cart arrived. We filled our bottles and took our rations and waited again. They let us into a ruined house where we got a smoke and at about 2 a.m. they fell us in and marched us to a turnip field where we dug in.'

Kenneth and his comrades had paused at an area known as Locality C, which lay on the track that ran along the Gravenstafel Ridge, just to the west of and a few hundred yards behind their front-line positions of a few days before. Sergeant McIlree recalled that as they marched off from the barn, he looked back to make sure his platoon was all in line and keeping up. Behind him, stretched out in single file, stooped over under their heavy packs, his men were silhouetted by the burning buildings and explosions in distant Ypres, a sight he remembered for the rest of his life.[88]

Whilst this manoeuvre was in hand, the Canadians conducted a counter-attack against a feature known as Kitchener's Wood that lay on a low ridge to the west of the village of St. Julien and away to the west of the 7th. At 11.45 p.m. the 10th Battalion, followed by the 16th, advanced up the slope in the pitch-black night to assault the wood. German machine guns mowed the attackers down, but they kept going. Casualties were severe but by dawn on 23rd April the wood was in Canadian hands.

Whilst the Gravenstafel Ridge was under pressure, the main German assault was taking place across a broad front to the west of St. Julien and onto the Pilckem Ridge. At 2.00 a.m. Brigadier General Currie, commanding the 2nd Brigade, responded to a

---

88   Records of The British Columbia Regiment.

Chapter 5 The Second Battle of Ypres

request by the 3rd Brigade to fill the gap in the Canadians' lines and redirected the 7th Battalion to do so, to the northeast of St. Julien. Leaving No. 1 Company under Captain John Warden at Locality C to reinforce the 8th Battalion, the 7th moved westwards and took up a position with its left on St. Julien, where the 15th Battalion was located, and its right on the foot of the village of Keerselaere.[89] Occupying some old artillery dugouts and along a hedge line, they again began to dig in.

By dawn on Friday 23rd April, the Canadian flank had been reinforced, but there were still some large breaches and one of these was on the 7th Battalion's right flank. Beyond this gap the besieged 13th Battalion, shelled and attacked by infantry, held on through the night. At 5.30 a.m., a further counter attack by the 1st and 4th Battalions, assisted by the British 3rd Battalion The Middlesex Regiment, was initiated on Mauser Ridge to the west of Kitchener's Wood. Again, the German artillery and machine guns subjected the attackers to a deadly hail of bullets and explosive, and despite capturing some ground, the advance was unsustainable. The Canadian survivors withdrew to the foot of the ridge and dug in.

As day dawned the position of the defenders remained critical. A small number of Canadian and British battalions that had been rapidly redeployed during the night, reduced by casualties, tired, thirsty and holding under-prepared positions were overlooked by a considerably superior German force supported by a huge quantity of artillery. Throughout the day, this artillery pounded the Canadians' line, blasting men out of their trenches, thwarting movement and preventing resupply. Fortunately for the Allies, the German Army under Duke Albrecht concentrated his attacks

---

89 Captain John Warden had been the Second-in-Command of the company to Major Guy Moberley. Moberley survived the war, serving in 1918 in the Canadian Board of Pensions Commission, and Warden also survived. Though he was badly wounded during the action on the Gravenstafel Ridge, he returned to Canada, raised and then commanded the 102nd Canadian Battalion on the Western Front.

Keeping The Old Flag Flying

that day to the north of the Ypres Salient in the Poperinghe area, where he met little success. Had he exploited the gap between Kenneth's battalion and the 13th to their north, he might have cut off the Salient. Kenneth describes his company's position:

'The turnips were old and run to seed, and we dug in among them each man making a hole for himself with his entrenching tool. We dug on till daylight and after, till the first aeroplane made us lie down quietly. They shelled us off and on all that day but could not get our range. Major Byng-Hall, who with the help of his batman had dug a deep hole for the two of them close to where I was, went to see the Colonel and came back saying the shells were bursting close to the Colonel's dugout.

In the afternoon, the Colonel went out with Major Odlum and an engineer officer to choose a site for the trenches. [90] They suddenly found themselves close to a German trench and in making for cover the Colonel was shot and mortally wounded. I did not know him well but have heard he was very nice and have since read that he was a great rifle shot. He was a chronic dyspeptic and had to have special food when on the Plains, I don't know how he got on at the front.'

Lieutenant Colonel Hart McHarg had found that his small reconnaissance party had been under observation by a large group of Germans located about 100 yards away. The Canadians ran back, but Hart McHarg was hit in the thigh, the bullet penetrating his stomach. Odlum managed to get back to the Canadian positions and he and the Battalion Medical Officer, Captain George Gibson, went back to dress Hart McHarg's wounds and stretcher bearers evacuated him when it got dark. Nevertheless, he died during the night, a massive blow, and Odlum took command of the 7th Battalion.

---

90 The engineer officer was Lieutenant Donald Mathieson of the 2nd Field Company, Divisional Engineers. Pay and Record Office op. cit.

Chapter 5 The Second Battle of Ypres

Whilst this tragic tale was unfolding, the Canadian Division had been allocated the use of the British 13th Brigade. A counter attack by this formation towards Pilckem was ordered and took place at 4.25 p.m. and included another assault by the 1st and 4th Canadian Battalions towards Mauser Ridge. The attackers were again mown down by the overwhelming German defence, the two Canadian Battalions losing some 858 officers and men. By dusk, the survivors withdrew.

During the night, the Canadians redeployed. The 13th Battalion adjusted its line rearwards to face northwest and, reinforced by two companies of the 2nd Battalion The East Kent Regiment, the gap between them and the 7th was effectively closed.

At 4.00 a.m. on Saturday 24th April, the German artillery opened up on the Canadian front line with devastating effect, causing numerous casualties. The bombardment was followed by another release of gas, nearly reaching as far as Locality C and enveloping the 8th and 15th Battalions along with the company of the 7th that had been detached to Gravenstafel Ridge. This barrage heralded the second phase of the Second Battle of Ypres; The Battle of St. Julien. Due to sheer determination and some rudimentary protection, typically improvised cloth face coverings soaked in water or urine, the 8th held on, despite taking many casualties.

The Germans advanced confidently in solid formations but were surprised at the vigorous defence they encountered from the 5th and 8th Battalions' machine gun and rifle fire. The attack wavered in this area but the 15th Battalion in between them was more heavily gassed and eventually the German infantry broke through and behind the Canadian line. Whilst some of the 15th were able to withdraw, many were forced to surrender, and the battalion suffered 671 casualties.

It seems that the 7th Battalion was not initially affected by the German assault. Indeed, the companies were enjoying a bright spring morning, the warm sunshine making the sodden grass and wild flowers steam. The trenches that Kenneth and his comrades had prepared the day before were somewhat shallow as, after a few feet of digging, the excavations started to fill with water. To compensate, they raised a parapet on the enemy side, reinforced with sand-bags that were found in an old artillery dugout. Four strands of barbed-wire were added, but all in all, it was a fairly insufficient defensive position.

Early in the day, a German aeroplane flew over, so low that the pilot could be seen clearly, but the soldiers had orders not to open fire and reveal their positions. Nevertheless, the Canadians had been spotted and the aircraft then dropped white pencils of smoke to show the enemy artillery where the trenches were.[91]

Kenneth describes activity in No. 4 Company during the morning:

'We had had breakfast next morning April 24th, and I had laid down in a nice dry place to sleep, when we got the orders to shift up the trench a bit. My new place was wet and muddy, it was quite close to the Major's [Byng-Hall's] dugout. Soon after we got the order to stand to and I heard the Major say, 'If we can hold this trench today we shall make our name alright'.

We had not a good field of fire where I was owing to a bit of slightly rising ground in front. Beyond that were some buildings and a sniper was spotted in them and we all fired at them. Occasionally, one saw a German passing among the buildings and then we let fly, our orders being not to fire unless we saw something to fire at.'

Whilst Kenneth was thus engaged, the Germans commenced attacking the northwest of the Canadian sector towards Keerselaere and St. Julien. Two positions held, but to their north,

---

91 Derived from: McClung, Nellie L. *'Three Times and Out'* told by Private Simmons. Boston and New York Houghton Mifflin Company, 1918. Simmons was in No. 3 Company.

Chapter 5 The Second Battle of Ypres

the German advance coupled with heavy artillery salvoes forced the 13th Battalion to withdraw. The penetration of the 15th and the withdrawal of the 13th now brought the enemy up to the positions of the 7th.

Experiencing the streams of gassed and wounded casualties passing their positions from the northern battalions, Major Odlum, commanding the 7th, tried on a number of occasions to contact the headquarters of the 3rd Brigade for orders, but was unable to get through, the telephone lines having been cut. Nevertheless, at 8 a.m., 'The enemy debouched from the wood in massed formation. The machine gun played on this excellent target and the Germans broke up and fled in disorder to the shelter of the wood.'[92] Kenneth takes up the story:

> 'Meanwhile further to our right on the road the Germans were attacking in their old close formation. One of our sections was sent to reinforce that point. We had had a good few casualties, but not much excitement. The words, 'Stretcher bearers on the double', would come down the trench and as soon as they had struggled past it would come from the other direction. At last the stretcher bearers ran short of dressings and could do no more. I might say that the standing orders were that the doctors were not to go into the front-line trench unless specially sent for, their lives being valuable.
>
> The Major [Byng-Hall] was in command of the battalion, as the Colonel was dead and Major Odlum was at headquarters. Although he once told us that one day he hoped to command the battalion, when it came about he grumbled rather at it. He had already made arrangements in case of retreat and told the officers which way to go.'

As Odlum sought direction from the Brigade Commander, the 7th was facing another major onslaught which was creating heavy

---

92 Scudamore op. cit.

casualties and was also being fired on from the rear by German troops who had penetrated the 15th Battalion's lines to the north. In the north of the Canadian Division's area, the pressure was intense and the scene one of carnage. The overwhelming waves of German infantry, supported by artillery, blasted their way into the Canadian lines. The defenders fought with determination and courage, but they lacked bombs and machine guns, their Ross rifles jammed after every shot and they were quite unable to make an effective reply.

At 11.45 a.m., Odlum ordered his battalion to conduct an ordered withdrawal, starting on the right, with those on the left providing cover. The intention was to fall back on trenches that lay in front of St. Julien. No. 2 Company covered the withdrawal but was soon overrun, and Kenneth's No. 4 Company made a run for it. They were also covered by the battalion's machine guns. The Machine Gun Section was commanded by Lieutenant Edward Bellew who personally manned one gun until overrun and captured. The other was operated by Sergeant Hugh Peerless who was killed. Bellew was awarded a VC[93] for his actions that day and Peerless was awarded a posthumous DCM.[94] Kenneth explains his part in this engagement:

> 'Suddenly things got a bit urgent and the Major and Captain Haines produced rifles from somewhere or other and took their places beside us at the parapet. Just then a man came running up from the rear, threw himself on the ground and said to the Major, 'Orders from Major Odlum to retire'. We at once began to retire to the left. I and some more put on our packs but a good many left theirs behind.
>
> Just to our left was a hedge running at right angles to

[93] The Victoria Cross; the highest British military decoration awarded for valour in the face of the enemy.
[94] The Distinguished Conduct Medal; an award to warrant officers, non-commissioned officers and men for distinguished, gallant and good conduct in the field. It is the second highest award for gallantry in action after the Victoria Cross, and the other ranks' equivalent of the DSO.

Chapter 5 The Second Battle of Ypres

our line, beyond the hedge our trench was set back a bit. It carried on more or less straight for some distance till it met another trench at right angles to it. This latter was some 300 yards long and another trench ran across its end at right angles again. I will call the first of these three the 'front trench', the second the 'communication trench' and the last the 'reserve trench' although I am not at all sure that they were not all intended for front trenches.

Our section was told to line the hedge to cover the retirement, but we had barely taken up our position when we were recalled by signal. We moved slowly along the trenches, halting at intervals. In one of these in the front trench I saw a sergeant I knew lying out behind, wounded. He kept crying, 'Don't leave me', and I decided if we moved on again to try and get him away, but two men got out and helped him off. I saw his name later as dead and one of the men who went with him as missing. The trenches were full of dead and wounded in all directions, but I saw only a few I knew. One chap was shot in the legs and men put him in the trench he was lying outside.

Thus, we went along slowly past the front and communication trenches. I came in the end to the reserve trench. On my left as I entered it, it ran some 30 yards and stopped. On the right, it went up to and beyond some buildings. I managed to get into it and just round to the left when we came to a stop. In front of me was a dead man lying on his face and beyond that a wounded man on his back. At Mürren [in Switzerland, where Kenneth spent time later in the war, as we shall learn] I met the man who laid them there, the dead man was Sergeant Muir who, then a corporal, had been in the first tent with me at Valcartier. He had been shot taking a short cut over the reserve trench parapet.[95]

---

95 17191 Scrgeant Duncan Muir, whose widowed mother lived in

Keeping The Old Flag Flying

We came to a stop as the leading men had come to the end of the trench and there was nothing beyond. Messages kept on being passed up from the Major to keep on but whether they reached the end or not, I don't know. I had a [better] position for firing at the Germans than in the front trench, but I was so close to the communication trench that those in it yelled me to stop, so I stood and waited. A number of men made a jump over the parapet at the gap they saw between me and the next man. We yelled at them to stop as they always landed on the wounded man and at last we hauled him up and a man got in next to me across Muir.

On the ground at the back were numerous men unhurt, wounded or dead. Our Sergeant Major was lying there and got caught by a bit of shrapnel in the leg.[96] Another shrapnel hit me in the mouth and made my lip bleed a bit and caught the man next to me on the forehead and hand; I bound him up. Then a shell passed through my waterproof cap cover. It fitted rather loosely and the shell cut it, so that it flapped over my face but without touching the cap, and buried itself in the parapet. I heard it sizzling and looking down the hole saw it some six inches down then it stopped and did not burst. As both these had come from behind I and another man knelt down on Muir, little thinking who it was, and got below the ground level.

Before we retired, our artillery, or what we took for ours, had started. The first shell burst short of the Germans, the next nearer them but the third was very near us and the Major said he wished he had a telephone and thought of sending back a messenger, but I believe now that it was all German guns, ours I believe had run short of ammunition.

Kilmarnock, Scotland. He has no known grave and is commemorated on the Ypres (Menin Gate) Memorial. He was aged 24. CWGC op. cit.

96 Presumably, this was still Company Sergeant Major Thomas Hepburn. It seems that he survived the war.

Chapter 5 The Second Battle of Ypres

With the Salient as it was, one could not be sure it was our own shells because they came from behind.

Finally, a message came along the trench, 'No officers left, every man for himself'. The man next me said, 'I suppose we had better surrender', and I said, 'Surrender be hanged I am going to beat it,' and I got out and cleared off. He must have followed me because I saw him later. I asked our Sergeant Major if he could manage and he said he could.

I went off at a left incline to avoid a fence and because the ground was lower. Another man I met in Germany, who was some 20 feet to my right, went straight back and ran into Germans. I kept on till I came to another trench, the men in it yelled me to get in it. I did so and followed its windings for some way till I got tired of it. The old feeling of annoyance came over me that I used to have during the blasting at Sydney and I got out and walked away.[97]

I was feeling very downhearted, I thought of Alderson's boast at Strazeele, 'The Canadians never budge'. I felt we had budged and the feeling of defeat was very, very bitter. I found after that the others felt so too. When we came back to talk it over that night we realised we had not retired till ordered to and had done all flesh and blood could. Later I came to see that if Ypres was saved, a mile or so of the Salient didn't matter and I wrote home to ask if it had been.

Later still in Germany, I saw an English paper and read that the whole Pas de Calais was ringing with what we had done. I read French's report, 'After a very gallant resistance by the Canadians the village of St. Julien was captured, our line now runs south of that point.'[98] Also, his telegram to

---

97 Sydney is in Nova Scotia, Canada where Kenneth worked in a steel works before the war. As we have already learned, he was often bombarded with frozen pieces of rock when the stock of iron stone was blasted.

98 Field Marshal Sir John French authored regular dispatches from the Front.

Keeping The Old Flag Flying

Premier Bordon [Canadian Prime Minister], 'No words of mine can describe the gallantry of the Canadians. Canada has indeed reason to be proud of her sons'. When I read all that, I saw that we had made our name all right as the Major said. But all that was in the future and just then the feeling of defeat was very, very bitter.

We were just wandering away like men do from a football match and it occurred to me to be thankful there was no cavalry after us. I came to a ditch with water in and the man in front of me walked through it. I did the same but at a different place and went in over my boot tops. A little further on I saw the Sergeant Major coming. As he was limping I waited for him and helped him along. He asked me where I was going, I said 'To the guns', that was my sole idea to rally round the guns, though I hadn't the foggiest idea where they were.

We went on till we came to battalion headquarters. In the road was the Adjutant. He sent the Sergeant Major onto the rear, he asked me if I was wounded and on my saying, 'No', he sent me to line the fence [at the] back of [the] headquarters. In a ditch were remains of our battalion and I found what was left of our platoon. Our Section Commander, Corporal Edginton and four others of our section, and one of another section.[99] The acting Platoon Sergeant I met later. They said some others had got away and had gone to the rear.

A man I knew in another platoon who had left his pack asked me to sell him a pair of socks, as his were wet. I brought out a pair and he insisted on paying for them and I was glad he did later. I noticed Edginton had not got his

---

His Eighth Despatch was printed in the Second Supplement to the London Gazette of 10th July 1915. Kenneth's quotation has not been discovered therein, but the dispatch lauds the gallantry and brilliance of the Canadians.

99   16884 Corporal Lewis Edginton, originally from the Isle of Wight in England. CEF 2nd Infantry Brigade Headquarters and Seventh Battalion op. cit.

Chapter 5 The Second Battle of Ypres

pack though I had seen him put it on. He said it had been pounded to bits by a machine gun. He had been knocked down by the blow but was not hurt.'

At the rendezvous, in front of St. Julien, Odlum collected about 100 of his men and a few stragglers from other battalions. But swept by German fire the position was untenable and after a meeting of the commanding officers of the 7th, 14th and 15th Battalions, it was decided to withdraw further 1,000 yards. This time, the 7th fell back in good order, still managing to deter the advancing Germans with well-aimed fire, but were pressed by the waves of enemy infantry, which, '... isolated small sections of trenches and then rushed them. They came on six or seven lines at intervals of fifty yards and seemed very uncertain of what they were up against'.[100] But as the 7th withdrew, the Germans 'descended like a gigantic tidal wave upon the village'.[101] Many of the 7th were cut off and either killed or captured. Major Byng-Hall, commanding Kenneth's company, was one of the latter. Kenneth takes up the tale:

'We stayed there some time and then were told again to retire. Edginton suggested that we should keep together. A little further on we saw the Durham Light Infantry Territorials coming up. 'Look at that, Foyster' said Edginton, I said, 'It's too late'. I was feeling very down.

The Durhams came up in the new artillery formation of four lines in open order and the shrapnel was playing on their front lines. As we passed through them I felt they must look on us as we had looked on the Algerians. They were, I heard, fresh from England and had only been out there three days.'

It seems that Kenneth had seen the advance of the 5th Durham Light Infantry, part of the 150th (York and Durham) Brigade which had only arrived in France on 20th April. They had been

---

100 Scudamore op. cit.
101 Cassar op. cit., Page 205.

ordered up to the village of Wieltje at about noon as part of a British force to be used to bolster the Canadians' lines. Kenneth and his surviving comrades continued to make their way back to the area of Wieltje:

'After passing through the Durhams, I could see no sign of the others. Whether they went back with them or not, the man who got my socks did, I don't know, I did not see them again.

I followed the scattered remnant of all our battalions and about a mile further, two lieutenants took charge of us. One of them told me they were all the officers left of their battalion. I don't know which it was. They took us to a trench at the back of the farm. This trench was not dug into the ground, but the sides were raised and turfed. In the middle was a covered room, this was full, so I went on to the trench beyond and lay on my pack.

Then they shelled us. I had not been scared up till then but then I was. There were three guns shelling us, two field pieces and a howitzer. The field pieces I didn't mind, the shell and report arrive together. If the shell is passing over, you hear the report and at the same time the scream of the shell passing. In this case we heard only the explosion. But the horror of the howitzer was that you could hear the shell coming. We had heard them often in the trenches at Fleurbaix. They sounded like an old street car rumbling overhead, they seemed to go slow and you could fancy you heard the jolt at the joints of the rails. We used to call them Railroaders.

But here it was different. There they were meant for far beyond us, here they burst when they got to us. I heard the devilish things coming nearer and nearer and huddled against the side of the trench knowing that when it got over

Chapter 5 The Second Battle of Ypres

me it would explode. Some shook some earth over us, one splattered me and my rifle with some inky fluid. Afterwards I saw the ground all around a mass of Jack Johnson [heavy artillery] holes.[102] There was one man between me and the end of the trench. He got up and ran around to the other end. I got the men behind me to move up and I edged as far as I could get towards the middle of the trench.

At dusk, when the shelling had stopped an hour or so, a lot of our officers and men came up. Major Odlum, the Adjutant, Captain Haines and another captain and one lieutenant were all I think that were left. The lieutenant I didn't see, he was killed a month later.[103]

I forgot to say that when we reached headquarters the Adjutant asked me where Major Byng-Hall was. I said, 'Dead or badly wounded' and gave the last word we had as my reason. I was very glad later to hear that the Major was captured unhurt, they must have been completely surrounded soon after I left.

Our officers gathered the battalion together and put us in a barn in the farm. In the yard, a chap was lying as if asleep, he had been killed by a shell while carrying a wounded man. The wounded man was in the barn groaning. I and our acting Platoon Sergeant Macelrey [sic – probably Sergeant McIlree] who I then met, and a man of No. 3 Company who I knew, got together in a corner of the barn and talked it all over. I took off my putties and boots and changed my socks which were wet from the ditch I had got in. Soon after, they called us to fall in. It took me some time to put on my boots and I had rather a bother to find the others. They only wanted

---

102 Named after heavyweight boxing champion Jack Johnson.
103 Probably Lieutenant Geoffrey Hornby who was killed on 24th May 1915 aged 35. He was the son of the late Robert and Lucy Hornby and is commemorated on the Vimy Memorial. CWGC op. cit.

to count us. There were 72 of us there though there were others beside those I had seen before. Then we went back to the barn. It was pitch dark now and we dared not show a light. After a hunt, I found a vacant place and, keeping my boots on this time, I got down and went to sleep.'

By the end of the 24th, the Germans were forced to vacate St. Julien due to accurate Canadian artillery fire and the village remained unoccupied all night. However, they still held an east-west line just to the north of it, including Kitchener Wood, and were pressing hard against Locality C on the Gravenstafel Ridge which the few Canadian survivors finally abandoned during the night. Between St. Julien and Locality C lay a diverse force of British infantry. To the east, the 8th Battalion held on grimly, their positions jutting northwards, their left flank open. The 8th's headquarters was situated in Boetleer's Farm, a set of buildings which lay on the Gravenstafel Ridge track to the east of Locality C, which also held many of the 8th's casualties. A new farm with the same name was built on the site sometime after the war and is still there.

So ended Kenneth's deeds on 24th April. The 7th Battalion's War Diary notes that it suffered 500 casualties that day.[104] Major Thomas Scudamore estimates the numbers of killed as 184 with 466 wounded.[105] During the night, the 8th Battalion attempted to obtain reinforcements with some success. Lieutenant Colonel Louis Lipsett, commanding the 8th, managed to find some 1,000 men from miscellaneous British battalions belonging to the 28th Division and used them to bolster his left flank to the west of Boetleer's Farm. His own battalion still occupied positions on the northern side of the Gravenstafel Ridge.

Meanwhile, at midnight, the Canadian Division's staff held a meeting with the brigade commanders of the 1st and 2nd Canadian

---

104 The numbers of killed, missing and wounded are not given, but it can be assumed that about a third of these died.
105 Scudamore op. cit.

Chapter 5 The Second Battle of Ypres

Brigades and the 150th (York and Durham) Brigade. The result was further attempts to stabilise the Canadian line. Amongst these was a requirement for the 2nd Brigade to use a composite unit formed from the survivors of the 7th and 10th Battalions to extend left to the edge of the Hanebeek stream, which lay to the rear of the 8th's positions. Kenneth describes the result:

> 'I should think it was about two hours after that they woke us, and we fell in again and marched out along the road. We came to some trenches, but they were all occupied. We came at last to some that were not, but there was not room for us all in them. So, the rest of us dug in beside the road with our entrenching tools. The object being to give us cover from shell fire, next day. They dished out rations – there were rations then for the whole battalion and only 72 of us – so we got plenty. We got a loaf of bread each and a tin of Maconochie, the first we were ever given, and could have two Maconochies for the asking, also we had a good tot of rum.
>
> It was raining then in a thick drizzle and we had just laid down in our holes when the Brigadier [Currie] came along. He said, 'Where is the 7th Battalion? It is the Brigadier speaking. I want the British Columbia boys'. We got up and then the order came, 'Fall in by battalions'. We fell in and he marched us back to the firing line. This was in the early hours of April 25th.'

This manoeuvre was an attempt by the composite unit, which numbered about 360 all ranks, to protect the exposed left flank of the 8th Battalion's line. The unit, led personally by Currie, set off at 2 a.m. and passed through a place called Bombard Crossroads, probably the junction of the St Julien to Zonnebeke and Wieltje to Passchendaele roads. At 4 a.m. they arrived on the Gravenstafel Ridge and Currie placed his force to the southwest of Boetleer's Farm, leaving Odlum in charge.

Meanwhile, the 8th Battalion Durham Light Infantry from the 50th Division appeared at the farm to reinforce the Canadian 8th Battalion. Immediately on its arrival the 7th/10th were attacked by the enemy and the fight continued all day on Gravenstafel Ridge, the unrelenting enemy artillery and machine gun fire taking a frightful toll of the already depleted British and Canadian units. In spite of being slowly blasted out of their trenches by artillery, the 7th/10th held on during the afternoon.

Also that morning, the British 10th Brigade of the British 4th Division arrived at Weiltje to launch a counter-attack onto St. Julien and Kitchener Wood. The attack, conducted within full view of the enemy, was bravely fought but did not succeed. The leading waves 'ran into such a tempest of fire that they were cut down like wheat before a scythe'.[106] Eventually the survivors halted and dug in. The attack had failed, but at least troops now occupied the St. Julien gap.

Kenneth describes his personal experiences during the day:

'As we went, the brigade officers counted us and as they passed back I heard one of them say, '300 men'. We must have gone some four miles as we had two halts on the road and were glad of them both. Just about a mile from the trenches, we came across a large poplar tree lying across the road. On one side of it was a motor ambulance and on the other we met an entire stretcher party.

We reached a farm with the trenches just beyond it in broad daylight. The trenches were all occupied, and we passed along up them to where there were no trenches at all. On our way, we came to a steep bank, our Adjutant was standing on the top helping the men up it. He grabbed me as I came, but just then his foot slipped, and we fell together into the ditch. My rifle got plastered with slime and

---

106 Cassar op. cit., Page 251.

Chapter 5 The Second Battle of Ypres

I thought it would want cleaning before I used it again, but I never did use it.

We came as I said to a place where there were no trenches. We were at the foot of a fairly steep slope with some ruined buildings at the top. They spread us out and told us to dig in quickly as we could as we should be attacked soon. I was reaching round for my entrenching tool. One carried it at the small of one's back and it was a bit awkward to get it out. Suddenly two men looking like Algerians appeared beside the ruined buildings. Captain Cooper of No. 3 Company shouted to them to, *'Venez ici, ici, ici'*, but as they stood still he levelled his revolver and shot one of them. The other turned and ran and he shot him too. It was good shooting as they were some 200-300 yards off. Some of our men began firing, others ran up the hill and came back saying it was a mistake and I heard Captain Haines say, 'But we know there are no French in front of us'.[107] Just then I saw to our left some men coming towards us in regular English open order. Then a burst of firing came from the buildings and about the first bullet got me in the arm.

I was standing struggling with my entrenching tool which had got stuck and the bullet went through my arm about three inches below the shoulder and could only have just missed the bone. I stood for a bit looking at my hand which was streaming blood and seemed to be in a different position to what it was and then it opened of its own accord. Then a bullet whizzed past my ear and I realised that although hit, I might be hit again and followed the example of the others and lay down.

It took me some time to make the men next to me understand that I was hit. By the time they had cut off

---

107 Some German formations had sent troops forward dressed in captured British uniforms the day before in an attempt to fool the Canadian defenders.

the sleeve of all the clothes I had on and had stopped the bleeding I had lost a lot of blood. A most horrid sensation came over me. As far as I remember I was sitting up and lying down all the time, which must have been awkward for them. When they had done, I said, 'I suppose I had better go back' and they said they would come with me. I got on my feet and the horrible sensation came over me again. I came to, to find them holding me up. I said, 'Did I faint?' and they said, 'Just for a minute'.

They soon found that only one man was of any use and the other went back. This man helped me along to the farm. I could only go some 10 yards at a time, then everything would swim before my eyes and I had to lie down. We got at last to the farm and he left me lying on a pile of earth out of the puddles while he went to find the dressing station. He came back and helped me into one of the barns of the farm.

This farm I was told was the 8th headquarters [Boetleer's Farm, which the 8th Battalion had vacated some hours earlier] and must have been the place where we used to meet the ration carts some two miles from our old trenches. The building I was in was built of stone and was a collection of pig pens. There was a passage down the middle with a door at each end, there was also the door I had entered by which opened from the yard into one of the pens in which I lay. A half wall divided this from the next pen and each pen had a doorway to this central passage. It was not the dressing station, but it was full of wounded. Had I got to the dressing station I should not have been better off as it was captured, doctor and all, and the wounded made to get up and walk as they were.

There was one other man in the pen with me. He was lying on a stretcher with his legs broken and had been wounded the day before. The stretcher bearers of the 8th

Chapter 5 The Second Battle of Ypres

had all been gassed and there were one or two volunteers looking after us. There was not much to do, they shared out the tea they made, and hot water was very scarce. I thought of the full water bottle and loaf of bread I had left where I was wounded and asked the man who brought me down to get them, but he said we had retired from there. So, I shared my chocolate which was in my greatcoat pocket with the other wounded man and was glad I had got it.'

Kenneth was probably wounded during the late morning. As he lay in the farm, the German attack continued, commencing to encircle the $7^{th}/10^{th}$ unit, decimating the Durhams and forcing both them and the 8th Canadian Battalion rearwards. The main German thrust seemed to be against Boetleer's Farm. Kenneth continues:

'We lay all that Sunday longing for the night and ambulance to come and talking of the fine time we should have at home. But there was one fly in the amber, and I wished we were the other side of Ypres. I had forgotten the fallen poplar and I didn't know the state of things behind us. I know now that Ypres was burning and deserted, that the roads were blocked with Jack Johnson holes and wrecked transport and ammunition wagons. When the Durhams came up, they had to come by the fields as the roads were impassable.

Our artillery, what there was of it, was without ammunition and helpless. We had seen them withdrawing one battery as we waited by headquarters the day before. I don't think there was much artillery in the Salient at the time. The Major had told us just before that our people were to make an attack at the Yser Canal and maybe they drew it off for that. However, we knew nothing of all this that Sunday and we hoped for the best.'

Finally, Alderson, the Divisional Commander, ordered a general withdrawal at 5 p.m. This was an exceptionally difficult manoeuvre in contact with the enemy, but it commenced as dusk approached and continued throughout the night. Nevertheless, some companies, including those from the 8th Durhams, had not received the order to retire and held on until they too were ordered back in the early hours of the 26th April. Kenneth describes the scene at the farm:

'In the afternoon, we saw our men retiring through the farmyard past us, and all the unwounded left. I wanted to go too but I didn't like to go alone after my performance in the morning. The other man said bitterly, 'I suppose it's every man for himself'. I said, 'I can't help you if I stay and I manage to get away'. When I asked one of the unwounded to give me an arm he persuaded me that I had better stay where I was and said the ambulance would be sure to come after dark. So, I went back and waited.'

The 7th Battalion retired to the area of Fortuin on 26th April where it held a new position and was heavily shelled. When it was relieved, the remnants of the battalion marched via Potizje to billets in Brielen, about a mile northwest of Ypres.

The Battle of St. Julien ended in early May. Despite its inexperience and inferior equipment, notably the Ross rifle, the Canadian Division had mounted an effective defence and according to many had 'saved the day'; three VCs had been won. But it seems that between 15th April to the 3rd May, when it was withdrawn, the Canadian Division had taken a severe number of casualties; 208 officers and 5,828 other ranks were killed, missing or wounded.[108] As stated earlier, about a third of these would have been fatal.

Kenneth knew none of this. He did not withdraw with the survivors but remained with the other wounded from a miscellany

---

108 Derived from: Crawford T. S., *'Wiltshire and the Great War: Training the Empire's Soldiers'* op. sit.

Chapter 5 The Second Battle of Ypres

of units in Boetleer's Farm. As Monday 26th April dawned, they waited to see what fate would bring:

'Sometime during the night [in fact at about 3.00 a.m.], we heard the Germans in the yard, they chatter like mad, and I could see three of them. One of them was shot and the others disappeared into a ruined building at right angle with ours shouting, *'Ambulance'*. Sometime after, some men came to the outside door of our pen and asked, 'Who is here?' We did not answer for some time as we thought they might be Germans, at last I said, 'Canadian wounded'. They came in with a run and the last was shot as they did so. They at once began firing at the Germans in the ruined building from the door and I thought it would be safer in the next pen and so I went in there.

Things quietened down after this, the new arrivals told us there was heavy sniping going on and no-one could get to us. But still I hoped and hoped until the first streaks of dawn showed all hope to be in vain, and with the daylight the Germans came.'

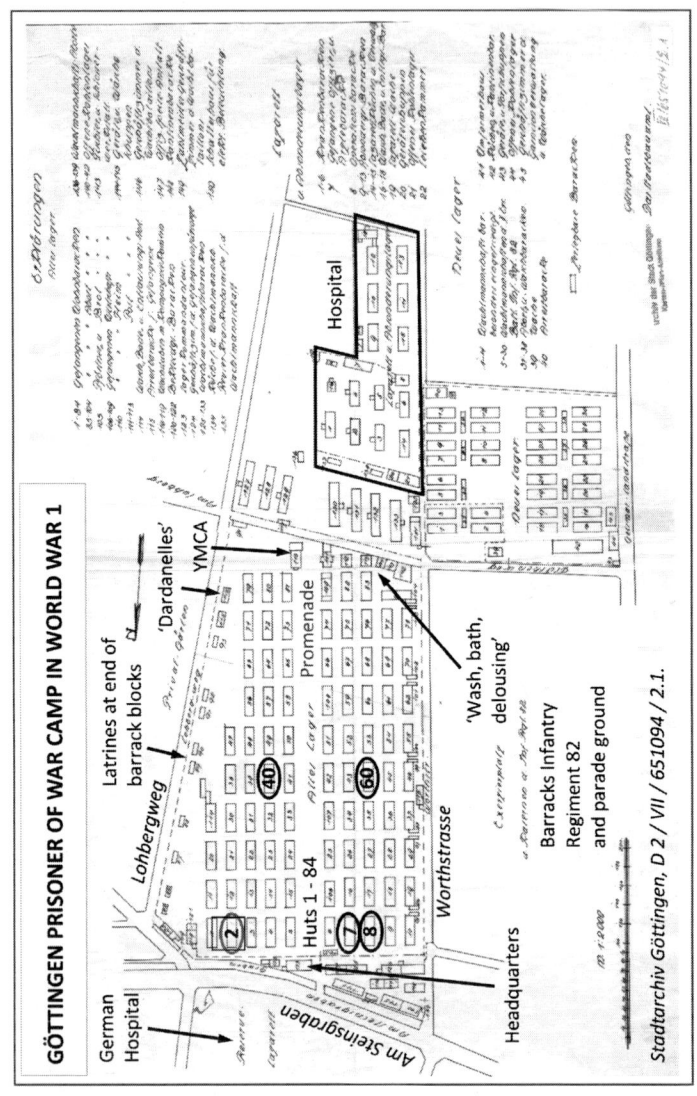

Chapter 6
Kriegsgefangener

On Monday 26th April 1915, shot through the arm, weak, bleeding, left behind and unable to escape, Kenneth waited in his farm hideout until dawn to see what the Germans would do:

> 'We heard them chattering outside the barn, and we all kept quiet. The man who was wounded in the night wanted to be turned over or something, but the others told him to keep quiet. Then all of a sudden, the pen on the other side of the passage was flooded with daylight and we heard, 'Hands up, *raus, raus* [out, out]'. After a bit, they came in and cleared us out. I was the last to leave and as I was going out a German pushed past me and went out. I looked around and found I was alone and darted back into the pen I came from. It was quite dark in there, the door was in one corner and I squatted in the other corner on the same side with my back to the passage. Then thinking that the small amount of light coming from the door of the shed in the next pen over the half wall shone on me, I moved across to opposite the door and huddled up in the dark there.
>
> A German came and stood in the door and looked towards me, another came and asked him in German if all were out, he said, 'Yes', and to make sure struck a match and saw me. He threatened me with his bayonet and I got up and left.
>
> There were a lot of Germans entrenched at the other

side of the ruined building next to us and more on the road beyond. They got us all together and marched us off. As we passed the trenches one German stood hitting each man as he passed with the butt of his rifle. An officer told him to stop before I got to him.

I had seen them drag out the wretched man with the broken legs, who I had spent the day before with. Two Germans pulled him along with his legs dangling, why they couldn't have carried him on the stretcher he was on I can't imagine. I think it was him I heard behind me as I went down the road being dragged along by two unwounded prisoners and saying, 'I can't stand it, I can't stand it'. We passed some stretchers after a time and perhaps they put him on one as I didn't see him again.

There were some unwounded among us including two officers. I heard one of them telling the other how he was caught. He was looking for some regiment, I think the Monmouths, he left his platoon and went on and shouted, 'Is that the Monmouths?' A voice answered, 'Yes, step forward'.[109] He did so and found himself surrounded by Germans, he said he was glad he saved his platoon.

The unwounded were helping the worst wounded. The rest of us paired off and got on as best we could. I had as a mate a man who had a slight wound in his leg and we clung to each other. We went very slow with frequent halts. Our guards were marine and some of them gave us a drink of coffee from their water bottles.'

The German infantry that approached the Gravenstafel Ridge were from the 2nd Reserve Ersatz Brigade of the 51st Reserve Division to the west, and the 38th Landwehr Brigade of the 1st

---

109 The 1st Monmouthshires from the 28th Division were in the line east of the Canadians.

Chapter 6 Kriegsgefangener

Landwehr Division to the east. However, the Saxon Sturmbrigade von Schmieden, a composite formation organized from battalions of the 27th Reserve Corps to exploit any progress on the left wing of the 26th Corps, was pushed through the 2nd Reserve Ersatz Brigade on 24th April, and it seems that the von Schmieden brigade took the area of Locality C and Boetleer's Farm on the 26th. The 'marines' were probably from Matrosen-Regiment Nr. 5, an infantry regiment made from reservist seamen belonging to the 4th Marine Brigade, another exploitation formation, which similarly advanced into the area on 25th April. This brigade seems to have relieved Brigade Schmieden on the ridge during the night of the 26th.[110] But during the day, it appears that they provided the prisoner guards to the rear.

Kenneth was now a *Kriegsgefangener;* a prisoner of war. He continues:

'We went about two miles and came at last to a village. It was full of Germans and what Belgians there were, were driven away. At frequent intervals along the street were large cook wagons with limbers. These consisted of large coppers with fires below for making coffee. Some were ready, and the Germans filled their bottles at them and some were being boiled up. There was a huge quantity of them.

Most of the Germans watched us pass in silence but one man shouted in good English and the most unparliamentary language that we fought for money not for our Fatherland. One couldn't make the obvious retort that he fought only because he had to and after all a mercenary was better than a conscript.

We went some way down the village and then stopped and they began sorting out those wounded in the legs and

---

110 Derived from: Baumgarten-Crusius, Artur. *'Sachsen in Großer Zeit'*, Leipzig, Akademische Buchhandlung R. Max Lippold, 1919, and Dominik, Hugo. *'Das Matrosen-Regiment Nr. 5'*, Oldenburg, Stalling, 1929.

putting them in a cottage. They passed me by. One of our officers said to me, 'You don't look as if you could go much further'. I said, 'No, but they won't let me go'. He said something to the Germans and one asked me if I could march another four kilometres. I said, 'No', and they let me go into the cottage.

They put us in one of the front rooms, the floor was covered with some flock stuff and on the door was chalked, *Gott strafe England* [May God punish England]. We asked for water and between us produced two water bottles. One German was kept busy carrying us water in these and a good sized can for quite a long time. A doctor came in to see us and examined our dressings saying, 'Poor man, poor man'. One of the men wanted to smoke so I asked the doctor, *'Ist rauchen verboten?'* [Is smoking forbidden?] (that much German I had learnt at Saarbrücken) he asked the guards and they said, 'Yes', because of the flock stuff on the floor.[111]

They asked for our papers and we handed them up and got them back. I did not hand over my diary and as they made no attempt to search us, I got it through unseen. I will tell in its place how I got it out of Germany again.'

Out of the front line, the Allied captured were now transported rearwards, through Belgium and into Germany and Kenneth describes his particular journey:

'They fell us in once outside and then sent us back. After about an hour we went out to a sort of train on tram lines in the street and in it went on to the station at Roulers [Roesalere, about seven miles northeast of Ypres]. Here we were met by some young Red Cross Germans who carried the worst cases on their backs to the train.

---

111 Saarbrücken was where Kenneth had worked as an industrial journalist before the war.

Chapter 6 Kriegsgefangener

We were put in box cars with boards across for seats. There were 38 in my car. A Red Cross youth chatted to us for a bit as well as he could, he said he came from Hanover. He told us we should have good beds in Germany and when we asked how soon we should get there we understood him to say 10 o'clock that night. Soon after they shut and locked the doors and we sat and waited but it was 10 p.m. before we started.

I shall never forget that journey. This was the 26th. We were in that car all day and night, and all day and night of the 27th. At intervals along the line they let us out for a bit and gave us food, but being all wounded together made it worse, if you touched a man he groaned. The food and water was not plentiful, and the place was so crowded the back rows hardly got any.

I was feeling worse and worse, and on the second night I could stand sitting no longer and I got down between the seats and got a sleep. It must be remembered that I had had none except about two hours since the night of the 21st. I don't think I slept long. I woke feeling suffocated to find the benches above me occupied. My struggles to get up only elicited groans. At last I rolled over and over to the open space in the middle of the car. We were all by this time in a bad way and apt to think only of ourselves. I had no sooner got there than I wanted a seat. I got the end of a form and managed to edge the next man along till I could sit down. The horror ended next morning when we were put into an ordinary German third-class carriage, bare wooden seats but heaven after that car.

I think then we had only got out of Belgium. We had gone so slow before with long stops. Now we went at a decent pace, crossed the Rhine at Essen and reached a place I believe named Altenburg [possibly Arnsberg] at about noon. Here they gave us all soup in a building against the station. Here I met some men I knew in our platoon and stuck to them after that. One man in our platoon got separated from us but three of us kept together. Here also I saw Captain Harvey.

After we had finished they began sorting us out, most of us were sent to hospitals in the town but 28 of us, including Captain Harvey and two other officers were put into a train and sent to Hofgeismar near Cassel, where we arrived after dark.

It was here I came across the German incapacity for counting for the first time. I never discovered it when at Saarbrücken. We were only 28 in number, yet they kept us 20 minutes while officers, doctors and men counted us and made it different each time. We said, 'The idiots can't count'. Later we found that to be quite true.

When at last the counting was over we marched up to a large house used as a hospital. We were accompanied all the way by staring crowds that huddled around the lampposts to see us better. At the drive gate to the house we left them behind.

When we arrived at the house we were given soup in the hall and then went a few at a time to get a bath. The other two and I got ours early. I had great difficulty in getting off my boots as my feet had swelled and I could only use one hand. The German would only stand on my toe which made it worse. I got them off in the end and got a bath and washed off the blood as well as I could. They gave us nightgowns and we went upstairs and at last got to bed and oh, how I did enjoy it. Three times has bed felt heavenly to me during this time; at Hofgeismar, at the hospital at Göttingen and the first night at Mürren.'

Kenneth's enforced travels between 1915 and 1919 were

Chapter 6 Kriegsgefangener

varied. How and when he moved from Ypres in Belgium to Göttingen and Mannheim in Germany, and thence to Mürren in Switzerland, we will discover in due course. He resumes:

'There were six in our room – three Imperials, my two friends and myself. It was an ordinary house with a small garden and a yard at the back. The doctor's room was on the ground floor and we had to go down to be dressed and for the frequent inoculations they gave us. The bath was in the basement.

They took our clothes and boiled them, caps and all, except the boots. These last were left for days in the yard and the sentries helped themselves to several including mine. The caps on being boiled, of course came to pieces. The khaki underclothing and some kilts were boiled together, and all the colours ran and mixed. One of the 15th [Battalion] Canadians I made a great friend with later, had a kilt which he kept as a souvenir, all the colour was washed out and run together with khaki mixed with it; a horrible looking rag. At this hospital, we had a piece of bread and butter at 8 a.m., 10 a.m. and 3 p.m. with coffee. We had dinner, mostly soup, at 12 [noon] and supper, soup or cheese, the latter often uneatably strong, at 6 p.m.

As soon as we could get our money changed, we three Canadians used to buy sugar and bread from the kitchen and other food. We shared out with the other three in our room and about ran out of funds. I think I had 40 pfennigs left when I got into hospital at Göttingen, I was glad of the money for those socks.

On April 30th, they gave us special postcards with a sort of form to fill in and a small space for correspondence. I gather they went quicker as there was a long time at home after they got my postcard before they got the letter. I wrote on May 2nd. It was here we first met that pretty little word *Kriegsgefangenen-sendung* or Prisoner's Post.'

Kenneth's postcard to his mother dated 30th April and sent from *Reserve Lazarette* [Hospital], *Hofgeismar bei Cassel*, was brief and reads, 'I am prisoner here with flesh wound in arm – couldn't write before above is my address – can only write two letters and four cards a month. Keep casualty lists for me. You can send parcels. Please send tobacco, chocolate etc., not perishable food as they take a long time – you can also send money – am not sure how by telegram I think, please send a pound a month, I will repay. Had hoped this wound meant nice time at home with you. Am ill and in hospital. Had long tiring journey here and much enjoy present rest. They are very strict here but treat us fairly well.'

The subsequent letter that he mentions arrived in early June and his mother circulated it around the family. It clearly mentioned something of the suspicion Kenneth had that the Canadians would be criticised for retreating, budging, during their time in the Ypres Salient as his sister Hilda stated that she was concerned that he did not know how splendidly people thought the Canadians had done.

Kenneth continues to describe his misfortunes:

> 'I was very weak and bad all this time and my hand was smarting, burning and very tender and now and then it used to keep me awake at night. On May 6th, I nearly fainted while waiting to be dressed. They gave the others some cotton trousers and let them get up and go out but would give me none. On the 9th I borrowed a pair and went out for an hour. I did not get any of my own until the 11th when I was warned to leave next day.
>
> On May 8th, Private Dixon of our battalion who had died there was buried.[112] They gave him quite a decent funeral

---

112 17216 Private William Dickson, son of William and Kate Dickson, of Beaver Creek, Alberni, British Columbia, who died on 6th May. He is interred in

Chapter 6 Kriegsgefangener

and a good many of the English went. That same evening Captain Harvey died and they all went to his funeral again, he had a hearse.[113] I did not go to either.

I was practically dug straight out of bed to go to Göttingen. My wound had healed but my hand was no manner of use and I was very weak still from loss of blood. Since I was captured I had let my beard grow and I looked a plaintive object.

We left Hofgeismar at about 9 a.m. and went to Cassel where we changed. While waiting we were put in a room in the station full of German soldiers. They were fairly good to us and one of them took a lot of trouble to screen the windows, so the crowd outside couldn't see in.'

Kenneth's journey ended at Göttingen, an ancient university town on the River Leine in Lower Saxony about 100 kilometres south of Hannover. The Germans set up a prisoner of war camp there in 1914 at a place called Ebertal, below the Lohberg Mountain on a wheat field next to a military barracks. They had planned for a maximum population of 10,000 prisoners, but by August 1915, the number of prisoners of war had swelled to twice that number, consisting of British, French, Belgians and Russians, the latter having been captured on the Eastern Front where Russia was fighting German and Austro-Hungarian forces.[114] Many of the Canadians taken at Ypres were sent to this camp, or to Giessen in Hesse.[115]

Niederzwehren Cemetery, Kassel. Pay and Record Office op. cit. and CWGC op. cit.

113 Originally reported as killed in action, Captain Harvey was in fact wounded and taken prisoner, dying later from his wounds. He is also interred in the Niederzwehren Cemetery, Kassel. CWGC op. cit.

114 Derived from: Polauke, Marina, *'Die Siedlung im Ebertal'* at: https://goettingensozial.wordpress.com. and Stange, Carl. *'Das Gefangenenlager in Göttingen'*, Louis Hofer, Göttingen 1915.

115 Most camps were pulled down after the war, but the Göttingen Camp was built more robustly than most. It was updated after the war and turned into low-

'We reached Göttingen sometime in the afternoon, it is a long walk up to the camp and when we were halted outside the *Kommandantur* [headquarters] in the sun I had to lie down. Some men who saw me coming told me later they were sure I would die. They kept us there some 10 minutes and then we were let into the camp and put in one of the huts.'

About 300 camps were instituted in Germany from early 1915 and during the war, some 2,400,000 soldiers of all nationalities were held by Germany. The conditions in some of these camps were appalling, others less so.

As Kenneth appraised his new home, news of his capture circulated around his family and it is worth diverting to summarise their activities. His widowed mother Adelaide was living in Aspley Guise. Elder sister Ada was with her vicar husband and children in Staverton, where she had become the Lady Superintendent of her local Red Cross branch. Brother Arthur was living in Pinner with his wife and young daughter, and he continued his work as a government ammunition inspector, also designing electrical systems for government buildings. Brother Hugh was still sheep farming in New Zealand and married to Amy, writing to the family to say how he hated being 'out of it'. The Reverend Lionel remained in Western Canada in his isolated parish, reading of Kenneth's capture in the Canadian newspapers.

By the time Kenneth was imprisoned, his younger sister Hilda had deployed to France with the Red Cross Voluntary Aid Detachment (VAD), starting work at Malassise Hospital at St. Omer, previously a monastery and later titled No. 7 General Hospital, where she was Quartermaster. She then moved to assist the doctors and nurses in a general hospital in Boulogne. The youngest, Philip, had joined up for full wartime service and was serving as a lieutenant in the Royal Engineers. In July 1915, he

---

income housing for homeless veterans and their families. The barracks stood until the late 1960s, when they were replaced with modern apartment blocks.

Chapter 6 Kriegsgefangener

was posted to the 85th Field Company and served in Gallipoli, but when this company left there he was laid low by dysentery and sent to Egypt that autumn to recover.

The family had heard about the brave activities of the 7th Canadian Battalion at the Battle of St. Julien, but had no news of it from Kenneth until his 30th April card arrived, though Hilda had met a soldier from the battalion in Boulogne on 25th April who had told her that Kenneth was 'OK'. However, it is clear that an official notification of his capture was received some time in May.

On 15th May, Hilda wrote, 'I am most awfully sorry about poor old K getting just what he dreaded, it is most tantalising to think that he would have otherwise come down here [Boulogne] with his wound – I doubt England – all the trains come through here and if men have friends or relations here they will put them off even if the train is going elsewhere. But we must look on the bright side of it and think of him as out of such severe danger now. All the Germans aren't such brutes, one can only hope he'll strike the best kind. I am going to write to him. I am very glad they allow them to write as much as that. I suppose he won't like to tell us how and when he got his wound. What a lot there will be to hear when the war is over.'

Hilda's remarks may reflect news of a number of atrocities actually committed by German troops during their advance through Belgium in 1914, and to the consequent British 'atrocity propaganda' which depicted the Germans as murderous monsters. Kenneth continues his saga by describing the people and the place of his new abode:

'I must now interrupt my personal narrative to describe the camp at Göttingen, the various nationalities in the camp, what things had been like there during the preceding winter, what they were like when we got there and how we used to spend our time.

The camp at Göttingen was situated at the edge of the

town on the slope of a hill. Across the road were a number of huts used as a hospital for wounded Germans. Below the camp was a barracks and parade ground, above the hill was wooded and was crowned at the top by a tower known as Bismarck Tower.

Down the centre of the camp ran a Promenade some quarter of a mile long. Part of its width was paved with sleepers lying skin to skin and two-abreast. On this Promenade at the side were water hydrants at intervals with concrete round them for washing on. On one side, the huts came up to the Promenade, but on the other was a bit of ground between the Promenade and the huts where they used to grow potatoes.

There were 84 huts, each hut was divided into two by a partition and there was a small room at each end called by us 'bunks' and generally reserved for sergeants. The bunks held five each and the larger rooms 55 each making 120 men per hut. The huts were numbered from the entrance gates, the other half being A. Thus 24 and 24A were the two halves of one hut.

The huts were arranged in rows extending through the width of the camp at right angles to the Promenade which by the way rejoiced in the name of *Hauptagestrasse* [possibly *Hauptstrasse* or Main Road]. The camp was divided into four companies, though there was no barrier between them. For some unknown reason No. 2 came first then Nos. 1, 3 and 4.

In the large room of each hut there was a stone and brick chimney in the centre and on each side of this an erection of beds. One of these held four on each of two decks and the other six on each of its decks. There were also beds divided by wooden partitions like fiddles on board ship along the

Chapter 6 Kriegsgefangener

outside walls. Except for this framework, beds were laid out on the bare floor. There were two tables and several stools to each half hut. The bunks were similarly arranged.

Each man had one mattress stuffed with some sort of chopped material, later they used to stuff them with paper, and two blankets, all of which were very dirty. One also had two bowls; a large one for washing and a small for eating, and a spoon. One lived and ate in the same room.

At intervals along the Promenade were the cookhouses, one for each company, a canteen and to one side the bath house about the only brick building, the rest being built of wood on a brick foundation. At the far end was the YMCA, newly built when we got there, also the parcel offices.'

Early in the war, prompted by its American branch, the YMCA mobilized on an international basis to assist war prisoners, irrespective of national origin or religious creed. YMCA huts supplied soldiers with food and a place to rest. When the German Ministry of War reached an agreement with the chief American YMCA negotiator in Europe, Archibald C. Harte, and the American YMCA to establish three huts in prison camps, Göttingen was among the initially selected sites and the YMCA building was opened in April 1915. Kenneth continues:

'Outside the camp at the entrance gates end was the *Kommandantur* offices and barracks or huts for sentries. There were more huts for sentries at the other end and beyond them was the hospital.

The hospital was in its own barbed-wire enclosure, it consisted of some eight or 10 huts with fairly good beds, mattresses, pillows stuffed with straw, sheets and a number of blankets in one cover. There was a place for disinfecting clothes in the hospital enclosure and a doctors' hut with kitchen, operating rooms etc. Each hut had a bath in it, and the first thing one did on coming in was to have a bath while one's clothes were steamed and disinfected.

I forgot to mention the paths also ran between the lines of huts in the camp. Later on, two paths were made between each row and each half row on either side of the Promenade was surrounded with wire netting with gates. This netting was double with a five-foot space between so that any half row was isolated from the rest.

The bath house consisted of a place for washing the clothes of the camp, but we usually washed our own in cold water as it was hard to know when they were coming, and they charged rather high for it. There was also the bath house proper. This was in three, a long room with 24 showers in it and two dressing rooms. Later they built a place for disinfecting clothes in. The bath was about the best thing in the camp.

The latrines were at the far top edge of the camp and each hut had one for use at night. Later when the half rows were divided up they only closed those compartments at night and made a latrine and water hydrant in each.

The nationalities in the camp were French, Belgians, Russians and English. The Russians were kept in separate huts as they had had fever among them when they first came, the others were pretty equally divided in each hut. At the end of August 1915, they put the different nationalities into different huts and in April 1916, they were put into companies by themselves. Nos. 1 and 2 Companies were Belgians, one being Flemings and the other Walloons. No. 3 Company was English and No. 4 French. When we got there the French were in the majority, later a lot got sent to work and Belgians were imported. A certain Professor Stange of Göttingen university got all the better class Belgians sent

Chapter 6 Kriegsgefangener

to Göttingen to try and turn the Flems against the Walloons and *vice versa* and to ingratiate them with Germany. This was towards the end of the time I was there and, so far as I could see, he was failing hopelessly.'

Professor Carl Stange of the University of Göttingen was very active in the German YMCA movement and sought to improve the conditions within the prison camp as his Christian mission. He wrote the book *Das Gefangenlager in Göttingen* [The Prison Camp in Göttingen] in mid-1915 as an overview of the facility and the German military's practices.[116] Stange worked with the American YMCA and helped get the YMCA building completed by April 1915. During the conflict, Stange worked with the prisoners, setting up correspondence courses so that college students imprisoned in Göttingen could resume their education, and establishing a library with some 10,000 books. The camp also had a chapel and a hospital.

In early 1915, the German Government started to see an opportunity to indoctrinate Flemish prisoners of war so they would support a planned post-war division of Belgium into a French-speaking part and a *Herzogtum Flandern* (Flanders Duchy) that was supposed to be annexed to Germany. On the whole, this indoctrination effort failed, and the Germans noticed that Walloon and Flemish prisoners of war were getting along better the longer they were imprisoned. When a prisoner of war exchange with France became possible in April 1918, most Flemish prisoners opted to be sent to France rather than stay in Germany.[117]

In characteristically forthright language, Kenneth describes the nationalities he encountered at Göttingen and the stories of them asserted by his fellow inmates:

'The French were not liked by us. It must be remembered that these were the *Poilus* [infantrymen] of the beginning

---

116 Derived from: Stange op. sit.
117 Derived from: Ibid and Polauke op. sit.

of the war, I know nothing about the men of Verdun and the Somme, and I am quite willing to believe that they were different. I am merely describing them as I saw them. They were dirty almost beyond description not only in their persons and clothes, but their habits were most insanitary. When we were at the front, no British troops who had taken our trenches from the French had a good word to say for them and we were no exception to that rule.[118]

Besides their filthy ways and habits, they had not treated our men right during the previous winter [at Göttingen]. They could get food when our men were starving but they never gave the English any. The English used to watch them peeling potatoes in order to get the peel and Frenchmen have been known to put it in the fire in order that the English might not get it. The same thing applied to cigarette ends. Of course, fights between the two nations were frequent in consequence.

The Belgians were cleaner by far than the French, but they had acted to our men in exactly the same way. It used to make our chaps mad to hear how the Belgian refugees were being cared for in England and to see them drawing parcels sent from England, and to remember how in their need these same Belgians now fed by our countrymen refused them potato peel or cigarette ends.

If ever an Englishman did anything likely to get him into trouble the French and Belgians were sure to give him away. If an Englishman had a row with a Frenchman or Belgian half a dozen others would set on him. Of course, then the other English would start and there would be a free fight. The French and Belgians being worsted in the fight used to complain to the Germans. At last the *Kommandant*

---

118 *Poilu*; an informal term for a French World War I infantryman, meaning literally, hairy one.

Chapter 6 Kriegsgefangener

[commandant] got tired of punishing the English for fighting and as the *Gott strafe England* regime was dying out he said the others must fight their own battles.

As against all this bad feeling I am glad to say we had a great liking for the Russians and the Russians half-worshipped us. They would stick to us through thick and thin, they had not much idea of what to do and what not to do, but firmly believed that what we did must be right. I remember a parade we had, they got each nationality separately and wanted them to volunteer for work. The French and Belgians volunteered freely, the Russians said, 'If the English go we will go, if they won't we won't'. When they came to us we all refused, the Russians refused too.

The Russians had no use for the French. The French used to try to sell them mouldy bread at exorbitant prices and would give nothing. We used to give away what we didn't want and sell the other things cheap, so we got their good opinion. There was always one price for an Englishman, another for a Russian and quite another for French or Belgians.

The English, or perhaps I should say British, but I have been using the term in its continental sense, to the Germans we were all *Englanders*, were mostly Tommies of the old pre-war Army. There were some Canadians, mostly of the 15th Battalion, who were captured when I was. I had had a short experience of Tommies when with the Hampshires, here I had plenty more. I had always imagined that the Army was recruited 'from the scum of the streets'. Nothing could be further from the truth. British Tommies represent every class to be found among our 'working classes' and some higher classes too. There are some 'scum' but they have been so altered by the army training that they can no longer be ranked as such.

The army training has raised all to a certain pitch of excellence. The most noticeable thing about them is their cleanliness. Their persons, clothes even the rags they had when I got there, bed places, huts, eating utensils all were clean. The ordinary Tommy washes his face, ears and neck two or three times a day, has a bath regularly when he can and keeps himself shaved. There is no such smell among them that one finds among working men as a rule. If their army training inculcates this cleanliness among all ranks of the New Army, it will be one more blessing the war has undoubtedly given us as a nation.

Apart from his cleanliness Tommy Atkins is kindness itself to those sick or wounded. I have had plenty of experience of this. They say the Tommies are callous to the dead but tender as a woman to the wounded. They will pile up their dead to heighten the parapet but will go without themselves to help a wounded comrade. When I first got to camp they used to make my bed and wash it out unasked. They brought me cocoa and grape nuts, and if I had wanted it I could have extra soup, and all this at times when parcels were rare and they themselves not well off. They gave us our Church Army parcels which had been sent to the camp. One man who had got a parcel asked me and my chums to come and share it with him. He used to make my Bovril and Oxo when anyone gave me any and generally looked after me. His name was McGuire.[119]

But apart from his good qualities as a man, Tommy was the best of soldiers. I speak in the past tense for that army has gone and I know nothing about the New Army. We

---

119 Probably 9673 Private John McGuire of the 1st Leicestershires who came from County Cork, Ireland. *'The Wooden City - A Journal for British Prisoners of War'*, No. 8 Göttingen, 15th October 1915, University of Pennsylvania. The Penn Libraries at: www.library.upenn.edu. It seems that McGuire also ended up as an internee at Mürren, but Kenneth does not mention him whilst there.

Chapter 6 Kriegsgefangener

Canadians who saw just a little of it can dimly realise, in a way people at home or later comers cannot do, what the Tommies went through during that first autumn and winter. The retreat from Mons, the awful fighting against odds and overwhelming artillery, the new made, half-finished and flooded trenches, I have had it all described to me many a time. As I said we saw a little of it and we can dimly realize, and these men stuck it all with a grin, they were smiling and singing when we were at the Front, and after what I shall describe shortly, they were smiling and singing at Göttingen. No wonder Kipling writes of Tommy Atkins as he does, no one shall run him down again in my presence without challenge.

There was a regular camp lingo [jargon] understood by all, it was a mixture of English, French, German and Russian. It had no grammar merely a short vocabulary and signs made up the rest. The French were always called 'Froggies', the Belgians 'Belgies' and the Russians 'Ruskies', which is what the latter called themselves.

Some of the Tommies got mixed over foreign words and phrases. One man always came to grief on that dear little word *Kriegsgefangenen-sendung* that we had to put on all our letters. He said to a friend, 'You might write that long word for me, you know, Krugers offended'. Another man used to stop Frenchmen on the Prom as we called it for short, though it is a loathely [sic] word, to ask for a light, and used to say to them, '*Fermer la porte*'.

Some words were corrupted down. *Quelle heure est-il* became 'Cloratile' and *Bonsoir monsieur* became 'Bonswar manure'. On the other hand, English was murdered too. A Frenchman was heard to remark, 'To spoke English is very many difficult'. We had regular words for some things, disinfection for lice was *nicht pone,* a mixture of German and French and pronounced 'nixpoo'. Of that more later.

The Ruskies made excellent servants. Sometime about July 1915, they started coming round to our huts and washing our bowls for us. The Germans used to chase them away at first but gave up in the end. They would talk to us with signs and camp lingo and tell us about their share in the fighting. Just before that in hospital a Ruskie had attached himself to me and used to insist on getting my grub for me, making my bed etc. As I did not want all the bread I got there I gave it to him and anything else I didn't want. One day he had done so well he seemed to think he ought to work a bit more for it, so he had a regular clean-up of all the bottles etc. beside my bed. He washed the stool they stood on, but he did <u>not</u> wash those of a Frenchman who shared the stool with me.

One day in hospital, I wanted him to wash my clothes, but he only did them in a parcel and put them under my bed, I was told that being Sunday washing was not allowed. I pulled them out next day to remind him and they were at once pounced on by another Ruskie who went and washed them to the great discomfiture of my own man.

At first when they came to our huts in camp we gave them German soup that we didn't want, then German bread and then money. Later when there was nothing to be bought in the canteen, we gave them regular English food from our parcels. In the end those in the camp got parcels of their own and were too well off to work for us.

They used to wash our clothes and dishes and do any odd jobs we wanted. In the winter 1915-1916 some Ruskies used to come to our hut with coal. Coal was scarce and this they brought was good hot coal. Where they stole it, I don't

Chapter 6 Kriegsgefangener

know but they used to come with huge lumps weighing a hundredweight under their coats. We paid them well for it. We made a subscription of 10 pfennigs to each from time to time round the hut and with the money bought food for the 'Coal Ruskies'. Anyone getting what he did not care for in a parcel sold it to this fund. Two of them came regularly for some time, then they stopped, after a bit two more came but did not last long, either they were sent away or could not get the coal. We took good care they were satisfied with the price and did not take it elsewhere.

The Ruskies seemed able to eat anything. Bread that had not quite got to that bright orange colour that precedes the black stage they seemed to enjoy, anyhow they came after it then when they had plenty to eat. At Mannheim they used to roam round our huts at tea time, saying nothing and watching for bread.[120] If they saw anything being thrown away they pounced on it. The bright orange they would not have but anything younger than that was acceptable.

They revelled in the raw salt herrings we used to get now and then. We never touched them if we could get anything else. They delighted in fish and also salt. In hospital, a Ruskie made a dish for himself – bread dipped in water full of salt, one of our chaps tried it and said it was worse than brine. 'Give it to the Ruskie' was quite a saying I have heard in Switzerland when the food was not to the speaker's taste. If the word went forth that the Ruskies were refusing the soup, we never thought it was worthwhile going for it.

On February 1st 1916, a whole lot of Ruskies were sent from Göttingen to dig trenches on the Western Front. Those that didn't get killed or who didn't escape returned on March 16th, starved, wounded and dying like flies. We

---

120 Kenneth staged in Mannheim after his sojourn in Göttingen, as we will discover.

made a subscription of grub and sent it into hospital for them. We were very well off just then and they got a lot. At our next concert, the Russian Committee thanked us for it. It was read out in Russian and English that we made this subscription for our starving Russian comrades who had been six weeks with practically nothing to eat. I wondered how the Germans present and who understood English, or they wouldn't come to our concert, liked it. I think it was while I was there the committees started. Each nationality had one and it looked after their interests.

In describing the various nationalities, one must not forget the Germans themselves. I will write of them as I found them and give their special misdeeds later. At first, they were confident in the result of the War. '*England kapout*', England done for, they would tell you, everyone was *kapout* in those days bar themselves.[121] At any and every victory, real or imagined, they put out all the flags.

They were especially triumphant during the Russian retreat in the Summer of 1915.[122] A Ruskie told a German there were more men in Russia than there were potatoes in Germany. We took no notice of them and their flags. We refused to believe any bad news until we got the English paper and by then it was stale. Thus, we heard of Townsend's

---

121 Kenneth seems to have used an archaic spelling of *'kaput'*, which has been retained.
122 Despite some Russian success in early 1915, German troops launched a counter-offensive in Galicia in May, which triggered the collapse of the entire southern flank of the Russian line. Hundreds of thousands of Russian troops were killed, wounded or captured. Further north, German troops seized Warsaw in early August.

Chapter 6 Kriegsgefangener

surrender[123], Kitchener's death[124] and the German report of the Battle of Jutland[125], we just didn't believe them any more than we believed in the Fall of Verdun[126] for which they put up their flags. As to the Battle of Jutland that was a great occasion of rejoicing, though one sentry who knew more than the rest told us he thought they had lost more than we had.

But towards the end of autumn of 1915, those who kept their eyes open began to wonder. The censor at Göttingen was standing outside his office one day watching the laden carts full of English parcels come in and remarked, *'England kapout, England nicht essen, England nicht brot, alles schwindel'* [England done for, nothing to eat, no bread, it is all a swindle].

In the beginning and during 1916, we used to twit [taunt] them. *'England kapout?'*, we would say, *'England nicht kapout'*, would be the sad answer. About that time the blockade was beginning to take effect, all food of certain sorts could only be obtained by tickets and we saw them lining up for it outside the shops.'

The British Royal Navy spent the war patrolling the North Sea, intercepting and detaining thousands of merchant ships thought to be harbouring cargo bound for enemy shores. The North Sea

---

123 On 29th April 1916, the 6th (Poona) Division of the Indian Army, under Major General Charles Townshend, surrendered to the Ottoman Turk Army at Kut-al-Amara in Mesopotamia, now in Iraq, having been besieged there for months.
124 Lord Kitchener was Secretary of State for War. On 15th June 1916, whilst travelling to Russia for a diplomatic meeting, *HMS Hampshire* on which he was travelling, struck a mine and sank. Kitchener and most of the crew drowned.
125 The Battle of Jutland is largely considered to be the only major naval battle of World War One. The British Royal Navy lost more men and ships, but the German Navy was not thereafter able to put to sea in strength during the war.
126 The long, bloody fight for Verdun continued throughout 1916. Though the defending French Army lost several forts, Verdun itself did not fall.

was declared a British military area on 3rd November 1914. The blockade strategy worked effectively as very few supplies reached Germany or its allies. This constant stranglehold wore away at the strength and morale of the German people and its Army and was an important factor in the Allies' success in 1918. Kenneth resumes his tale:

'On March 3rd 1916, a friend of mine saw children in Göttingen, which was a wealthy town without any slums, crowding outside the barracks for the spare soup and he saw a hose turned on them to drive them away. On April 5th 1916, the German paper stated that they were beaten by famine. While we were at Mannheim we were told on three occasions, I think, that there had been a bread riot in the town the night before.

The sentries used to cadge for our bread, that is our German bread, which we only eat when all else ran out, and which we generally used for fuel. They would do anything for a loaf of it and they used to sell what they got in the town. Many of us would refuse to give it on principle.

The sentries were certainly not well fed, we knew that. They used to come in for a working party having only had coffee, of sorts, for breakfast. They would find us sitting down to a sumptuous meal of more than they eat in a week and have to wait as we absolutely refused to go out without our breakfast. This was in the later days when we had things our own way. If we were annoyed by a lot of Germans staring at us through the wires, we would bring out and open our parcels to make their mouths water and that generally drove them off.

On our way to Switzerland [where, as we shall see, Kenneth travelled later in the war], we had some brawn for breakfast in the train and gave some to the German sentry.

Chapter 6 Kriegsgefangener

He gulped it down and sat watching for more, which he didn't get, just like a dog does.

Krieg nicht gut [war no good] they used to say. The following story emphasises that. When a German is killed his relations get a telegram, I don't think they heard anything else of them. There was a German widow with twelve sons all of them at the front. She got eleven telegrams and then wrote to the Kaiser asking that her one remaining son might be sent home to support her. Her request was granted, and orders sent to the front for him to come home. But before these orders could be obeyed, she had got a twelfth telegram. Her last son was dead, and she died too.

Germany's shortage of men showed itself in many ways. When we got there, there were sentries at intervals all along the Prom and along the top of the camp as well as inside the wires. On April 26th 1916, there were no sentries on sentry go inside the wires. In the early days, there had been three sentries to each hut, who did nothing else and when we got there, there was one per hut. When we left each sentry had charge of four or five huts and often had to do sentry go as well. One-eyed sentries were common. One at Mannheim had lost his right eye, which would quite incapacitate him from shooting.

The Germans hated going to the *Krieg* as they call the front. To send them was the worst punishment they could be given. They have been known to weep when passed by the doctor and ordered to the *Krieg*. Sometimes they used to tell us that they would surrender as soon as they got the choice.

The chief fault of the German Army from the German point of view was the lack of comradeship and the bullying. Any German would give another away if he found him doing anything. They could not understand the English sticking together. It was in this way that we English prisoners finally beat them and got more or less our own way. The English would behave as one man and we could play off one German against another. As to the bullying, everyone bullied those below him. They could not understand English privates refusing promotion, as they often do. To them promotion meant less to bully you and more for you to bully. Like all continental armies they had to salute everyone from *Unterofficier* [corporal] upwards. They used to make us do the same, but we got it limited to officers in the end.

As to training, the following seemed to be what they got, judging from what we saw going on on the parade grounds. They were taught to salute and taught it thoroughly. Then they were taught the 'goose step'. They did it in every sort of position and in every sort of uniform, they did it singly, they did it in pairs, they did it in squads, it took days and days. When they had so mastered the goose step as to be able to do it under any conceivable circumstances, they were set racing over high wooden walls, given a little open order training, this we only saw at Mannheim, a few route marches, and taught to cheer while charging, then they played the Dead March over them and sent them to the Front. We saw it again and again. We would hear them cheering and charging, next day was the Dead March and on the next a new lot learning to salute.

One thing, we found they did, they break step when 'marching easy'. It is a fatal thing to do. It is the step and only the step that keeps one going when one is dead beat, you get going mechanically. No wonder they couldn't catch up with us in the retreat from Mons. When 'marching to attention' they keep very good step, but the NCOs do not keep step with them. They used to sing as they passed our camp, one particular song ended up short. Our chaps got

Chapter 6 Kriegsgefangener

hold of the air, put their own words to it and made fun of it. There was a great row once they caught us.'

Before Kenneth and the Canadians arrived at Göttingen, those captured earlier in the war had suffered a harsh regime. Kenneth was told about these times by prisoners that had been incarcerated then and now pauses to describe what he heard:

'I now come to a description of the 'Dark Ages' as the Tommies call the first winter of the war [1914]. Of course, these stories I am going to give are at second hand. I am merely retailing from memory the stories as they were told to me and in details they may be a bit inaccurate. But of the main truth of them I have not the slightest doubt. I have heard the same stories over and over again from all sorts of men, some of whom did not know each other and so what I have heard has plainly proved the truth of it all. As I used to listen to these stories my blood used to boil. I will give the stories as accurately as I can.

I will start with the capture of the Leicesters as it was among them I was placed when I came to Göttingen. The Leicesters held a part of the line in front of Fleurbaix, in advance of where we were afterwards. They had been holding back some five times their number for days. They got orders to retire, but these orders did not reach some of them with the consequence that they were left behind and after a gallant resistance, surrounded and had to surrender.'

The 1st Battalion The Leicestershire Regiment took part in the First Battle of Ypres in 1914. The Battalion held a railway embankment at Armentieres between 23rd and 26th October facing many times its own strength, as the Germans tried to break through with sheer weight of numbers. In the early hours of 25 October, D Company was overrun.[127] Those men not killed in

---

[127] Derived from: *'The Story of The Royal Leicestershire Regiment'* on the website of the Regiment at: https://www.royalleicestershireregiment.org.uk/

the hand to hand fighting which followed were marched away as prisoners of war, at least some such as Kenneth's friend Private McGuire, to Göttingen. Kenneth continues:

'One would have thought a civilised race would have shown honour to such gallant foes, this is what the Germans did. They took their greatcoats, jackets and woollen sweaters, cut their belts and braces, slit their trousers down the back, so that they had to hold them up and marched them between a double line of men who kicked and punched them with their rifles. Some of them were wearing these slit trousers, sewn up again, when I arrived at Göttingen. After this they were marched to Lille being kicked and pounded all the way by any Germans they met. The Germans took particular delight in hitting one man who was crippled with rheumatism and generally fell down when struck.

At Lille, they were put in a building, then someone asked for a volunteer to draw bread. A man named Weston volunteered and was taken before a German officer who spoke English. He asked how long he had been in the Army [and] Weston told him. He said, 'Don't you know better than to fight against Germany? How dare you fight against Germany?' He then demanded to know the whereabouts of our artillery. Weston said he didn't know, no more he did. He was sent back for an hour and told if at the end of that time he didn't tell he would be shot. Weston was so tired that when he got back he went to sleep and slept undisturbed till morning.

Men of other regiments were made to march for miles with their hands over their heads and when they dropped them from fatigue, they were pounded and kicked. They were herded into box cars and locked up with only a couple of small barred windows for ventilation. At rare intervals,

history-of-the-regiment-2.

Chapter 6 Kriegsgefangener

they were given some watery soup. In the case of the Leicesters this was doped, which with the entire lack of sanitary arrangements, produced a state of things such that it is a wonder that it did not raise a fever.

After some three days of this, they arrived at Göttingen dressed in their shirts and trousers. This was the end of October, and they were captured during the First Battle of Ypres on October 24th. Göttingen Camp was then only being built and they were put into dugouts. They were given one thin blanket each which they draped over their shoulders to keep themselves warm. They used to fasten them with nails, but this was *verboten* and anyone with a nail in his blanket got punished.

No-one at Göttingen spoke English, but one of the Leicesters, a sergeant major by the name of Wheeler, spoke French and so interpreting was done through him and the French *Dolmetscher* [interpreter].[128] There were numerous roll calls, at all hours of the day, they were lined up and counted. Wheeler as *Dolmetscher* did not fall in with the others on one occasion and the Germans were one short. He explained that he was the one, but they couldn't understand it. They put them in fives, they put them in 10s and counted again and again, always they were one short. Finally, Wheeler fell in with the others and then at last they saw where they were wrong.

After a while some huts were finished, and they were put into them. The camp at this time was a sea of mud. The food they got was coffee, watery soup with one or two minute

---

128 Kenneth may be partly mistaken. The only sergeant major of the name of Wheeler found to have been at Göttingen was 5716 Company Quarter Master Sergeant, later Company Sergeant Major, John Wheeler of the 2nd Wiltshires. *'The Wooden City - A Journal for British Prisoners of War'*, No. 4, Göttingen, 15th August 1915. The Penn Libraries op. sit. Wheeler later became an internee in Holland.

pieces of cabbage for dinner and coffee at night. They were given a small loaf of bread once every three days. They soon got ravenously hungry. They generally ate the whole loaf as they got it and went hungry the other two days. They used to line up outside the cookhouse for extra soup and often had the hose turned on them. The dish it came to them in and their bowls were scraped absolutely clean with their fingers.

On one occasion, a man named Johnson was just getting some extra soup at the cookhouse when the *Kommandant*, the same one as when I was there, appeared. The crowd outside had failed to salute him, and he drew his sword and burst into the cookhouse shouting, or 'barking', at the top of his voice. Johnson dropped his bowl and fled.

We always called the particular raucous shouting of the Germans barking. The higher they were in rank the better they used to bark. The *Kommandant* at Göttingen, a colonel, was pretty good at it, but a friend of mine heard the *Kommandant* at Mannheim, a general, once bark at a Ruskie for not saluting him, he said it was a 'royal bark' quite outdoing the Göttingen Colonel. I should like to hear the Kaiser bark, it must be worth hearing.

In one of the camps at this time, things were about the same in all camps during the dark ages, the Ruskies stole the *Kommandant's* dog and ate it. One Ruskie angered a German at Göttingen and the German drew his revolver and fired at him about 10 yards range and missed him. The Ruskie turned round and said, *'Ruskie nicht kapout'* and then fled.

They used to round the men up in gangs and drive them off for *Arbeit,* or work, on the new huts. One man got his shoulder cut by an officer's sword for being too weak to

Chapter 6 Kriegsgefangener

carry the number of bricks the officer thought he should carry. One man was rounded up with the rest one day, he was wounded in the leg and lame. They made no difference between wounded and unwounded. In consequence, he could not keep up with the others, the sentry swore at him and hit him and finding that did no good, he finally drew back and shot him dead. I have been shown the spot where he fell, it was on the Prom some 50 yards from the *Kommandantur* and in full view of its windows. The other English went to pick him up but were driven off and he was carried away by Frenchmen. A German who was standing by laughed and handed the sentry another cartridge in place of the one he had used. Where they buried him we never discovered.

Just before I left Göttingen a deputation went to the Inspector at the hospital who was there at the time and asked where he was buried as they wished to put a cross on his grave. The only answer they got was, 'He was buried'. 'Yes, but where?' 'He was buried'. Not an Englishman there at the time but has the whole incident well implanted in his memory, and I think the fear of being held responsible and of possible reprisals made the *Kommandant* more cushy [easy] with us later on.

Our men then as later used to dodge this *Arbeit* as much as they could, but at that time the place teamed with sentries and if you ran from one you ran into another.

One night the Germans got it into their heads that someone had escaped, and in the middle of the night everyone was turned out, literally kicked out, for the long business of counting. Our poor chaps thought and hoped peace had been declared. The method of calling them in the morning was to kick or prod them with rifles. When the electric light was installed, as soon as it was turned on anyone who was awake woke the rest to avoid this daily ill usage.

There were then three sentries to each hut and they used to come in one after the other. The first saw the men were awake and cleaning the hut. The next saw that the first had done his work, and the third saw that the first two had done theirs.

All the winter long, our men were dressed in practically only a blanket and it was a cold winter. They had only this watery soup, more like dishwater than soup they told me, and bread every three days. Most of their time was spent hunting for food. They used to sell their shirts and socks and boots to the French to buy bread at the canteen. All their money, watches and valuables had been taken from them when captured.

One common practice was known as 'raiding the spud cart'. They used to watch for the cart bringing potatoes to the camp and though it was surrounded with sentries, they used to make a rush at it at the risk of their lives, grab a few potatoes and cook and eat them. At other times, they would roam about looking for potato peelings and other garbage and eat that.

One mad hid in the bread store, he had got on the fatigue for handing in the bread and he hid behind it and got locked in. When the Germans had gone his friends came to the window which he opened and handed out to them some 40 loaves. Then he himself escaped through the window. The Germans never found out who did it, but they made all the English stand out in the snow, some with no boots and some with blanket and trousers only, for four hours.

The general punishment at that time was to tie men to

Chapter 6 Kriegsgefangener

posts for hours at a stretch, sometimes for next to nothing, and some were so overcome that when released they could hardly stand.

Another method of getting food was to raid the canteen. A man would go in and ask for a loaf of bread, and when he had got that he would ask for something else, while they were getting that he would bolt with the bread. Another method was to get a stick with a nail in the end and hook the loaves through the window.

Even if a man tried to make his bread, when issued, last three days someone else would probably take it, starving men don't stick at trifles. One man was saving his loaf up for Christmas, when on returning to his bed he found it had gone. He had noticed the man who slept behind him munching bread in a quiet corner and taxed him with it when he confessed to having taken it. The man who had been robbed didn't want to say anything about it, but a corporal said that if he didn't tell Wheeler who was *Chef de Barraque* [the NCO in charge of a hut], he would do so. So, the two went together to the bunk and told Wheeler. They did not tell the Germans as the wretched man was not strong and would only have been tied to a post, so Wheeler reprimanded him, and it was arranged that he should give his loaf to the other man at the next issue.

Smoking all this time was forbidden and no tobacco was obtainable as a rule, but the men used to smoke whatever they could get and even peat which the foundations of the huts were filled with.

One man was taken on a fatigue down the town to carry some bags of coal or something. He was too weak to lift them and the sentry, extra soft-hearted for a German, did it himself. When they got back this sentry gave him some bread and got him extra soup from the cookhouses.

Certain fatigues were rewarded with soup and there was a regular scramble to get on these. Cleaning the Germans' huts was rewarded by their leavings, the scrapings of their plates etc., and this was much sought after.

Any spare soup going at meal times there was a scramble for. One day an Englishman got shoved by the press behind him right on to the dixie [cooking pot] of the soup. The German hit him three times in the face fetching blood each time. Hardly any fuel for fires was given to them, they did their best to keep a small fire on and used to huddle round it. One day two men saw a German civilian going along with a ladder. They followed him and he went up on to the roof of a hut to do some job up there. No sooner was his back turned than they took the ladder and fled and in a very short space of time it was broken up for firewood.

Often in better times I have seen men point to a dirty bit of food lying in the mud and say, 'That wouldn't be there long last winter'.

They had no medical attendance and the wounded in camp had no attention at all. There were no baths, and all were alive with lice. 'Doing nixpoo', i.e. hunting and killing lice, was a nightly occupation. They all grew beards they had nothing to shave with and at intervals they were clipped all over like a horse.

The first guards they had were Prussian guards. They were the worst of the lot. They had not been to the front themselves and when they saw our men lousing themselves they called them *Schweinerei* [a mess, derived from the word for pig]. Somewhere about the New Year a fresh lot

Chapter 6 Kriegsgefangener

of guards came that were better and when I got there, there were a third lot that were better still.

They were very fond of that word *Schweinerei* about the worst epithet in the German language I believe, they used it freely when I was there. Later its use was *verboten*. Then if a sentry called you it, you replied, 'Me *nicht Schweinerei, me Englisch gefangene,* you *Kommandant morgen'* [Commandant tomorrow], which always brought them to their knees, and they used to explain that it was the floor or some other inanimate object that was the *Schweinerei,* not you. The song 'Why do they call me Archibald?' was very popular at Göttingen in the summer of 1915 and there were many parodies. One was 'Why do they call me *Schweinerei*?'

At last just a little before Christmas the parcels began to arrive a few at a time. At first, they had to line up for them outside, the lists being put up the day before. One man, Corporal Beck of the Wiltshire Regiment, told me the story of his first parcel.[129] He was on the roll and on the strength of it he finished off his bread the day before, and lay all night dreaming of good things to eat. He lined up in good time and waited hours in the snow until all the parcels were given out and his name had not been called. Then he went to Wheeler, who from the first, managed the parcel office, and asked if there wasn't one for him. Wheeler said he thought there was a small one and after hunting through the waste paper produced a parcel containing a St. John Testament. No doubt the good lady who sent it meant well, but on the horrible irony of giving a Testament to a starving man; asking for bread and getting a stone with vengeance.[130]

---

129 Probably 8557 Corporal Percy Beck of the 2nd Wiltshires. *'The Wooden City - A Journal for British Prisoners of War',* No. 8 Göttingen, 15th October 1915. The Penn Libraries op. sit.
130 A reference to The Gospel of St. Luke Chapter 11, Verse 11.

Keeping The Old Flag Flying

Christmas Day 1914. I am afraid I can't do justice to it, as they did not speak much of it. Christmas 1915 I will describe in its place and the contrast should be noted. In 1914 the day was not much if any different from the rest. I think the bread issue had been the day before, they got the same dirty water masquerading as soup and the acorn coffee morning and evening. They huddled round their small fire clad in their blankets to try to get warm or they roamed round the camp looking for any garbage to assuage the pangs of hunger.

I say the contrast should be noted, with this in mind, that in 1914 the Germans had plenty of food had they chosen to give it to them. There was absolutely no lack whatever in any German household that Christmas. In 1915 the blockade had begun to tell a bit, but they gave us a meat meal which we ate, though we had parcels galore. More than that, in June 1916 we had to live for a fortnight on German grub at Mannheim and though not by any means overfed we were never hungry. It is true we bought stuff at the canteen, but this was mostly jam and things like that, yet in June there were several bread riots and German civilians had months before been glad, in the salt mines, to pick up and eat crusts thrown away by prisoners.

Why was all this? In 1914 [the Germans] were sure of winning, it did not matter what they did in Belgium or to their prisoners, they would never be called to account any more than they were in 1870. They could indulge their bent for cruelty to the utmost. But later on, those high up at any rate began to doubt and to fear reprisals, and orders filtered down to stop it. Bit by bit we noticed that as they got it worse in the field, they treated us better. An individual burst of temper there might be, but bad news for the Germans from the front always resulted in better treatment for us.

Chapter 6 Kriegsgefangener

They tried to wipe out their past misdeeds, but we saw through it, took all they gave us without thanks, and without abating one jot of our hatred for them.'

Having told us the stories passed on to him about the regrettable fate of prisoners of war in 1914, Kenneth returns to 1915 and to describing his own experiences at Göttingen. First, he gives some detail about the regime there:

'When we got there [in May 1915] things had improved past all knowledge. It may have been Neuve Chapelle, for the last month or six weeks it had got better and better.[131] Parcels were coming fairly regularly though far fewer than they were after. Men no longer were dressed in blankets. The Germans gave coats to those who had none and those who had no boots got clogs. The men lived largely on German soup, but the soup was better, was issued twice a day and looking for garbage and raiding the spud cart had ceased entirely.

We were locked up every night at 10 p.m. Smoking was allowed outside from 2 p.m. to 8 p.m. On July 21st, it was allowed at all hours. It was never allowed in the huts, but we smoked there all the same. Some Germans used to spend their time creeping around trying to catch men smoking in the huts, they were generally smoking themselves. Now and then they caught one and he generally went to the 'Dardanelles' [see below] but we kept scouts out and had warning words the commonest being 'Vandoon'. During the first Summer, the Dardanelles were full of people smoking, but later as labour got short in Germany and they wanted prisoners to work there were so many cases of refusing to work that such minor offences as smoking were overlooked.

---

[131] The Battle of Neuve Chapelle took place from 10th to 13th March 1915 and as we have seen, the Canadians played a supporting role. The British broke into the German lines but lacked the resources to exploit their success.

Keeping The Old Flag Flying

In my account of the camp I find I have omitted to mention the *Arresthaus* [arrest house] or Dardanelles as they were called by Germans and prisoners alike. They were situated at the top of the camp. I can't describe them very well as I had the good fortune to avoid them. The cells were small, about 8 feet x 6, I believe. Later they used to cram three men into them. The windows had shutters that let in air but kept out light. Smoking used to take place even there as cigarettes were smuggled in and the men hid them and blew smoke up between the boarding.

Every Sunday morning, they had a parade at which we were counted. This was by companies as a rule but every now and then they had a *Kommandant's* parade when all the camp were out. Later they started making us parade on Sundays with some article or other, our bowls or underclothing or spare pair of boots or something of that sort. The occupants of each hut were counted every night at bed time by the sentry.

Most men spent a lot of time dodging *Arbeit*. I was saved this as being a cripple, I was rarely taken. There were several ways of doing this, they used to dive through the windows and fly round the huts. In one half hut when they came for *Arbeit* they were told there was a *Dolmetscher* in the other half and while the Germans were there the first half quietly emptied.

Nos. 2 and 2A were filled with English in the summer of 1916. These huts lay way up from the Promenade and there were always men sitting outside at each end. If they saw any sentries coming, they ran through the hut giving the alarm and cleared off. When the sentries arrived, there was no-one there. These huts had previously been full of Russians and were under a small man generally known as *kleine Posten* [small sentry]. He used to be a regular brute to the Ruskies

Chapter 6 Kriegsgefangener

and tried the same game on with the English, but they tamed him. How they did it I don't quite know. One night they hustled him rather and threatened to duck him in a big tub of water which stood in each hut in case of fire, the next night he turned up with an armed escort. But later on, he got quite tame and would do anything for the English and especially for those who had been in his hut.

The Germans never could understand the English. Our 'old soldier' tricks used to beat them every time. A sentry would leave a hut with a dozen men, before he got to the gates he only had two left. Perhaps he would see one clearing off and give chase, when he not only failed to catch that one but lost all the rest and would have to go to the other huts for more as the ones he had been to would be empty. Some men used to get up early and hide at the other end of the camp till all the fatigues had started. It was not fear of work so much as the objection on principle to working for Germans.

Later the *Chef de Barraque* used to warn the men in turn our night for fatigue. This was a fairer way as in the old way some men got taken again and again. The *Chef de Barraques* were the senior NCO of the half hut, there being two per whole hut. Later when the nationalities were separated they got more authority. These fatigues were all sorts of small jobs down the town or round camp and also the 'quarry', as we called a new road they were making up the hill above the camp.

More serious was the warning to go away on *Arbeit*, which meant going away to work on farms or in salt mines. Taken as a general rule the *Chef de Barraques* would have nothing to do with this but let the Germans pick their men and warn them themselves. Many men refused to work, especially at jobs like mines etc. which they reckoned to be helping the German Army. For this many have suffered all sorts of punishments. If you were caught trying to escape you got 14 days, the least you got for refusing to work was three weeks. Men were given sentences of six months to five years in prison at Cologne and other places.

When we left Germany all cruelty at the camps had ceased entirely, but on those working parties where Americans and others never came they were still continued.[132] In March 1916, some men were kept some five days in a dark cell on water only for refusing to work. These parties were often under some *Unterofficier* or corporal, who could do what he liked.

There was one, a perfect brute, at Göttingen. He used to kick and knock the men about and he finally left to our joy at the end of October. But he had gone in charge of the salt mines at Salstead. There he was a regular autocrat. He hit a French Canadian with an iron bar and maimed him for being sick one morning. The English there wanted to write and complain to the *Kommandant*, they asked the Belgium interpreter to write a letter for them. He not only refused but when they wrote it in English he told 'Mick Adams' as we called him, about it and he got hold of it and tore it up.[133] Later this all came out and the English Committee at Göttingen took it up with the result that Mick Adams got a court martial. I don't know what he got but I hope it was something severe. I hated the sight of the man.'

'Salstead' is possibly Sarstedt near Hannover, which had such a mine. Work in the salt mines was extreme and inhumane, the shifts were long and the conditions harsh. 'Salt was blasted into

---

132 This probably refers to inspections carried out by the then neutral United States, which had taken on the role of 'protecting power' for British prisoners in Germany.
133 Possibly a reference to the London bantamweight boxer Mick Adams, who was knocked out in his only bout in the early 1900s.

Chapter 6 Kriegsgefangener

large heaps of sharp, jagged crystals, which prisoners loaded into carts with their bare hands'.[134] Apart from almost daily beatings and repulsive sanitary conditions, 'prisoners discovered some of the nastier features of salt mining, particularly the boil-like salt sores which developed whenever fragments of salt lodged in the skin or entered wounds or open sores.'[135] Kenneth goes on:

'The men had various dodges for getting sent back to camp. To give offence either by refusing, trying to escape or striking a civilian would get you sent back to face trial or imprisonment with sometimes months in camp before and after it. One man had the best way of all. He looked half-witted, and as he always acted up to it, many thought he was. We knew him better. He would grin stupidly at the Germans when told to do things and generally got sent back in disgust as *Dum* or mad. He got to Switzerland that way in the end.

Another poor chap who really was mad was not so lucky. He was in hospital with me at Göttingen. Later he was sent to another camp and from there sent on to *Arbeit* where he was so ill-treated that he died.

One of the Socialist members of the Reichstag once protested that the English prisoners did more harm than good. He was about right as they used to do all the damage they conveniently could. One man, Pallett by name[136], was sent to Salstead. There was a Belgian electrician there who knew how to damage things but dared not do it himself as he would invariably be found out. So he used to tell Pallett what to do when he himself was out of the way and very

---

134 Morton op. cit., Page 86.
135 Ibid.
136 Probably 7051 Private Frederick Pallett of the 1st Leicesters. *'The Wooden City - A Journal for British Prisoners of War'*, No. 9 Göttingen 1st November 1915. The Penn Libraries op. sit. and 1914-1918 Prisoners of the First World War, ICRC 1WW Archives at: https://grandeguerre.icrc.org/en.

much damage they did between them, wrecking trams by removing rails, upsetting the electric arrangements etc.

Some other men were put to sowing turnips on a farm. They put half a pint of seeds in one place then nothing for 100 yards and finally put large stones down the drum of the threshing machine and broke that.

In early 1916, a man was brought to Göttingen in a dying condition. It was said he had struck an *Unterofficier* and had been shot and as this is quite allowable by German military law nothing was said. Then a Russian from the same working party was brought in for refusing to work. He told the English Committee the whole story. The man had gone sick and the German had first prodded him in two places with a bayonet and then shot him. All the Russians had thereupon refused to work and this man as ringleader was sent back. The *Unterofficier* had begged the Russians not to report him as he had a wife and family, but they said he should have thought of them before. The English Committee got this Russian before the *Kommandant* to whom he told his story, with the result that the *Unterofficier* was court-martialled, I did not hear what he got.

[After the man died], all the English choral [sic] sang at his funeral and there were representations of all the nationalities in camp. All nationalities also sent large and beautiful wreaths. [The] Russian told the English Committee he didn't care what happened to him so long as he could get the *Unterofficier* punished.

Up to the middle of July we were all lousy. I came out of hospital clean, but soon got as bad as the rest as the mattresses and blankets were alive. I will tell in its place how we got rid of them at last. Before the Germans used to try what we called *nicht pone* powders, but they were

Chapter 6 Kriegsgefangener

no use. One man caught an extra big louse and kept it in a match box as a pet and used to feed it on their powders and it seemed to thrive.

Both before and especially after it was all put right, the '*nicht pone* blokes' used to come round. A band of Germans would surround the hut and everyone had to take down his clothes and be examined. Later on, they never found anything on the English but often on the French.

On August 10th [1915], stoves were forbidden to be lighted in the huts and we used to make our tea etc. on methylated spirit stoves. Later they had no spirits in the canteen and used to provide us with hot water from the cookhouses. In 1916 things were different and when the order against stoves came out we simply ignored it.

In 1915, there was one *Unterofficier* who was particularly busily on the look-out for infringements of the rule. We called him 'Shrapnel' because of the way he used to dart about. He was an extraordinary man. He would be walking fast down the Prom when he would remember something. He would then put his forefinger to his forehead, give it a twist, turn round and go back.

We used to love to fool him. On one occasion, he saw smoke coming from a chimney and darted into the hut in question only to find the stove cold. He couldn't make it out. What had happened was this, at the back of the chimney was a door for removing the soot and we had put brown paper in there and set it smouldering. Another time he felt a stove and burnt his hand badly as it was nearly red hot. Another time he saw them through the window putting a bowl of water on the stove. We used to boil the water in our large bowls. He darted in with a jug of water, opened the stove to find a methylated spirit lamp inside. Unlike Mick Adams he never bore a grudge.

He left about the end of November and the man who got his place was still more harmless. Mick Adams and Shrapnel had liked to creep around a hut spying out smokers. They found that if everyone stood to attention when they came in they couldn't catch them, so they discountenanced all that. This man was out for all his corporal's rank would give him and cared nothing about the smoking.

The first morning he came in no one took any notice of him, so he went out and fetched the *Chef de Barraque* and interpreter and told us that in future when he came in someone was to call out, '*Achtung*' [attention] and all were to stand to attention. Then he went out and shut the door and after a pause threw it open with a flourish. Someone yelled, '*Achtung*' and we all stood up and he walked quite pleased with himself, down the hut in true shop-walker style, he was a Göttingen draper in civil life. He never came oftener than once a day, generally he shouted, '*Achtung*' himself and stood in the doorway till all got up, when he continued his triumphal progress. I wonder what it is like to have a mind like that. So long as we stood to attention when he came to the hut and saluted him outside he left us quite alone, barring the saluting parades.

The saluting parades were the joy and pride of his poor, childish little soul. The idea was, I think, exercise. With Shrapnel, it had been physical drill. The Germans loved to drill us but couldn't. In the dark ages, they tried but as none of our chaps knew what the orders meant, they each did what they thought best and after a time it occurred to the Germans to make our own NCO do it. With '*Achtung*', as we called him, the parades consisted of marching backwards and forwards saluting him. He used to take a nationality a

Chapter 6 Kriegsgefangener

day in turn, but he never could get the English. It was bad enough saluting the poor idiot when we met him so when it was our turn we went to the YMCA. The sentry of our hut, who liked it as well as we did, used to declare that we were all on *Arbeit*. Achtung said the English were all *Schweinerei* and contented himself with the others.

I said that bad news often brought about individual displays of temper. Shrapnel was very much taken this way. If he appeared 'on the rampage' we generally found there was good news for us. On March 1st 1916, I was walking on the Prom when a *Feldwebel* [sergeant] of another company rushed up to me and took my name. Later I saw him driving a herd of his own Frenchmen along, half-drawing his sword and slapping it back, and a little while after he was barking at some Germans on parade. As he disappeared soon after, I gathered he had been warned for the *Krieg*.

The *Kommandant* at Göttingen was, as I have said a colonel.[137] There was a major too who was always on horseback till they took his horse away. We used to see him parading six Germans, mounted on his horse and all got up as if for a review by the Kaiser. The officers wore their sword, spurs, gloves and all on every occasion, I imagine to distinguish them from those below. The *Unterofficiers* were a thing of beauty and the *Feldwebels* had swords, so an officer had to have his spurs and gloves to show what he was. There were a few more officers about. There was a *Feldwebel* and two *Unterofficiers* to each company.

When the exchange of prisoners started, we got the benefit of the good treatment of Germans in England.

---

137 The *Kommandant* at Göttingen in 1915 was one Colonel Bogen, who seemingly ran his camp efficiently and well. It appears that he was a strict disciplinarian but dealt fairly with the prisoners. Derived from: Gerard, James W, *'My Four Years in Germany'*. New York, Grosset and Dunlap, 1917. Chapter X.

When they heard from returned prisoners how their own countrymen were treated in England I think the Germans had the grace to be a little ashamed of themselves. One of these told us that the women of England were sorry for the German prisoners, but the women of Germany were not in the least sorry for us.

In the end, also our cleanliness our comradeship and the way we hung together got us better terms and when I left Germany we were far better treated than the other nationalities, and in some camps, Göttingen among them, the English had it pretty well their own way. But more and more were sent away on *Arbeit*. We had to pass the doctor at intervals and those well enough to work were sent off. There was nothing very much to complain of in the treatment at the camps when I left but some of the working parties were still, I believe, hell.

I now come to describe how we spent our time. Firstly, in reading. I don't know how I could have got on in Germany if I could not have read. I had books sent me from home and in addition there was a good library in camp. This library was in the YMCA and grew and grew until it got unwieldy. They used to send large parcels of books and magazines out to working parties. Each nationality had a library of its own.

Those of us who could not work used to get our exercise by walking up and down the Promenade, which as I have said was about a quarter of a mile long. In 1915, one might make a round there as there was a path along the top and another between huts below the Prom. But when they put up the wire netting one had only got the Prom to walk on and a dull job it was too. During the summer of 1915 they made a lot of seats along the Promenade and they were generally full in the summer time.

Chapter 6 Kriegsgefangener

A good many men used to kill time by knitting. They used to pull out old socks and stockings for wool and knit socks, belts, sweaters and all sorts of things. A later idea was to embroider designs on handkerchiefs or any piece of white stuff. It became quite a craze. The design was nearly always the flags of the allies with the Union Jack shield shaped or their regimental crest in the centre. One of these sold for over 200 francs at an exhibition in Switzerland.

There were in the camp numerous tailor and cobbler shops, one I think for each company. Also barber shops; an English and a French. One of the sentries started photographing and there was a craze for being 'photoed'. He got a Canadian who understood it to help him and many groups and single portraits were taken.

The YMCA building was new-built when we got there. It held the libraries and also staged the concerts. The French being most numerous in camp managed the theatrical part and used to give four or five performances a week. Every nationality had its day or days. Our time was Saturday night.

I believe I was at the first English Concert. It was held on May 13th, the *Kommandant* was there and from what I have been told, I think it was the first. There was then just a bare stage and men were called up from the audience to sing. Later things got much more elaborate. They got a curtain and scenery, programmes and numbers of turns put up. On September 4th, the French started a disappearing electric sign outside advertising their programme. At first, they charged admittance to English concerts, but afterwards only reserved seats were paid for, the rest being free. At first, they used to have a lot of boxing with songs etc. but later they developed into sketches, some really good with occasional dumb-bell and Indian club or gymnastic displays or various kinds of dancing.

Keeping The Old Flag Flying

Our greatest effort was the Christmas revue. It was written by a man in camp, the songs being imported from home and staged by a professional actor, Kennedy by name, who was on the Army Reserve.[138] It was really good, the girls in it were boys and were dressed in clothes either from home or hired in the town. I have photos of them and it could be hard to tell them from real girls. The camp orchestra played for us at concerts. Later the English got an orchestra of their own. All instruments were hired and everything we had we had to pay for.

'I believe Kennedy is making arrangements', I wrote in November 1916, 'to stage the Christmas revue in London after the war. He is not at all afraid of what the other camps can show. The last tableau is to be the girls first with, and then without, their wigs. It should take alright if it can be arranged.' There was also at intervals a meeting of what was called the 'International Athletic Association' which held its first meeting on September 10th 1915. This consisted in boxing, wrestling etc. The theatrical artistes were excused *Arbeit* for some time, but they were beginning to take them when we left.

The great thing in our lives were the parcels. My diary is full of them – what I had got, the fact that they hadn't come etc. We practically lived on them alone. Once when we were dependant on hot water from the cookhouse and it was not hot, we told the Germans outright that boiling water was all we asked from them and not that if we could boil it ourselves.

---

138 Probably 7714 Private Thomas Kennedy of The Buffs (Royal East Kent Regiment) who was a prolific concert performer at Göttingen. *'The Wooden City - A Journal for British Prisoners of War'*, No. 7 Göttingen, 1st October 1915. The Penn Libraries op. sit. and ICRC op. cit. This interesting individual was interned in Mürren in Switzerland in 1916, repatriated to England due to sickness, and ended the war in the Labour Corps. The National Archives UK, British Army WWI Service Records, 1914-1920.

Chapter 6 Kriegsgefangener

Lists would be posted up of the parcels to be distributed at certain times. As our names were called we went and saw the parcel opened, censored and then carried it off. Despite all the censoring, going to even slitting up packets of tea and sugar and cutting open loaves, English and French papers were smuggled in regularly. One method was to wrap the parcel in two sets of brown paper and put the paper between, another man got his wrapped round the inside of a tin containing tea or loose sugar. Another man I heard of got a map and compass sent out in jam jars with a false bottom, but he did not catch on till the second came and he had lost the first.

The English in the camps as a rule at the end had plenty of parcels. Some were called 'charity'. I don't know what the definition was, but I think anything was charity that did not come from a relation. If a man got a parcel we used to tease him by singing, 'Why do they call me charity?' or singing, 'Oh, the dear kind lady'.

The Evening News used to send parcels in a special green box that were called 'Green Linnets'. Anyone getting one of these was generally followed down the Prom by people whistling and everyone in the hut used to whistle when he arrived there. The cream of the joke was that it came from the 'Lonely Soldier's Fund' and the recipient was called a 'charity-faced old hypocrite'. I don't want it to be at all understood that we got too many or that the Tommies were 'pulling the legs' of the public at home, all this was our fun and as it often made individuals angry it was of course continued. Whilst on the matter of parcels I may say that had it not been for the public at home, many of us prisoners would not have survived, and the majority of us recognised that fact and were extremely grateful to them.

We were allowed to write two letters monthly and a postcard every Sunday. The letters we received were given to us as soon as they were censored. They started putting on our letters home that we were only allowed one a week in answer. This was pure bluff as they had no means of telling how many we got and never tried to keep any back. But we could not write home and say so.

Another favourite occupation in the winter was snowballing. It was always the English versus French. If we and the Ruskies were alone, they and we would snowball each other, but if there were any French or Belgies around, the Ruskies always joined forces with us. The French had a knack of putting stones in the snowballs, but they generally got the worst of it. A Froggie found at that game was unmercifully pelted by all the English. Generally, then they lost their tempers and stood and said bad words in French until an extra good shot hit them in the mouth and stopped further utterance.

The last thing I have to mention is our church. At first it was held in the YMCA. It was held at 10 a.m. on Sundays and taken by Sergeant Winyard of the Hussars.[139] This man ran the church services from the time they started. When the Switzerland business came on he went up with the rest and passed. But finding there was no one to take his place he had his name taken off the roll and stayed at Göttingen.

There was also a service on Wednesdays taken by the German Pastor of Göttingen. He used to take the funerals also. His English was not very good. At the end of the service he used to give the war news as he knew it. I didn't often go as his news was so garbled and as he used at one time to call us *Schweinerei*. I put him down as bad as all the rest and all he did as 'soft soap'. On September 19th,

---

139 Probably 4756 Sergeant Ernest Winyard, 15th (The King's) Hussars. *'The Wooden City - A Journal for British Prisoners of War'*, No. 3 Göttingen, 1st August 1915. The Penn Libraries op. sit. and ICRC op. cit.

Chapter 6 Kriegsgefangener

they started services on Sunday evenings as well, these had to be held in an empty barrack as the French had a concert on Sunday nights. On Christmas Day, we had a grand service with the English orchestra present. Usually we had a harmonium and Winyard used to preach.

On February 9th 1916, we got a half hut given us for a church, the French had got one before us. Mr. Williams got his sister to send us altar cloths and hangings etc. from England and we made quite a nice church of it. Mr. Williams was I believe the only English parson in Germany. He got leave to go round the camps and used to go to all, including the men in prison at Cologne etc. He came to Göttingen twice while I was there; November 11th 1915 and February 25th 1916. He came to Mannheim while I was there, but I could not go. He used to hold Holy Communion after the service. He was a very amusing man and he used to tell us funny anecdotes in his sermon, the place was always packed, many going then who went at no other time.

One thing I omitted to say, we used to make shelves and cupboards from the boxes our parcels came in and put them up in our huts. If a photo has been taken of any English hut, it would have made an excellent advertisement for Hudson's soap. For the number of Hudson soap boxes that came and their convenience for the purpose made them general everywhere.'

It is believed that 'Mr. Williams' was The Reverend H. M. Williams, who had been in charge of the English Church in Berlin, but since the outbreak of hostilities, he had been placed in a German internment camp at Ruhleben. It seems he was allowed to visit different camps and hospitals, but this consent was later withdrawn.[140] The prisoners then had to organise their own services.

Kenneth has mentioned Switzerland a number of times thus far and some explanation is required. The Hague Conventions of 1899 and 1907 were multilateral treaties that addressed the conduct of warfare. Amongst a raft of measures, they encouraged belligerents to make their own arrangements to exchange severely wounded prisoners of war. During the Great War, after some negotiation, French and German casualties were being exchanged via transportation provided by the Swiss Red Cross, and the rate reached some 500 per month by 1916. In late 1915, Britain and Belgium sought a similar arrangement, and this was achieved, usually via neutral Holland.

This agreement only concerned the most severely sick and wounded. The Swiss Red Cross advised that the Swiss Government might offer to hold as internees those prisoners from either side that were less severely wounded or unwell. Prisoners would remain in Switzerland throughout the war and any who escaped would be returned by their own side. This proposal suited the Swiss Government. As well as consolidating Switzerland's neutrality, the prospect of filling holiday hotels, emptied by the war, with persons whose governments would foot the bill was an attractive one.

With encouragement from the Pope, the first batches of French and German prisoners arrived in Switzerland in early 1916. Britain then became involved in the scheme, suitable prisoners insufficiently incapacitated to justify repatriation being selected by Swiss and host-nation judges. The first Canadians reached Switzerland in May 1916, but 'the process of selection could be anguishing. Acceptance by the commission seemed to promise virtual release from captivity, rejection meant more months and even years of crowded huts, barbed-wire, and monotonous manual

---

140 The National Archives UK, Records Created or Inherited by the Foreign Office, FO 383/180 and FO 383/206.

Chapter 6 Kriegsgefangener

labour.'[141] One of those interned in December 1916 was Major Thomas Scudamore, who served as a company commander with the 7th Battalion and had also been captured at St. Julien. He was sent to Switzerland where he was promoted to lieutenant colonel and held an intelligence job for the duration of the war. Thereafter, he wrote 'A Short History of the 7th Battalion C.E.F.', from which some of the notes appended to this memoir are drawn.[142]

Kenneth and his comrades became aware of this initiative in the spring of 1916 and as we shall discover in due course, its tantalising lure would thereafter prove hard to ignore.

Having described the Göttingen routine, Kenneth returns to his own circumstances:

'I will now resume my personal narrative. We arrived at Göttingen on May 12th [1915] and were put into No. 8 hut. The Tommies crowded round us and listened to our story and told us theirs. 'Telling the old story' as we called it was, is and will be while this generation lasts, a favourite occupation.

As I have said I had lost my boots at Hofgeismar, they had given me a pair of German boots, but they hurt my feet. One of the Tommies gave me a pair of leather clogs and I wore them until a pair of boots came from England on August 24th. That same day I got a civilian jacket, as my own had the sleeve cut off. I had noticed that any Canadians who saw me came up and asked what battalion I was in etc. I wondered how they knew I was Canadian until someone pointed out that our jackets had stand up collars whereas the Imperial ones turned down.

The next day, I went with McGuire, who had already begun to look after me, to what I believe to have been the

---

141 Morton op. cit., Page 122.
142 Scudamore op. cit.

first English Concert. McGuire was in 8A and next day [14th] when we had got our Church Army parcels and he had got a parcel, I spent most of the day in his bed. Otherwise I lay in my bed all day reading. We had to put our mattresses and blankets out of doors, so I generally lay on the bare floor. I was so weak that after the shortest walk or exertion I was quite exhausted.

On May 22nd, I had a bath. We used to go on appointed days, a hut at a time, later we could go when we liked within certain hours. It was while waiting outside the bath house that a man persuaded me to try and get into hospital. It had been suggested to me before but as I had only just come from hospital I didn't want to go in again. He told me I should get better food there, and as I knew that was what I needed, I determined to do so.

So, on Monday May 24th, I reported sick and went to see the doctor who told me to come next day. I had been feeling pretty bad on the Monday, but on the Tuesday I felt better. I told the doctor what was wrong with me and he said he could do nothing. As I was turning away he asked what I wanted him to do for me. I said I wanted something to make me stronger. He told me to strip, tested me and finally to my joy sent me to hospital. Arrived there, I had to undress and leave my clothes outside, I then had a bath and went to bed. Again, for the second time that bed was like Heaven and I lay all the morning thinking how much better it was than lying on the bare floor in the hut.

Next day 26th, an orderly came in from another hut. He was on the reserve but had been in Canada when the war broke out and I had a long talk with him. On the 27th I was put on No. 2 diet with extras. This meant two white rolls of bread per day, coffee in the morning some rice pudding at 11 a.m., soup at 12 [noon] and soup in the evening. The rice was rather filling and coming such a short time before rather spoilt the dinner, but I crammed it all down.

On the 28th, my clothes came back from being *nicht poned*. They used to steam them with super-heated steam and though it tended to rot them it undoubtedly destroyed all the vermin. I was then told I could get up and did so. I felt wonderfully better and much stronger than I had felt since I had been wounded. On the 29th I got my first parcel. It was from the American Embassy at Copenhagen and was addressed to some other man, but the name had been altered to mine.

I used to get up after breakfast and have a smoke. Smoking was allowed at all hours but only outdoors. I had got some money from home about now and had bought some German tobacco. Before this I had been too ill to want to smoke. After a smoke, I generally went to bed again when the sun got up as we were having very hot weather just then and there was no shade outdoors. After dinner, I had another smoke and lay down till evening, when I used to go out again. The afternoon sun shone on my bed and it was hard to keep cool.

My hand had been giving a lot of trouble smarting and burning and at last began to swell. I showed it to the doctor and he ordered some stuff to put on it. On June 30th, they daubed some black stuff all over it and bound it up. The German orderly said it would be right in two days. When at the end of two days it still hurt though the swelling was gone he took no more interest in it.

I showed it to the doctor again on June 2nd. He ordered some pills for it and said something about water. So, on the 5th I tried cooling it by dipping it in water and found it

Mürren in the early 1900s.
(Library of Congress, Prints & Photographs Division,
Photochrom Collection LC-DIG-ppmsc-07039).

The ice rinks opposite the Palace Hotel des Alps at Mürren, taken after the war.
(Published by G. D'Aguanno-Zinsli, Interlaken).

Chapter 6 Kriegsgefangener

Group of internees at Mürren.
(Photo Max Amstutz, Chalet Alpina Mürren).

General view of new YMCA hut, Mürren. Mr A. Brauen and
'Mons' (possibly M.) Buriner in foreground. The former was
a representative of the National Council of the YMCA.
(Cadbury Research Library: Special Collections,
University of Birmingham YMCA/K/1/9/136).

Alfred Brauen, Robert Whitwell and John Hobday
in front of the YMCA Hut, Mürren.
(Cadbury Research Library: Special Collections,
University of Birmingham YMCA/K/1/9/144).

Chapter 6 Kriegsgefangener

Mürren Internees' Dinner
(Cadbury Research Library: Special Collections,
University of Birmingham YMCA/K/1/9/140).

Kenneth and Totum.
(Private collection).

Kenneth in Canadian Scottish Regiment uniform after the war.
(Private collection).

Chapter 6 Kriegsgefangener

7th Battalion Dinner 26th April 1924 in the
29th Battalion Drill Hall (Dunsmuir and Beatty Street).
(City of Vancouver Archives VLP 64).

Kenneth (left) and 'Mr. Brother' at the Bilton House School,
Vancouver in the late 1920s.
(West Vancouver Archives 1329.WVA.RAH).

relieved the pain. All the rest of the summer I kept a bowl of water by me and dipped my hand in it at intervals.

On June 8th, I was put on No. 1 diet. This consisted of some brown bread of a better quality than we got in the camp in addition to the two rolls, and also a little butter. I did not then get the rice and the soup was not so good, often they gave us raw salt herrings for supper which we gave to the Ruskies. On that same day, I got a parcel and letters from home and so was not so dependent on German food.

The nails of my bad hand had not grown at all since I was wounded but on the 9th they had started to grow again. They became a nuisance. I had written for nail scissors in my first letter home, the parcel enclosing them went astray and when I got it the scissors were missing. So, I bought a pair in town per our sentry, I kept these for some time and then they vanished. I got another pair and they went too, so I gave up till I got to Switzerland. I used to keep the good hand down by biting them and had to borrow scissors for the others.

On the evening of June 12th, we were all driven in early. We used to be in generally at 9 p.m., this evening we were sent in at 7 p.m. We found that one of the doctors wanted to do a flirtation outside. He had some female with him and they sat on a seat and drank beer together.

On June 19th, Wynne, one of the English in our hut died.[143] He was no sooner dead than they brought in a coffin put him in it and carried him out. They had taken no notice of him as he lay dying but waited till he was quite dead.

There were about six English in the hut the rest being

---

143 10892 Private Patrick Wynne of the 1st Battalion Royal Welsh Fusiliers. He is interred in the Niederzwehren Cemetery, Kassel. CWGC op. cit.

Chapter 6 Kriegsgefangener

Frenchmen and Russians. We could do nothing for Wynne, he was unconscious and delirious. A good many men in hospital were simply saved by their comrades, the Germans never bothered, if a man wanted to die they let him. On June 21st, I returned to camp and went back to No. 8 hut. I was quite strong and well in myself then, but my hand was no better. It was always smarting, and I could not bear it touched. I used to keep it quiet by putting it in water. If I was lying down, any jar on the floor set it tingling and for months after, reading a story of a hairbreadth escape would make it tingle.

I asked one of the men in my platoon who had come with me from Hofgeismar, if I could 'muck in' with him and his 'school'. They were agreeable. The school consisted of White,[144] Good also in the 7th Battalion,[145] and Corporal Christie of the 15th Battalion.[146] We had all been at Hofgeismar together. A 'mucking in school' was a small mess and shared all their parcels etc. If one wanted any help, as I did, one's mucking in chums were supposed to supply it. They were your particular chums and all they had was yours and all you had was theirs.

I came in as rather a boon and a blessing to the school. They had been very short, had been living on tea leaves given them after being used once and German grub. Tea leaves were quite a commodity then, in the Dark Ages they used to use them three or four times, and then dry and

---

144 Probably 16946 Private Frank White from Victoria. Derived from: *'The Wooden City - A Journal for British Prisoners of War'*, No. 3 Göttingen, 1st August 1915. The Penn Libraries op. sit. and The Canadian Great War Project at: canadiangreatwarproject.com.

145 Probably 21698 Bugler Harold Good from Saskatchewan. *'The Wooden City - A Journal for British Prisoners of War'*, No. 5 Göttingen, 1st September 1915. The Penn Libraries op. sit. and ICRC op. cit.

146 Probably 27983 Corporal Campbell Christie, originally from London, England. Pay and Record Office op. cit.

smoke them. At this time people were often glad of once-used leaves, later of course we wouldn't look at them. I had plenty of money and had just had a parcel and the school was well set up. I generally financed the whole thing and in return they made my bed and did my chores.

On June 22nd, I had a bath, the first since entering hospital four weeks before. My hand had been getting white and the skin hard from so much water and on the 22nd, I rubbed Vaseline into it. Next day I tried some oil, said to be good for stiff joints. Later I got Lanoline from home and used to rub that in every night until it got all right. For months, it never perspired and used to be like parchment in the mornings.

White had been very seedy and on July 1st we persuaded him to go sick and he was sent to hospital. Later in the day they said he had a fever and we were quarantined. The hut was locked up and no one allowed in or out. This was supposed to last a fortnight, but they let us out on the 9th. The hut was very full at the time and we used to get awfully stuffy and all the fresh air we got was by leaning out of the windows. Also, we could not get any exercise. Our parcels etc. were brought to us and handed through the windows.

The muscle of my thumb had by this time quite sunk in and on July 7th, I made a small pad and used to grip it. It restored the muscle a bit and kept the hand so comfortable that I used to carry it until I got to Switzerland.

My second lot of money had meanwhile arrived. In hospital, they gave us the lot at once, but in the camp, they would only give 10 marks per week. When I went for the second instalment on July 12th I got all the balance in stamps.

From now on these stamps became the currency of the camp and we were not supposed to have *Gelt* [money]

Chapter 6 Kriegsgefangener

in our possession. The stamps were about half the size of a postage stamp, were perforated and gummed on the back. The mark stamps were yellow, 20 pfennigs blue, 10 pfennigs red, 5 pfennigs green and one pfennig brown. When anyone left the camp, they could get them changed for *Gelt,* generally in notes.

On July 14th, we had our first *nicht pone*. We had all been lousy up till then, but this cured it and we were never lousy again. But it was the most miserable day I ever spent. The weather was wet and very cold. We had to strip and spent all day from 9 a.m. to 4 p.m. with only a towel, greatcoat and a pair of clogs on. Our clothes and blankets were taken to the hospital and there steamed. It was a slow business and we only got them back at 4 p.m. Meanwhile the hut was thoroughly scrubbed out by a fatigue party while we shivered round the stove in No. 9.

On August 27th, we were *nicht poned* again. This time it was all right. They had made an addition to the bath house for it. We took our mattresses as well this time, had a bath and waited naked in the warm room next to the bath house till our clothes were done and all was over in an hour. But that first *nicht pone* I shall never forget. There was a third on Sept. 21st, but as we had had a bath the day before I dodged it. After these *nicht pones* there was no excuse at all for being lousy and the English were all clean from that time onwards. I hope I then ended my experience of lice, I don't want to get them again.

Somewhere about this time, I have not got the date in my diary, I determined to get rid of my beard. I got a Frenchman in the hut to take it off. He only had a pair of scissors and so could only cut it short first and his razor was blunt. The result was agony. It took him half an hour as I could only stand it being done piece meal. On July 19th, I started to go to the French barber's shop and used to go there three times a week and I soon got over the soreness of my first shave. I was dependent on barbers till I got to Switzerland and got a razor from home. I might have written for one but at Göttingen there was no trouble in getting a shave and at Mannheim when there was, we were continually expecting to leave. On the 22nd I was presented with a German jacket. They were giving them to everyone who had not his own uniform. It was a thin black thing with yellow braid round it and a '7' on the collar.

On August 2nd, everyone in our company had to go before the doctor and all except those wounded or sick were passed for work. I was rejected but Good and Christie were passed. Christie got off it being a corporal, but Good left on August 4th with nearly all the English and others in 8 and 8A and went to Salstead. Christie and I were left in our school and we mucked in together till February. We were a small party left in the hut some twelve or fourteen each in 8 and 8A. We moved the centre beds against the wall and we put our beds along the opposite wall. It was a peaceful time and no one bothered us for fatigue as we were all certified *krank* [ill].

On August 9th, we as *nicht Arbeiters* [not workers] were ordered to attend the funeral of a Canadian who had died in hospital.[147] It was the only funeral I went to in Germany. The cemetery was a long way from the camp, some two miles I should think. We had to wait some time for the German pastor. He read the English service and when it was over we were marched back. One portion of the cemetery was kept for prisoners and just before we left they were getting up a subscription to put a monument there. We saw lots of German women in black visiting graves in the other parts.

---

147 Probably 27448 Private Angelo Barchi of the 15th Canadian Battalion, originally from Cheshire, who died on 6th August 1915. He is interred in the Niederzwehren Cemetery, Kassel. CWGC op. cit.

Chapter 6 Kriegsgefangener

Most of the graves were enclosed and had seats inside the enclosure, a curious idea.'

Göttingen Military Cemetery was begun by the Germans in 1915 for the burial of prisoners of war who died at the local camp. After the war, it was decided that the graves of Commonwealth servicemen who had died all over Germany should be brought together into four permanent cemeteries. Niederzwehren was one of those chosen and in the following four years, more than 1,500 graves were brought into the cemetery from 190 burial grounds in Baden, Bavaria, Hanover, Hesse and Saxony.[148] Kenneth continues:

'On August 14th, the proceeds from our concert went to provide surgical appliances for British wounded. Next day Sunday an American YMCA man who was in camp attended our service and preached.

We heard White was to come out of hospital on the 16th and hoped he would get back to our hut, but the hut was filled with a crowd of wounded Frenchmen mostly with wooden legs and who had come to Göttingen recently, and White was put into another. I was never in the same hut with him again. One of these one-legged Frenchmen was a particularly lively person. He used to dance, stand on his head and do more with his one leg than we could do with our two. One day he was particularly lively and we heard that he had just heard from his wife who was in Lille, the second letter he had in nearly a year. Most of them were exchanged a month or so later.

On August 12th, we had to parade before a cinematograph which the Germans insisted on the American I mentioned taking of the camp. We were taken strolling about, drawn

---
148 CWGC op. cit.

up in line and marching past and then I and several more escaped.

On August 24th, my boots came. We were rather short of grub at the time and Christie was very disgusted when he found what my parcel was, but I was delighted with them. On August 30th, we were all moved into No. 7 which was thereafter kept for English only. It was very nice not to have any foreigners in that hut. At this time, each nationality was put into separate huts.

On September 2nd, I got my first Swiss bread. We Canadians were the first to get it and it was a treat. Bread from England often came bad in the hot weather but if the Swiss bread came direct it was always good. Later everyone almost got it and it became a drug on the market. But though familiarity bred contempt as it always does, we were often very glad of it and never again, when it came regularly as it soon did, did we eat German bread at Göttingen. Often, we did not trouble to draw our German bread, and if we did we used it as fuel. I believe it was largely composed of sawdust and it certainly made excellent fires. The Germans were furious when they caught us burning it, but we seldom let them catch us.

On September 11th, I got my first parcel ordered from Messrs. Fortnum & Mason and from this date I had plenty. Christie drew the parcel for me and he met me after the concert and told me I had a glorious parcel and what was in it. Our mouths watered at the thoughts of it. This and the following night they did not lock up the huts, but as people were walking on the Prom at all hours they locked them again on 13th.

From September 26th to 30th, my diary is full of the 'glorious news from the Front', some of it was rumours and much better than the truth. It was news of the battle of Loos and the advance then made. I had given the war at the start not less than six months and not more than 12, and I had an idea that all would be over by my birthday, October 12th. So, when this news came through I thought I was right. There was an intense excitement over it in the camp and we all crowded round the maps hung in the YMCA and excited Frenchmen were pointing out to all and sundry where the places mentioned were. But after a few days of expectancy it all died out and we settled down to our dull life again.'

The mining village of Loos is in France, to the northwest of Lens. The Battle of Loos took place from 25 September to 18 October 1915 as the British element of a major Allied offensive. It was the first fully large-scale British offensive action of the war and, due to its size, it was referred to as The Big Push. The flat ground was not chosen by the British, and stocks of ammunition and artillery were deficient, but they attacked with six divisions and initially achieved success, using chlorine gas for the first time in the war. But British casualties were heavy, they were unable to exploit the gains with reserves and the battle deteriorated into trench warfare once again. One outcome was the replacement of Field Marshal Sir John French by General Sir Douglas Haig as Commander of the BEF. Kenneth goes on with his narrative:

'On October 2nd, they started the issue of coal, or rather coke. It was not much they gave us – about two shovels full of coke and two or three sticks of kindling. We generally saved it up till we had enough to keep the fire going all day. On other days, we fixed the grate at the top of the stove and each school supplied the fuel to boil its bowl. This was provided from the wooden boxes of parcels or else cardboard or paper. We burnt all the headboards, boards fixed at a slope at the head of the bed frames for pillows, the struts of the centre beds and the spare bed frames. It was the one thing we were short of and when on December 5th the Ruskies brought us coal it meant a nice warm hut to go into.

On October 11th, a Russian doctor passed me for light *Arbeit*, but it was little I did. I got sent down that day with a gang to fetch gravel for the side paths. I merely walked there and back, a nice walk of four miles. On the 23rd, I was on a coal yard fatigue in the camp. As I could do nothing I was soon sent away. On the 26th, I was on a fatigue in the coal yard of the town barracks. It was a bitter, cold day and I nearly froze as I could not work. I think these were all I was ever on. I said they were welcome to anything I could do with one hand. I could not use my bad hand at that time and anyhow I was determined not to use it in Germany.

On October 20th, I got a parcel of underclothing from the Canadian Red Cross, as this was thick I was a good deal warmer afterwards. On November 8th, they found we had burned the broken leg of one of our tables, so they took the tables and stools away for eight days, and we had to eat as best we could.'

The onset of winter weather threatened to add to the prisoners' woes. Kenneth describes this and the adjusted winter routine:

'On November 11th, there was a long parade. They divided us up into groups and then had a lengthy argument between themselves as to the sum of 55 + 7. One *Unterofficier* declared that it made 61 and that they were one man short and the others did not seem at all sure he was not right. After about an hour of counting and reckoning they came to the conclusion that 55 + 7 made 62 and that all was right. Next day the parade was continued. This time as it was raining they put us into different huts. We found out it was to find out how many were employed in camp and how many were *Arbeiters* etc. We who were *nicht Arbeit* were

Chapter 6 Kriegsgefangener

then inspected by a doctor.

On November 11th, Mr. Williams came. On November 14th, another parson came and they said he was Swiss, but I believe he was a German. He told us that as an infant he had been a prisoner in 'Magdalein' during the Abyssinian War in the 60s and was rescued by the English.[149]

On November 16th, the electric light in our half row of huts went wrong. It did the same on one or two other occasions. We had to go to bed by the light of what candles we had, but we had a longer lie in next morning.

In the summer when we first came they used to get us up at 6 a.m. in the winter it was 7 a.m. The hut sentry used to come round and shout, 'upstand *raus*!' It depended on the sentry whether you needed to get up then or not. Some were apt to throw water on you if you didn't.

The nights were cold about now and I was by no means warm in bed with the two thin blankets. On the 19th, a rug came from home, followed next day by a beautiful blanket from the Canadian Red Cross which was more than twice the size and thickness of a German one. I was not cold after that. Another blanket and three quilts followed from home and these I gave away. They were most gratefully received. Some men had got spare blankets, but they used to search for them at intervals and take them. They did not take mine as I was entitled to two German ones and the others were my private property.

On November 28th, I could tell by the squeaking of the

---

[149] The Battle of Magdala was fought in April 1868 between British and Abyssinian forces in what is now Ethiopia. It was conducted to release some diplomats and a group of missionaries who had been seized by the Abyssinian Emperor. The British force, mounted from Bombay, made its way inland to the fortress town and won the battle. The Emperor committed suicide.

snow in the morning that it was below zero. It was the only day I noticed it as cold as that.

On December 10th, we all had to wear large number cards. Before we had been supposed to be labelled with the numbers of our hut and bed. Now we had to wear on jacket and overcoat a card the size of a postcard. This was divided into four. In the top two squares were the number of the army corps and of the camp, XI and VII respectively, and below the numbers of hut and bed. We had similar cards at Mannheim. When crossing Switzerland in the train, the Swiss orderlies told us to tear them off saying, 'That is Germany, this is Switzerland'.

On December 17th, the men started kicking footballs on a bit of ground at the back of the bath house. This was continued till they wanted the ground to put potatoes in. It wasn't a good pitch being ploughed and on a slope.

As Christmas approached, we had more and more parcels and our larders were full. Christie got one parcel with seven plum puddings in. One I got pleased me very much. It was from the CMS [Church Missionary Society] at Sydney, of which I had been Secretary at one time.[150] It was an extra good one but besides that it was very nice to be thought of. I also got a splendid one later on from the choir at Aspley Guise.[151] They had devoted the proceeds of their carol singing to sending parcels to all Aspley men, I am sure we all appreciated them. Each Canadian got a parcel of games from the Red Cross. These were chiefly draughts, and consequently draughts boards were a drug on the market. I got a game of wall quoits and a pipe.

On the evening of the 24th, the hut remained open and

---

150 Kenneth lived in Sydney, Nova Scotia in Canada from 1911 to 1912.
151 Kenneth's family home, where his widowed mother lived.

Chapter 6 Kriegsgefangener

the light on till 1 a.m. I thought it a nuisance rather than otherwise. The light was too bad to read by and if one wanted to read one had to but with candles. At 12 they came round and said we mustn't sing any more.

On Christmas Day, we got up at 8.30. Church was at 10. It was a specially grand service with the orchestra. At 11 a.m. we all lined up at the cookhouse and got a dinner of meat, for a change, and potatoes. It was not at all bad. We had had a pail on the fire all morning boiling our plum puddings, so we had quite a decent dinner. Contrast this, as all the Tommies did, with 1914.

On New Year's Eve, the hut was open till 12.30. An officer came round and wished us a Happy New Year – very kind of him – we should perhaps have thanked him if he had not behaved as he had a year before. At midnight, we all shook hands and we all said, 'May this be the Peace year'. We all firmly believed it would be yet! It is as well one can't see the future. In moments of depression I used to wish I could know the date when it would end, but I am glad now the wish was not granted.

The Christmas revue's first performance was given on December 27th. I have mentioned it before, but as it formed a distinct part of the Christmas festivities I must not omit it here. There were several performances reaching into the New Year and I went to several of them.

There is one thing I forgot to mention and that is our paper at Göttingen. The French started one first called '*Le Camp de Göttingen*'. Some little time after I came out of hospital the English started 'The Wooden City'. It used, I think, to come out twice a month. I have one or two numbers of it, one being the special Christmas number.'

In mid-1915, the camp *Kommandant*, Colonel Bogen, agreed

to allow Professor Dr. Carl Stange to offer the British the right to produce a newspaper, considering the French and Flemish newspapers already published for French and Belgian prisoners of war at the camp. The British one was titled 'The Wooden City – A Journal for British Prisoners of War', which helpfully lists many names of the prisoners that were incarcerated there. This fortnightly publication first appeared on 1st July 1915, and Bogen even wrote an introduction and contributed his portrait photograph to the first issue. After stating his hope that the journal would obtain a 'beneficial influence', provide 'an intellectual centre' and 'raise the knowledge of all', he wrote, 'In a word, it will be some day when Peace will have succeeded to War a lasting souvenir of the present days.'[152] How right he was.

Since the Battle of Loos, there had been few major offensive actions on the Western Front, though fighting around Ypres for tactical advantage continued, and as 1916 dawned, Allied operations elsewhere were unpromising. The Ottoman Army was besieging a British division at Kut-Al-Amara in Mesopotamia and the evacuation of the British Army from the ill-fortuned campaign in Gallipoli was all but complete. Such details did not affect the lives of Kenneth and his companions inside their wire cage, where life was dominated by the minutiae of existence, as Kenneth illustrates:

> 'On January 8th 1916, I got a pass to see the dentist. It was a long job, I had to go sick, go to the hospital and hang around till I could see the head doctor and get it from him and it took me all morning. I went down the town with some other men to a dentist, but we could not see him. At last on January 21st, I went down to a dentist. He could speak no English, but he drew three teeth with injections and told me to come the next day with a *Dolmetscher*. Next day I could

---

[152] A set of the newspapers, a source of much information about the camp and its inhabitants, is held by The University of Pennsylvania in The Penn Libraries and published at: www.library.upenn.edu.

Chapter 6 Kriegsgefangener

not get a sentry and after that they would let no one go to the dentist. Later on, a Belgian dentist started in camp but by then the Swiss business had started. I got seen at last in Switzerland and I got false teeth sooner from having had those three out so long before. This war had cost me six teeth. I have no doubt they could have been saved but for neglect, not a large price to pay at all.'

In early 1916, Kenneth may have been wondering whether he would remain at Göttingen indefinitely or perhaps be found acceptable, as other wounded soldiers had been, for internment in a neutral country; the Swiss business. Kenneth had spent some 10 months incarcerated at Göttingen and whilst life, in terms of food and entertainment had improved, the confinement and wearisome routine was hard to take. His wounded arm was still bothering him and caused him pain, but it was somewhat a blessing in disguise as it prevented him from taking part in *Arbeit*, such as working in the dreaded salt mines.

As we have already pointed out, by international agreement and by courtesy of the International Committee of the Red Cross (ICRC), some wounded prisoners were allowed to spend the rest of the war in neutral Holland or Switzerland instead of their German camps. As he was wounded, fortunately as it turned out, Kenneth was a candidate:

'On January 13th, the Red Cross clothing began to arrive. Our government had sent previously to the *Kommandant* of each camp enough kharki [khaki uniform] for the British then, but in all but a few cases they had not got it. At the same time complaints came from the front of parties of Germans dressed in kharki trying to get into our trenches. So, they sent by private sources and addressed to each man individually a black uniform and underclothing. Some men saw large stores of our army 'grey-back' shirts at Göttingen and a German officer was seen arrayed in kharki standing on the steps of the *Kommandantur*. The

Canadian stuff came per the Canadian Red Cross. We got the uniform, underclothing, boots and a kit bag and they were much wanted.

On January 29th, the cripples were examined for exchange [and thus to be interned in Switzerland] and left on February 1st. I did not think it worthwhile going up and I was sorry after that I had not. But it would have been no use. They had another exchange on March 27th which I tried for and failed. The first exchange got home all right but the second hung around Germany for some months and finally went to Switzerland.

On February 3rd, the privates were all moved into 7A, the No. 7 being kept for NCOs. Christie and I were thus parted. I then mucked in with 'Tiny' Dutton of the 15th Canadians,[153] so called because he was over six feet high, and 'Jock' McClure of the Royal Scots Fusiliers.[154] Sometime later Tiny was sent away on *Arbeit* and Jock and I were left alone.

On February 3rd, the *Kommandant* inspected all the huts in our company. He inspected the whole camp about then. He said the English huts were the cleanest. Some French huts were punished for being dirty. On February 10th, I was passed by the doctor for *Arbeit*. He did not inspect us at all and nearly everyone got *Arbeit*. But the men in my hut, seeing I could do nothing, agreed that I should not take my turn on fatigues.

On February 16th, they made the NCOs do sentry on the

---

153 Probably 27469 Private Fred Dutton. *'The Wooden City - A Journal for British Prisoners of War'*, No. 3 Göttingen, 1st August 1915. The Penn Libraries op. sit. and ICRC op. cit.
154 Probably 6845 Private Alexander McClure of the 2nd Royal Scots Fusiliers. *'The Wooden City - A Journal for British Prisoners of War'*, No. 8 Göttingen, 15th October 1915. The Penn Libraries op. sit. and ICRC op. cit.

Chapter 6 Kriegsgefangener

dustbins. These were large concrete boxes placed at intervals along the Prom. At first, we put all waste material into them, then they provided wooden boxes and we had to put all tins in one and all rags in another. The NCOs were responsible that this was done. We thought they were making bombs of the tins and stamped them flat, but I expect they were melted down. Later on, they used to keep the cardboard boxes the Swiss bread came in. They had always kept all the string of the parcels.

Mr. Williams came again on February 25th, on the 27th and again on March 10th. I got my photograph taken and I sent one home, and then for some reason it was stopped. On March 27th, the Russians who had left camp for the trenches on February 1st returned in a starving condition as already mentioned. On March 28th, a large party of French left for Russia. There was a medical inspection of the whole camp on March 30th. I got '3'. What it meant I did not know but I think it was merely a report of the health of the camp. At this time, the English were the best treated of all the nationalities. As I have said this was due to our cleanliness, the way we stuck together and refused to do what we did not like and to the way the Germans in England were treated.'

Kenneth now tells us how the tantalising prospect of internment started to become a reality:

'The first mention of the rumour that all sick and wounded were to go to a neutral country in my diary is on March 6th. Switzerland was the first country mentioned, then Holland, then again Switzerland. A Swiss Commission had already been and had passed a lot of Frenchmen and they were still waiting to leave.

At 3 p.m. on April 10th, we paraded before the German doctor in hospital to be passed for Switzerland. Our

Feldwebel had combed out those with nothing the matter with them but some of the companies turned up *en masse*. I was passed, my name taken, and we were told unofficially that we should leave in about a fortnight. As I went back down the Prom it was all I could do to keep from dancing with delight. I did not then know that I had still four months of Germany before me – the worst four months I spent there – and I should curse the name of Switzerland and wish I had never heard it, before I got there. Had we then been told that we should not leave till August, I think we should have been quite happy. We could have lived through the intervening period all right, it was the continual putting off that made things so bad.

Next day April 11th, all the English moved to No. 3 Company, the NCOs and Swiss party from the other companies being put into 40A. McClure was in 41A, but we still continued to muck in together. They began taking our names and particulars and it looked like an early move. On April 18th, all the Swiss party were put together in 62A. I did not like the idea of this move as it looked as though we should not leave on May 1st as we had been told officially, but it was a quiet, out of the way hut, and we were not disturbed at all and used to lie in in the mornings as long as we liked.

Jock and I parted company and I went on my own, it did not seem worthwhile to start in with anyone else. Lots of things did not seem worthwhile. What was the good of writing home a letter with nothing in it, when in a few days one would be in Switzerland and be able to write all one wanted? They used later to have parades daily with clean underclothing and as we were leaving so soon it did not seem worthwhile getting the dirty washed.

On April 19th, a sentry came in, rounded up about a dozen

Chapter 6 Kriegsgefangener

of us, myself included, and took us to be examined by the doctor. We were very downhearted as though we were to be rejected but we found they only wanted to make a statement of our cases. Some of the men he found nothing wrong with, all were inspected on this and the following days.

They were particularly hard on the heart cases. Formerly when the sentries had gone to be examined for the *Krieg* some of our chaps had put them up to some old soldier tricks, such as taking soap pills etc. to make their hearts appear bad. Now these Germans told the doctors about this and all heart cases were suspect.

On the night of 23rd, the *Chef de Barraque* gave out, 'The following are not for *Suisse*' and read out a list with my name among the others. I had heard a rumour before but refused to believe it. Oh, the horrible disappointment! I was miserable, perfectly wretched. I did not know how much I had built on it till now. We had to parade, those who like myself could do nothing or were employed in camp were dismissed and the rest sent away to farms. The others had daily parades to see their clothing was in good order etc. They grumbled a lot, but I used to think I would be quite content if I could be with them.

One man among the rejects was wounded in two or three places, there didn't seem to be any method in it, and we noticed that all were rejected who had gone up that first day. I was miserable for four days, then on the 27th, I heard a rumour that we, and some French, had been taken off the Swiss roll for exchange home. This cheered me up wonderfully. I did not dare to attempt to verify it, I was content that I regained my spirits.

Then the doctor came back from a holiday. The English Committee had been to the *Kommandant* about the man I mentioned, and the doctor was asked why he had rejected him; he declared he hadn't. It was found that the papers of all those who went up the first day had been mislaid. The 'methodical' Germans had kept no list and a paper lost meant the man rejected. On May 1st, we were all on the roll again except those the doctor had found nothing wrong with and who had known their fate all along. One man had been sent to a farm and was sent for back. Some other men went up again and some got on this time.

Then we had our daily parade in earnest. We had to clean up as if for a review, our jackets had coloured bands let in the sleeves, our trousers had to have stripes and our greatcoats brass buttons which we had to get as best we could. We soon found these parades an infernal nuisance. We could not get the black clothes clean without something better than water which was all we got and some of the Germans delighted in finding fault. We had to show a clean set of underclothing daily and but was hard to get the others washed. In the end, I could wait no longer and borrowed some while mine were washed and dried.

On May 22nd, we were again inspected by the doctor and 10 were rejected. I was not rejected again after that first time. I was truly sorry for those who were then and later, the later it was the worse it must have been.

On May 25th, I joined Kennedy's school being tired of being alone. The school consisted of Kennedy of the Buffs, the professional actor I mentioned before, Blunsden, and Sergeant Rust of the Wiltshire Regiment.[155] They had had another sergeant of some Irish regiment with them, but he

---

155 Possibly 8609 Private Richard Blunsden of the 2nd Wiltshires. *'The Wooden City - A Journal for British Prisoners of War'*, No. 3 Göttingen, 1st August 1915. The Penn Libraries op. cit., and 8270 Sergeant Frederick Rust of the 2nd Wiltshires. ICRC op. cit.

Chapter 6 Kriegsgefangener

had been transferred a short time before for Limburg and got to Switzerland with the first party at the end of May.'

Limburg Camp was in Hesse, north east of Koblenz. The Germans moved over 2,000 Irish prisoners there to help encourage them to join Sir Roger Casement's Irish Brigade, which was supposed to travel to Ireland to help the fight for independence. In fact, Casement only recruited some 50 and the idea was defunct by mid-1916. Kenneth resumes:

'On May 28th, they started to put more on the roll. They put 18 on that day and on the 30th some others who had been sent in from working parties were included. These they said were to go to Mannheim to be passed again there. We should leave later, pick up those who had passed and go right through to Switzerland. We were told we had passed finally and were not to be inspected again.

I forgot to say that on May 9th, after the French had left, they had examined our spare kit and locked it up. We only then had one change of washing left and this had made the washing problem harder. When they examined our kit, I noticed that they let us put it back in the bags at a side table, so I put my diaries in my pocket and when mine had been examined, I put them into the bag. Other men got their kit out again when they found we were not leaving as soon as expected but as I had got my diaries in I left mine locked up.

All this time and all the time to follow we expected to leave either 'at the end of this week' or 'the beginning of next week'. It used to run Tuesday, Thursday, Saturday then Tuesday again. The Mannheim party left on May 31st and we left on June 2nd. The day before they told us we should only want food for 36 hours 'as we were going right through', this was official.'

It seems that Kenneth and his school anticipated a swift train ride to freedom in Switzerland and their tails were up. But yet again, the war was to disappoint them. Kenneth tells us how:

> 'We left Göttingen in the early morning, we had quite a send-off from the English. I had had a very bad night and we were called at 4 a.m. In the train, our school got together, and we had in our carriage as well Lloyd of the Cameron Highlanders,[156] who then joined the school, and a Canadian sergeant. We were in high spirits, Blunsden went on saying we were to spend the night at Mannheim and we told him to shut up and not be a fool.
>
> On the map in the carriage there were three lines running south from Frankfurt, one passing through Mannheim, one through Heidelberg and one missing both. According to the stations we were on this middle or last-mentioned line and it was with disgust that we found ourselves at Mannheim.'

Mannheim is on the Rhine in Baden-Württemberg, about 45 miles south of Frankfurt and some 175 miles south of Göttingen. The prisoner of war camp was laid out on a big manoeuvring field two miles northeast of the city centre and could hold 10,000 men. By this time, it was used as a clearing centre for British prisoners of war going to Switzerland. Of interest, the chlorine gas that the Germans first used during the Second Battle of Ypres in which Kenneth was captured, was manufactured in nearby Ludwigshafen. French aircraft had bombed the factory in May 1915; the first long-range bombing mission of the war. Kenneth continues:

> 'There was no sign of the other party and after a long halt during which the *Feldwebel* in charge went away for orders, we went to another small station and there to our despair left the train and went to the camp.

---

156 Probably 4391 Private George Lloyd of the 1st Queen's Own Cameron Highlanders. *'The Wooden City - A Journal for British Prisoners of War'*, No. 8 Göttingen 15th October 1915. The Penn Libraries op. sit. and ICRC op. cit.

Chapter 6 Kriegsgefangener

I forgot to mention the *Feldwebel* at Göttingen. The first we had was not a bad sort, he left about the New Year and the new one we called 'Old Bull Neck', he looked like a dog and barked like one. He had a grand bark, but he had practically no bite. He used to bark at his Germans as well as us and they hated him. I have seen him run yapping after a man just like a dog does and he used to put his face to yours as if he was going to bite your nose. It was a damp performance too as he spluttered. One Englishman after being barked at, wiped his face with his handkerchief, the *Feldwebel* looked daggers but could say nothing, the days of sword drawing had long since passed. The one in No. 3 Company was particularly nice but allowed himself to be ruled by his *Unterofficiers*. This one who brought us down belonged to the artillery in charge of two guns trained on the camp in case of mutiny. He was quite good to us during the journey.

Old Bull Neck had a great respect for the English but hated the French. On the day we left his company, the French were paraded first. They examined all our kits to see we had no company stuff. Bull Neck was in a roaring temper that day and he went in among the Froggies, who mostly went about with sticks, some wanted them, others did it to escape *Arbeit,* knocking their sticks from under them and producing general devastation. They chased one Englishman with a long pole, but [Bull Neck] was quite harmless to us and we laughed at him. We spent the morning washing out our old hut and smuggling most of our kit away into other huts. When Bull Neck saw the huts, he posted off to our new *Feldwebel* and told him to treat us well. The English he said were good fellows, they had washed out their huts without orders, but, he added the French were *Schweinerei.*

Keeping The Old Flag Flying

Mannheim is set on a dead-flat sandy plain. The camp was outside the town. It was bounded on one side by the railway, on another by a tram line which here goes up an embankment to cross the railway, on the third by a parade ground and on the fourth, the hospital and bath house beside a road with open fields beyond. The camp was divided into compartments. These were in pairs. There were three or four companies in each compartment and the company offices of two compartments were so arranged that you could pass from one compartment to the next through the office passage. Each compartment was I suppose 120 yards by 60 yards wide. The huts some eight in number were at one end and the cookhouse, canteen and wash house etc. at the other. The rest was open space. One compartment had huts of canvas wood-lined with small double-decked bedsteads in them. The other huts were built of wood and had just bare floors. We were given a mattress, one blanket, one small bowl and a spoon.

I was never in the hospital. The bath house was on the same plan as Göttingen, as we could only leave our compartment with a sentry, we only got baths at stated intervals generally once in 10 days. One noticeable feature after Göttingen was the number of sentries in the camp. They had them all round the outside and one for each set of gates – the compartment gates were placed four together. There were others doing orderly work in the compounds. I don't know whether the fact of Mannheim being in Baden and Göttingen in Hanover had anything to do with it. As to the officers – The *Kommandant* was a general, there was a captain over each compound and a *Feldwebel* over each company. I saw very few *Unterofficiers* at Mannheim.

Every day except Sunday a party used to go from each company to draw bread. It was a long business as one had

Chapter 6 Kriegsgefangener

to wait about so much. We went across the parade ground to a large bakery with armed guards over it and got the bread there. The Germans got the same, we used to see them drawing it. It was quite superior to what we got at Göttingen. The parcel office was a corner of the camp and when our parcels came a party used to go down from each compound in the afternoon to get them. At Mannheim, we had three parades for counting daily, at 7 a.m., 1 p.m. and 6 p.m. as a rule. On Sundays, the midday one was omitted.

As we passed through the camp on our way in, we passed the compound where our other party was. They told us they had had no inspection and our hearts sank. In the next compound to us were men from other camps who had been to Konstantin [Konstanz] and been rejected.'

Konstanz is a university city located at the western end of Lake Constance in the south-west corner of Germany, bordering Switzerland. It was the place where all prisoners destined for internment in Switzerland were concentrated. Kenneth resumes:

'As soon as we arrived, we wrote to Göttingen for our own parcels to be sent on but they did not begin to arrive till the 16th. We had to live as best we could on German stuff and what we could buy in the canteen. I came to Mannheim with about 40 marks [about £2, perhaps worth about £120 today], I only had about four when I left. Some men from other camps never got their parcels sent on to them at all. We managed somehow, though we did not like it. One could live on German grub as it was far different to the Dark Ages. There was a cooking stove in each compound and we did our best. We found that the raw salt herrings boiled in two sets of water with potatoes were not bad, and Kennedy and Lloyd used to make some rather nice dishes with them. One thing was they used to give us lots of potatoes. But when our parcels came all was right again.

Our compound was against the tram line, the sentries' huts and the railway. Our chief occupation was watching the trams go by, not very exciting! There was a small theatre in the next compound and we used to get up concerts. They were not so bad but nothing like we had been used to in Göttingen. The Germans here went in a lot for keeping tame rabbits and chickens and there was generally some in each compound. Later on, we used to amuse ourselves in the evening by catching the cockchafers of which there were lots and giving them to the chickens.

On June 9th, we were inspected by the doctor for *Arbeit* and he passed all who did not say they were hurt in arms or legs. We caught on to this and a good many men limped up to him and got off. After this they tried to make us work, but we wouldn't. They wanted us to help in the cookhouse but when our men were put on peeling potatoes they peeled them all away and they didn't bother us after that.

The camp contained, not counting the Swiss parties, only half a dozen English, the rest being away at work, and a lot of French and Russians. Some of the French were for Switzerland but many were not. There were some of each nationality in every compound. There were a few Belgians also. The first Swiss Commission came to Mannheim at last and we were examined on June 13th. Blunsden got turned down and so did a lot more. After that we hoped we were going at last, but we hung on and on.

During the year I was at Göttingen the phrase, 'Oh, I am so sick of this life' or, 'How long will this last?' occurs only about twice, but during the time at Mannheim it comes again and again in my diary. Before the Swiss business started I had settled into a sort of groove living day by day, week by week, month by month without bothering much,

Chapter 6 Kriegsgefangener

except in moments of extra depression. But hope deferred maketh the heart sick, and too much of it tends to insanity.

During the month of July and at the beginning of August, I began to fear my reason would suffer and I tried to shut out all thoughts of Switzerland. We all of us wished we had been let alone and the whole thing had never been mentioned. The Germans used to tell us it was the fault of our government, but our people say, and I believe them, that the Germans did it on purpose.

On July 1st, we were moved into the compartment of tents. It was not half so nice as the other. The huts were full of sand fleas, crowded and ill-ventilated. Here some Belgians used to work for us as the Ruskies had done at one time in Göttingen. We got plenty of parcels and fed them for it. On July 2nd and the following days, it rained hard and the whole compound was flooded. They used to dig holes to drain off the water, but it would come down in torrents and flood it again. It added to our discomfort living like this on top of a lake. On July 12th, the second Swiss Commission came and more men were turned down. We dreaded these inspections we never knew if we should pass or not. Now we thought we must be leaving but we still stayed on.'

As these frustrations continued, a Franco-British offensive was taking place on the Western Front, the Battles of the Somme that lasted until November and caused huge British casualties, particularly on the 1st July, the first day of the assault. The Western Front had become a war of attrition where technology dominated the battlefield. It would be another two years before the lessons, most agonizingly gained, would be put to effective use. It is unlikely that Kenneth and his fellow prisoners knew anything of this as they strove to progress beyond Mannheim:

'On the 16th, the French who had passed this last

commission began to go. They took part at a time. They were taken to another compound, stripped naked and put into a hut while their clothes and kits were thoroughly searched. I gave up all hope of getting my diaries through. Of course, my stratagem at Göttingen was no longer any use when we got to Mannheim. At last I evolved a plan. When at Göttingen, I had made a précis of my diary and sewed it into the lining of my greatcoat. I now took this out and did it up small to drop in some corner and I meant to hide the diaries in a building. As all compounds were built alike, I could make my plan perfect beforehand.

On July 18th, we all moved back to our original compound, next day Blunsden and the other men rejected returned to their camps and still we stayed on. On the 27th, another party came from Göttingen. These had been passed by the first commission when it visited Göttingen, had gone to [Konstanz] and passed the second commission and came back to Mannheim.

In searching the French, the Germans had found on one man 20 German gold 20-mark pieces hidden between his toes. How he got them I don't know, but as it was then a crime for even a German to possess gold there was a great row. The Frenchman was set to prison instead of Switzerland and the money confiscated. On August 6th, they searched us all for money, *Gelt*, and found none.

We had changed our stamps when leaving Göttingen, but at Mannheim we had been made to change to stamps again. At this time, we handed in what we had left to be changed a long time before and were short of cash. We used to ask for it back daily, but they wouldn't give it to us until just before we went when we got *Gelt*.

At last the time came to go. We moved on August 10th to

Chapter 6 Kriegsgefangener

the tent compound once more to be searched. I had not been there five minutes before my diaries were safely planted. But I need not have worried as our *Feldwebel* was a good sort and he never searched our pockets. We had handed in all our books, papers and photos to be censored and it was a long time before we got them again. The search over we went into the huts. The fine weather since we had left his compound had brought on a regular plague of sand flies. One could pick them off men's necks as they stood outside, we were covered with them. Fleas don't bother me much and I soon got rid of them after, but they stuck to some men for days.

As I wandered round the compound that evening I thought of the time we had been there before, and it seemed too good to be true that we were going at last. I tried to get a bit of sleep but did not succeed, most men wouldn't lie down at all because of fleas.'

Keeping The Old Flag Flying

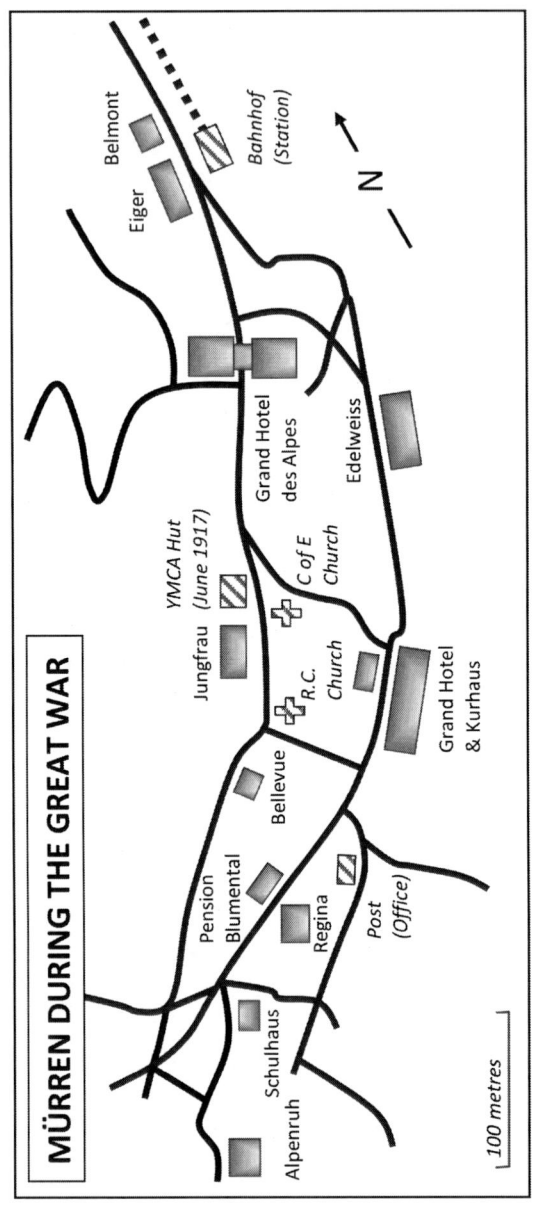

Chapter 7
Switzerland

The two months Kenneth had spent at Mannheim were wearisome and prone to the extremes of hope and disappointment. At last, he and his comrades were on the move:

'At midnight [on 10th/11th August 1916], they gave me hot water for tea and at 2 a.m. we fell in and went to the train which was on a siding next to the camp. The carriages were ordinary German third-class ones with plain wooden seats. The train started at last at 4 a.m. The party who came on the 27th followed 24 hours after us. We had a good journey. We got out at one place for a wash and food. We picked up our officers at Heidelberg.

We arrived at Konstanz at 4 p.m. We waited a long time in the train. Then we got out on to the platform and the train was shunted out and again we waited. At last the Swiss train was shunted in and we got in it. Such a contrast, it was comfortable, cushioned seats and nice and clean. We did not leave Konstanz till 8.30 p.m. The Swiss orderlies came through the train saying, 'Don't cheer till you cross the frontier, this is a German order, not ours'. We sat quiet, but we had hardly left the platform when we heard the children shouting, '*Vive l'Angleterre*' and then we let ourselves go. We cheered and cheered and sang and shouted till we were hoarse. Whenever we saw a house or person or a station we yelled like mad and it was days before our voices got quite right again.

All through Germany the train had crawled but here it went at express speed. I suppose the German lines have not been properly looked after through want of labour as they daren't go fast on them. All along the line were crowds cheering us, though it was a wet cold night. We reached Zurich at 9 p.m. and had a great reception. All the English colony was there and numerous others besides and they loaded us with every imaginable thing: tobacco, cigarettes, picture postcards, flowers, fruit, chocolate, everything. We decked ourselves with flowers and flags and we sang and cheered like madmen.

We got to Berne at 1 a.m. and here again this station was crowded. Here they gave us a meal with titled ladies to wait on us and overwhelmed us with more gifts than we knew what to do with them. The carriages were littered with them. At about 3 a.m. the Swiss authorities tried to drive the crowd away from the train but without success. They shunted it but some of them followed.

We left Berne at 6 a.m. and now could see a little of the Swiss scenery though most of it was covered in mist. We had thought the Black Forest scenery fine the day before, but it wasn't a patch on this. At Interlaken where we changed into the mountain train we had another reception. From here we went up the cogwheel line to Lauterbrunnen. Here we were addressed by the British Minister for Switzerland, then we had breakfast at cafés and went in parties on to Mürren.[157]

I and Rust went with the first party. One goes up a steep funicular railway to Grutschalp and from there in a short

---

157 The British Ambassador at that time was Sir Evelyn Mountstuart Grant Duff KCMG.

Chapter 7 Switzerland

tram to Mürren. We had another reception at the latter place and finally got settled in the Regina Hotel. We had dinner and went up to our rooms to lie down. Rust and I shared a room at the top of the house. We lay in our beds and gazed at the superb scenery, but two nights without sleep and the heavenly beds were too much for us and we knew nothing till someone called us at 7 p.m.'

Lying 15 miles south of Interlaken, the breathtakingly beautiful village of Mürren lies in Bernese Oberland, some 1,650 metres above sea level and overlooking a precipice which drops about 3,000 feet to the valley below. To this day it is unreachable by road, and visitors must take similar modes of transport to those Kenneth used 100 years ago. The funicular consisted of two small cars, holding about 50 people, one of which was fastened at each end of a long steel cable. These were dragged up and down the mountain over a mile-long, 45-degree track.[158] The village had been a skiing resort since the late 1800s and remains a popular winter sports destination today. In 1916, the many hotels in Mürren were empty and the Swiss Government was delighted to rent them to the World War 1 combatants for the purposes of internment. We shall become familiar with the names of some of these hotels, and their competing attractions, as our story proceeds.

Kenneth and his comrades were the first batch of internees to arrive at Mürren. Though no longer prisoners they were still confined, governed by Swiss and military law, and prevented by the agreement between the combatants from leaving until the war's end. The major challenge now was to fill the time with interesting and stimulating diversions, and the internees threw themselves into a host of activities with gusto. Many of these were focussed on the church or Christian organisations, as we will see.

On the Western Front, the Battles of the Somme, which started so disastrously on 1st July were still in progress. Again, Kenneth

---

158 Derived from: Douglas op. cit.

Keeping The Old Flag Flying

may not have been aware of such developments, but his own fortunes had taken a turn for the better. His existence had become more stable and agreeable, and he had a number of good friends. But the presence of so many differing personalities living cheek by jowl in confinement created the opportunity for disagreement and conflict, often over petty things. In the following pages, we will learn what life was like for the internees, meet an eclectic selection of intriguing characters and find out how they prospered. Kenneth introduces us to his new mountain home:

'Mürren is situated on the edge of a shelf of rock. On one side is the deep Lauterbrunnen Valley with its straight sheer sides and beyond that are the snow mountains; Eiger, Mönch, Jungfrau and the others in one long chain. On the other side are lower grass-covered hills. There are some nine hotels, one was occupied by the officers and six by the men. There were about 400 British officers and men at Mürren. I stayed in Mürren over two years.

My hand had been getting better fast during the last few months in fact alarmingly so, and I had been afraid that it would fail in getting me out of Germany. As soon as I got to Mürren I started to use it and on October 20th, I started a course of massage for it, and in the course of a few weeks it was as good as it had been before. I reckon I was lucky to have a wound that got me out of Germany and then did not disable me further.

I will now give a description of some of the principal people who were at Mürren at the time. First there was the SBO, Senior British Officer, Lieutenant Colonel Neish of the Gordon Highlanders. The Gordons appear to have had two colonels, but Colonel Neish, though the junior, was I believe really responsible for what happened to them. In the retreat from Mons they lost their way in the dark and walked right into the Germans. I saw it stated in one book that so

Chapter 7 Switzerland

narrow was the way of escape that it was only surprising that more did not do the same. Colonel Neish was a fine old man of the old school. He was affability itself with the men but had a great idea of keeping the junior officers in order, and during the summer of 1917 he had his hands full in that respect. He had a room in the [Hotel] des Alpes and was always visible there before 11 a.m. He knew everyone by name, I believe though at one time there were 800 in the Garrison. One man coming from the hospital was accosted by the Colonel who asked after each man in that hospital by name and mentioning their complaints.'

Colonel Francis Hugh Neish had commanded the 1st Battalion of The Gordon Highlanders. This battalion fought in Belgium, being positioned south of the Mons Canal on the 23rd August, and successfully engaged the mass of advancing German infantry. They took few casualties, but received the order to pull out along with the rest of the BEF.

After three days of wearing withdrawal, the battalion made a stand near the town of Le Cateau. They repelled the advancing Germans but did not hear of a further order to withdraw until after nightfall, by which time the Gordons had become isolated. An incensed dispute broke out between Neish, who wished to await the order to retire, and his Second-in-Command, Major and Brevet Colonel William Eagleson Gordon VC, who vehemently promoted immediate withdrawal. [159] In due course, and collecting troops from other cut-off battalions, the Gordons moved south but, coming under fierce fire and sustaining many casualties, they were forced to surrender. Some 500 were captured, including Neish and Gordon.[160] Kenneth continues:

---

[159] Brevet; a former type of military commission conferred especially for outstanding service, by which an officer was promoted to a higher rank without the corresponding pay.

[160] Derived from: Royle, Trevor *'The Gordon Highlanders: A Concise History'*, Edinburgh, Mainstream Publishing, 2007. Chapter 6.

'Next to him came Major Charley of the Royal Irish Rifles. He at once started organising shops and classes, or 'institutes' as the whole thing was called. The organisation was really splendid. By degrees we got tailors, boot-makers, carpenters, hairdressers, watch-repairers and printer shops, and classes in motoring, blacksmithing, woodcarving, French, Spanish, German and Russian.

In January or thereabouts an army schoolmaster arrived from England and during the summer there were added cinema and surveying classes. But Charley had an unfortunate tactless way with everyone. He got repatriated with the first lot in September 1917 and after some time at home got sent out again but in charge of all institutes in Switzerland. About October 1917, he started classes at Meiringen and Seeburg where they taught all sorts of trades and had experts from home to teach them.'

Major Harold Richard Charley served in the 2nd Battalion Royal Irish Rifles. He was wounded in 1914, captured on 21st March 1915 and in 1916, he started workshops for interned British servicemen at Mürren. In 1917, he was Officer-in-Charge for Technical Instruction for servicemen interned in Switzerland, then Commissioner British Red Cross Society Switzerland in 1918. Kenneth goes on:

'Another prominent person was the *Commandant de Place*, Captain Llopart, or Loppy as he was generally called. He was the Mürren doctor and used to attend all the villages round. At first, he was excessively disliked but afterwards he got used to us and we to him, and then he became equally popular. Sometime in the autumn we got another Commandant, not a doctor, and Loppy became Chief Medical Officer.

Commandants came and went and the doctors who

attended us lasted only six weeks each, but Loppy remained. When half the Garrison went to Interlaken in October 1917 he remained at Mürren as Commandant but finding the work too much for him, he was then *Commandant de Region, Commandant de Place* and local doctor. He got another *Commandant de Place* sometime about March 1918.'

Llopart was a young Swiss medical officer and as Commandant, he was responsible for discipline. The British newspaper and publishing magnate Lord Northcliffe visited Mürren during the war and wrote, 'Our prisoners, of course, are under Swiss discipline, and our officers and non-commissioned officers only hold their rank by courtesy of the Swiss authorities. So far this extremely delicate arrangement has worked admirably.'[161] Kenneth resumes:

'There were three chaplains in August 1916. The C of E was Reverend Campbell Bell.[162] At first, he seemed shy and mixed only with the officers; later he got in with the men, of him more later. The Presbyterian Chaplain was an old man who was quickly followed by Mr. Blake and he again by Mr. Matheson.[163] Neither of the former stayed long enough to get much known but Matheson was there some time. He and his wife were a pair of old women and he generally managed by his tactlessness to get into hot water with everyone, but he meant exceedingly well. He was very great at debates; committees at which he made some most foolish suggestions. But his great work was in founding the Ramblers. The full title of this club was The Mürren Temperance Rambling Club and later, The Mürren

---

[161] Lord Northcliffe, *'At The War'*, London, Hodder and Stoughton, 1918, Page 237.

[162] The Reverend George Campbell Bell served for many years as Chaplain to the Lahore Cantonment, a British garrison in India. In 1915, he was sent to Mürren as Padre. Obituary in the Yorkshire Post and Leeds Intelligencer, 29th September 1920, Page 8.

[163] The Reverend D. Matheson MA.

Total Abstinence Rambling Club. Members paid 50 cm [centimes]. Every 10 days and at intervals they went on excursions, the first taking place on I believe February 8th 1917. Any member found taking a drink was at once kicked out. As I did not approve of the thing at all or the way it was run, I never had anything to do with it and knew very little about it.

The third Chaplain was the RC priest. I think Father Fahy [Fahey] was there from the first, he was there most of the time, except when he was ill as he was now and then. I got to know him fairly well over the church lighting and he was the broadest-minded priest I have ever had the good fortune to meet. He was also a very nice man and a great walker.'

The Reverend Denis Fahey DD PhD C.S.Sp. was a priest, philosopher and theologian. It appears that he was Professor of Metaphysics and Dean of the Faculty of Philosophy at the Holy Ghost Missionary College at Kimmage in Ireland for some 40 years.[164] As Kenneth declares, Fahey served as a priest at Mürren during the internment. He was given to bouts of migraine which rendered him unfit and may explain Kenneth's comment on his health.

In June 1916, the dentist Joseph A. Woods MDS LDS was inspired to offer the British Government free treatment for internees in Switzerland. Appointed Head Dental Surgeon, he immediately closed down his private practice at Liverpool and travelled to Berne. He made Mürren his centre, and though he only intended to stay for three months, he remained until the end of the war, delivering quality, individual service ably assisted by his wife,[165] as Kenneth relates:

'Very soon after our arrival Mr. Woods and his wife came

---

164 Derived from: The Catholic Standard, 29th January 1954, Page 4.
165 Derived from: Picot, Lieutenant Colonel H. P., *'The British Interned in Switzerland'*. Edward Arnold, London 1919, Pages 115-116.

Chapter 7 Switzerland

out. He was one of the best dentists in England and quite a swell in his profession. He had a large practice in Liverpool and came out as his share in war work. At first, I think it was entirely at his own expense, though afterwards I believe the Red Cross helped him with drugs materials etc. I don't know when they arrived, but I went to see him on August 20th and later got a set of false teeth from him. At first, he only intended staying a few months but finding so much to do he stopped on practically all the time. He went home on May 29th 1917 and returned some months later, I don't quite know when but sometime in September I think. Both he and his wife were very nice people and used to take part in our activities as well as his professional work. Periodically they used to make him presents of plate etc. He was a Quaker and also, like Matheson, a rather bigoted temperance reformer and a leading spirit in the Ramblers.

Next, I must mention Mr. and Mrs. Lunn. Mr. Arnold Lunn, son of Sir Henry Lunn of the Lunn Hotel Company, was Manager in Switzerland of the Lunn Hotels among which there were the Palace and Des Alpes in Mürren. He was a peculiar individual, a great mountain climber and perfectly mad on skiing. They were both young. A short time before the war, Lunn had had a fall while rock climbing in Wales and still had an open wound. He had been refused by the military authorities five times and so had settled in Mürren with his wife and small boy.

Mrs. Lunn, a tiny little lady, I was first introduced to on October 22nd when we found we had many mutual friends. They were both very nice and I shall have occasion to mention them again. Lunn and Woods never got on together and were generally at daggers drawn. Lunn took a great part in our debates during the winter 1917-1918 and as

Keeping The Old Flag Flying

he could prove black was white when he liked, he was a useful member.'

Sir Arnold Lunn was a British slalom skier and international authority on skiing, who in 1922 created the modern Alpine slalom race. He had married Mabel Northcote in 1913 and went to Flanders with a Quaker Ambulance in 1915. Thereafter, he failed to obtain a commission, as Kenneth describes. Lunn founded the Ski Club of Great Britain and the Alpine Ski Club and held many exceptional international skiing appointments including Chairman of the International Downhill Ski Racing Committee. He was knighted in 1952 for service to British skiing and Anglo-Swiss relations. Kenneth now describes the next of these colourful newcomers:

'Early in the winter Mr. and Mrs. Jebb-Scott arrived. What he was no one quite knew. Some people declared he was an ex-army officer, but I don't think there was any truth in that. She, I believe, had all the money, and like Mr. Leo Hunter in Pickwick, he might be described as Mrs. Jebb-Scott's husband. He was a fussy individual who went in for little else than curling in the winter and spent most of the summer at Kandersteg [about 10 miles south west of Mürren] leaving his wife at Mürren. They came to Switzerland for Mrs. Jebb-Scott to run the Bread Bureau at Berne, but after some time there finding it one mass of graft they chucked it and came to Mürren.[166]

Sometime after their arrival they were followed by Tyler, a private in the 5th Canadians, who came through in the May party and had been working with Mrs. Jebb-Scott at Berne.[167] He became her Secretary in some Red Cross work

---

166 This may be a little unfair. The Scotts were involved in the receipt and dispatch of clothing and their 'able management added to the efficiency of the executive branch, and enabled it to keep abreast of the ever-expanding work.' Picot op. cit., Page 69.

167 Probably 13347 Private Bernard Tyler of the 5th Canadian Battalion, a

Chapter 7 Switzerland

she was doing, but later they had a row and from being fast friends became the greatest of enemies. I shall mention them again.'

As this diverse band set about its business, Kenneth introduces his daily routine and portrays further the British officer who was responsible for all the Swiss internees:

'Having described the chief actors in the scene I will now give an account of our daily life. We were supposed to get up at 7 a.m., of that more later. Breakfast was at 8, dinner at 12, supper at 6. Everyone had to be in at 9.30 and lights out at 10. On the 1st, 10th and 20th of each month, we received four francs from the Swiss authorities, at least these were the dates on which it was due, but we hardly ever got it then and once it was a week late. At first, we could get as much as we liked from home or our paymasters, but later on at the instigation of Colonel Peko [Picot] this was limited to £2.10. a month and an application signed by the SBO had to be obtained to get that.

This Colonel Peko [Picot] was an old military attaché who had settled in Switzerland. He got boosted into the job of Military Attaché at Berne, got the sack for incompetence and finally got put in charge of the British interned. He was the most incompetent old woman imaginable, but he hung on to the job till sometime in 1918 when he was superseded by General Hanbury Williams.'

Lieutenant Colonel Henry Picot was Military Attaché in Berne, and British Officer-in-Charge of the Interned in Switzerland. From 1893 to 1900, he had been Military Attaché at the British Legation in Teheran, Persia and previously, as an Indian Army officer, he had taken part in the 2nd Miranzai Expedition of 1851,

---

newspaper inspector, born in Nottingham in England. He had been captured in May 1915 and housed at a German prisoner of war camp in Munster. Records of The North Saskatchewan Regiment.

the Haraza Expedition of 1888 on the North-West Frontier and the 2nd Afghan War of 1878-1880. He wrote a detailed report of his experiences in Switzerland after the war,[168] and was awarded a CBE for his work as British Representative, Prisoners of War, Switzerland.[169] His daughter Henrietta was awarded an MBE for her work as 'Assistant, Bread Bureau for Prisoners of War, British Red Cross Society, Switzerland'.[170]

Kenneth's comment on how Picot came to leave Berne, as far as can be determined, is uncorroborated. Picot attributes his change of jobs in Switzerland to a favourable interview that he had with Lord Kitchener, then Secretary of State for War, where he presented the Swiss view on the internee situation, which Kitchener appreciated. Kenneth continues his financial review:

> 'It used to take a month or six weeks to get money from home and when the frontier was closed longer still. Early in March, an interned Canadian officer managed to arrange for the Canadian pay sheets to be sent to Berne and from that time we could get ours in a few days. At first, we were allowed unlimited free postage but in October, this was limited to one letter on each of 10 specified days each month.
>
> We used to be inspected by a doctor about once a month and weighed at certain intervals. I did not see a doctor till September 5th. Later when most of us got quite well these inspections became a farce and a nuisance.'

Having described the scene and the cast of anomalous characters

---

168 Picot op. cit.

169 Commander of the Most Excellent Order of the British Empire (CBE). Recorded in The Gazette (London Gazette), Supplement 6738, 4th June 1918, Page 6691.

170 Member of the Most Excellent Order of the British Empire (MBE). Recorded in The Gazette (London Gazette), Supplement 30730, 7th June 1918, Page 6738. It would appear that her work extended beyond this remit as she was Honorary Secretary to the Red Cross Special Branch for British Interned Prisoners from 1916 to 1918 in Berne.

Chapter 7 Switzerland

who had been brought together above the Lauterbrunnen valley, Kenneth goes on to describe the events in the microcosm of Mürren in 1916:

'On August 15th, we were given kharki [khaki], it was grand to get into it again, and later we were issued with complete kit. They used to hold kit inspections at intervals. Certain unscrupulous and impecunious individuals used to sell their kit and there was a regular market for some things such as grey-back shirts, boots and puttees. The chief emporium for this illicit traffic was the café of one John Staeger, which was generally known as The Telescope from a large telescope he kept outside for visitors to view the mountains with.

One of Staeger's best customers was Private Burns, generally known as 'Billy-born-drunk'.[171] On one kit inspection, he showed a solitary sock which having lost its mate was unusable. His underclothing consisted of a pair of pyjamas for which there was no market and he used to go about occasionally with one of the strings hanging out. But Billy's greatest exploit was as follows. Captain Llopart used to live in the Grand Hotel and Kurhaus [Spa] when it was open, and when it was closed, in the Regina. One night his dinner, a chicken, was missing and it was discovered that Billy had eaten it. He was transferred to the Alpenruch [Alpenruh]. The activities of these gentry were merely amusing until they took to helping themselves to other people's kit and selling that. This got so bad at one time that everyone had to lock up his room.

On August 20th, there was a Thanksgiving Service for C of E and Presbyterians in which both chaplains took part. In

---

171 Whilst there are a number of contenders, Private Burns has, perhaps mercifully, not been positively identified. There is a *Restaurant Stägerstübli* in Mürren to this day.

order to have more room, this was held in Des Alpes. This was the first of the compulsory church parades that were held weekly for each creed all the time Colonel Neish was at Mürren. Church parades are an abomination and I don't believe any chaplain worth his salt has ever been found to defend them, and these caused more grousing than even the celebrated snow fatigue in the winter. But the Colonel was one of the old school and a compulsory church parade was a *sine qua non* with him.

Another of his foibles was the abhorrence of football or cricket on Sundays. In the winter, he and other officers freely went curling and everyone went skiing, skating or tobogganing, but he would not hear of football in the summer. I only remember one football match on a Sunday and that was a special occasion. They wanted to play a Swiss team who could not come on a weekday. None of the officers dared to tackle the old man, so Tyler as Secretary of the Football undertook to do so. After being threatened with dire punishments for daring to argue from curling in the winter, he at last got an unwilling consent. After the Colonel left, the church parades gradually died out.

I forgot to mention the orderly officers. One or two officers were appointed weekly for this job and used to inspect the rooms. Some contented themselves with a cursory inspection, others were satisfied if one certain thing was as they wished. To one of these all was right so long as the water jugs were full, to another the one thing needful was a clean looking glass and so on. Others again went out of their way to look for trouble. They used to crawl under the beds to find dust, come around at 7 a.m. to see everyone was up, attend the roll call supposed to be held at 7.15 and try to catch the men smoking in their rooms, which for some unexplained reason was strictly forbidden, though no one

Chapter 7 Switzerland

ever did or ever could stop it. For these last we found a splendid specific. We used to tell [The Reverend] Campbell Bell, who at once complained to the Colonel, who had the officer in question 'on the mat' and said things to him that in civilian life could only have been wiped out in blood.

The chief offender was the Mine Sweeper, a naval chief petty officer and the only representative of the Navy in the Officers' Mess. On his second appearance on the mat, he was told that he was not fit to do Orderly Man let alone Orderly Officer. On his third appearance, he was informed that if it occurred again he would be sent to the Sergeants' Mess. When Campbell Bell left we had lost our 'power behind the throne' and by degrees the orderly officers came into their own again but for a time we had them so scared they hardly dared look at anything.

On August 24th was the first concert in my diary and I describe it as 'very good'. These concerts run by a select few who thought they had a sort of monopoly got feebler and feebler. The first may have been very good for that time, but as they always charged admission and never rose above a level far below what we attained at Göttingen, and as they were always the same, some of us at least decided to show them how these things should be done with the result that I shall relate in its proper place.

On September 10th, a lady accompanied by the Colonel came round the hotels with a message from the King. This introduces one or two stories about the Chief of Establishment, or Senior NCO of the Regina at that time. Sergeant Cane was not what might be called learned or even moderately educated, and at the end of the lady's little speech he felt he was called upon to do something, so he bawled out, 'Three cheers for HMS the King'. On another occasion, he announced that the fire alarm would be, 'Three concessive blasts on the gong'.[172] Later he was sent in charge of a place called Signal de Bonge [Signal de Bougy, which is near Lake Geneva] where habitual drunkards were sent and where by all accounts they were allowed to booze in peace and quietness!

On September 25th, a large party of officers and men went on a trip up the Jungfrau, Jock and I went with them. The railway runs up as far as that, the war having prevented its being continued at the top. It is a fine excursion and we much enjoyed it.

About this time the YMCA was opened. It was situated on the ground floor of a vacant hotel, the Jungfrau. In it one could buy tinned milk, cakes and other refreshments. It was run by a Mr. Whitwell, a singularly harmless and hopeless old gentleman with a wife, who came out later, who was one of the greatest snobs and bores ever imagined. Their daughter had married the Duke of Bedford's son and was always referred to by her mother as 'the Future Duchess'.'

This was Robert Jowitt Whitwell B.Litt., a British medievalist who made significant contributions to lexicography. How he came to be at Mürren has not been discovered, perhaps he was 'doing his bit'. He was married to Louisa, née Brown, and in 1914 their daughter Louisa married Hastings William Sackville Russell, who became 12th Duke of Bedford in 1940, Louisa being styled as Duchess of Bedford thereafter. Kenneth resumes:

'Poor old Whitty, an old Oxford Professor, was not a man of business and got things into an awful hash. Once he got a consignment of cigarettes and sold them beautifully cheap to find after they were gone that he had to foot a large bill of duty on them. He used to sell ham sandwiches at a price that covered the bread and a little more. He had a delightfully

---

172 Possibly 9420 Sergeant Herbert Cane of the 2nd Royal Scots. ICRC op. cit.

simple method of squaring his accounts, when he had a large deficit he used to write a cheque and when the money came from the bank put it on the credit side and so make all right.

His chief delight was in the evening when he used to hold a small service. As so few stopped for this he used, as a bait, to read out the war news from the Swiss papers. The men would stop for that, and old Whitty would drone out, 'The English Communiqué says ... the French Communiqué says ...', then snatching a Bible from under his arm, 'and the Lord says ....' at which there would be a regular stampede for the door. When she was there, Mrs. Whitwell would assist by blocking up the doorway and saying, 'Oh do stop, Mr. Whitwell is going to pray, and it will be so nice to hear him'. Sometime in the winter Whitty was superseded by a much more efficient person, but he hung on till the following autumn, making mistakes and getting in the way, then he drifted home and the authorities wisely prevented him from coming out again.'

Kenneth was now in for a most pleasant surprise. Possibly through public subscription, the British had created an arrangement whereby internees' wives were sent free of charge to spend two weeks with their husbands in Switzerland. If a man was not married, his mother could visit instead. In this manner many couples were reunited after years of separation.[173] But before this scheme commenced, Kenneth found that he had a caller:

'On October 6th, Ada came out on a visit. She had glorious weather which was very lucky, on the night before she left, the 16th, we had our first permanent fall of snow.'

As we have already discovered, Ada was Kenneth's 38-year-old sister, married to The Reverend Edmund Wethered and the

---
173 Derived from: Douglas op. cit., Page 179.

mother of four children. It seems astonishing that families could take the ferry to France and transit to Switzerland by train at the height of the war, but they did, and many wives and relations stayed out there for a while. Kenneth was amazed to see Ada. The telegram announcing her journey had yet to arrive.

Ada reported that Kenneth, 'looked so well in every way, just like his old self, though perhaps he is balder.' She also reports that his hand was practically well, though with some stiffness for which he would have 'electric treatment'. Staying in the Regina, Ada spent 10 agreeable days there getting to know the local area, Kenneth's associates and the hierarchy. Ada had beaten the rush, as Kenneth now explains:

'On October 27th, the first party of wives and mothers arrived and everyone in the garrison went to the station to meet them armed with all the cow bells, gongs, hotel bells and mouth organs obtainable. They were great occasions at first. Those whose relations were coming out met them at Berne or Interlaken. They stayed three weeks and a fresh party arrived every 10 days. Gradually fewer and fewer came to meet them and the excitement died out. Foremost on these and similar occasions was Private Cassidy of the Argyll and Sutherland Highlanders, who was quite a character in his way.'[174]

As visitors came and went, 1916 was reaching its end:

'On October 30th, the first debate was held. These debates took place in the YMCA. The thing was started by Corporal Williams[175] and was carried on all that winter and the next and led to other things I shall tell later.

---

[174] Possibly 3/5480 Private Daniel Cassidy of the 1st Argyll and Sutherland Highlanders, who had been a prisoner at Göttingen. ICRC op. cit.

[175] Probably 10439 Corporal George Williams of the Welch Regiment. ICRC op. cit. and The National Archives UK, British Army WWI Service Records, 1914-1920.

Chapter 7 Switzerland

On November 21st, the C of E Men's Society held its first meeting. This was got up by Campbell Bell and I was Secretary. It had only been going a month when Campbell Bell left. I managed to keep it alive during the interregnum that followed and under Canon Woodward it flourished. Mr. Bulstrode with his long prayers and his books on missions made it a regular bore and after July 17th it was allowed to drop. When Mr. Cready came I tried to revive it but he was unsympathetic and after one meeting on November 6th, I let it go. Campbell Bell and Woodward looked on it as a sort of Church Council and we used to discuss and arrange all sorts of things.'

This is the first mention of Canon Woodward and Mr. Bulstrode, but we will read about them in more detail later on when they formally make their appearance. 'Mr. Cready' was presumably the new Chaplain. Later in his memoir, Kenneth describes him as 'McCready'.[176]

'One day we were discussing the church lighting. Though electric light was cheap and plentiful in Mürren, neither church had it. The RC church was lit with candles and the C of E with hideous oil lamps. It was suggested that a subscription should be got up from the interned to light both churches with electricity in memory of their stay in Mürren. The RCs were approached and readily agreed. Sergeant Scott, an RC, was asked to do the work and I was to help him.[177]

---

176 In 1917, the Chaplain General appointed British Army chaplains to the Swiss internment centres and the newcomer was probably the Reverend David Frederick McCready, who saw service as a chaplain in the BEF from 1915-1916 and then was on the staff of the Chaplain General from 1916-1919. From 1920 he served as British Chaplain in Geneva. Derived from: All Hallows' Church, Leeds website at: http://allhallowsleeds.org.
177 Possibly 6661 Sergeant Thomas Scott of the 2nd Royal Scots Fusiliers. ICRC op. cit. and The National Archives UK, British Army WWI Service Records, 1914-1920.

We started the preliminary work on December 7th and having got estimates from Interlaken, and used them to beat down the Lauterbrunnen people, we started work on December 22nd. We got both churches done by January 24th at a cost of 740 francs. This including a brass plate for each church stating who had put the lighting in. These tablets were put up on April 14th, when all the money had been collected.'

One hundred years later, the brass plaque that they placed in the RC church is still in its position. It reads, 'The Electric Light was installed in this church by the British Interned at Mürren 1916-17'.

Being Switzerland, the winter heralded snow. Mürren had been a popular winter sports centre before the war and was to become so again at the war's end. However, Kenneth's snowy experiences were not so glamorous:

'On November 29th was the first snow fatigue. It came about in this way. That morning they asked for volunteers to help make the skating rink. No one turned up. Personally, I was busy and quite meant to go in the afternoon and there may have been many more like me. Anyhow, Major Charley called a compulsory parade for the afternoon and we were paraded up and down trampling down the snow. Of course, a lot of the men on this never intended to do any skating, and he and it did not gain popularity on that account.

By degrees it became a regular thing, every morning and sometimes in the afternoon as well, everyone but cripples and those 'garrison employed', that is working in shops offices etc. had to parade and work either on the skating rink or the toboggan run or clearing the snow from the railway. I believe this was an arrangement come to by the British Government. The consequence was that those on snow fatigue had little time for anything else and it came about

Chapter 7 Switzerland

that those who did not work got the sport and those who did the work got none.

Things came to a climax on January 10th. On that day it was snowing hard, the railway people said it wasn't fit for anyone to be out, the toboggan-run people said it was useless to do anything until it had stopped snowing, so the snow fatigue were put to clear the rink, quite the most futile job of the three. They cleared it in the morning, but in the afternoon it was just as bad as ever. By then it had got bitterly cold and was snowing harder than ever, in fact it was a brute of a day. When they wanted them to clear the rink again they refused.

The fault of the whole thing lay with the Chief of Sector, Senior Sergeant Major (SSM) Ingram, and the Adjutant Captain Johnstone [neither identified]. They ought to have had the sense to see it was useless to work on the rink and that the weather was quite unfit to be out in. When the men refused, the Sergeant reported to the SSM and he to the Adjutant with the result that 38 men were reported to the Commandant for mutiny and got various sentences of imprisonment.

After this incident, the snow fatigue was run on more reasonable lines, but it held on all the winter and even during the summer when a few men were told off daily to pick up paper etc. With the repatriation, all this ceased. When the second winter began Loppy said there was to be no snow fatigue. The rink and run were made by volunteers and the hotel people agreed to keep the line clear with civilian labour. Only on one occasion in March when Mürren was isolated for three or four days were any men warned to help clear the line. The railway job though necessary was the most objectionable as the civilians used to tell our men they were doing them out of a job. I thought the snow fatigue was a mistake from start to finish.

New men arrived from Germany on December 14th [and] 21st which doubled our numbers. On the first of these two dates, there was great excitement. There had been a heavy fall of snow during the night and everyone turned out early and cleared the paths. The Regina contingent were some 20 cripples, we dragged them on to sleighs to the hotel, carried them down to dinner and up to their rooms. The second party were hale and hearty and did not require this attention. They all looked very bad, far worse we were told, than we did on our arrival.'

Whilst Kenneth was involved in snow business, his younger brother Philip was still engaged in active operations. We left him recovering from dysentery in Egypt and, instead of returning to his engineer field company that was now in Salonika, he was posted to the 86th Field Company in the 11th Division that had just arrived in Egypt and was manning the British defences on the Suez Canal where the Ottoman Army was threatening British-controlled Egypt. But soon the 11th was on the move again, this time to the Western Front and the Somme area to join the British offensives that had commenced there on 1st July. The 11th Division occupied a variety of sectors as the successive offensives continued during the autumn, the 86th Company conducting engineering work, mainly to the rear.

By late November, the company had moved up and was near Theipval, which the British had recently captured. The front line lay about half a mile to the north of the town. Here they carried out revetting work, improved communication trenches and worked on a causeway over the nearby River Ancre. The company's casualties were light but on 6th December, two officers were severely wounded by shellfire. One of them was Philip. After treatment at a nearby medical unit, he was evacuated to a British hospital at Le Touquet suffering from a shrapnel wound in his upper thigh. After a few days, he developed gas gangrene.

Chapter 7 Switzerland

As his mother was too frail, his sister Hilda travelled to France, near to her old VAD station, to be with Philip, and he sadly died on 16th December 1916 aged 28. He is buried at the Étaples Military Cemetery.

It is not clear when Kenneth heard the distressing news of his brother Philip's death, but he does not include it in his memoir. We will now resume his narrative and in Mürren, Christmas 1916 was fast approaching:

'On December 23rd Campbell Bell left. I have already described how he used to persecute the orderly officers, but he went rather too far and fell out with the Swiss authorities too. He certainly had something on his side. It was over the question of punishments that they came to blows. The 'clink' or prison was first of all situated in an outhouse and was later moved to a cellar below the Des Alpes. Campbell Bell protested against this and against the severity of the sentences. Things came to a climax when he released a man on his own responsibility who said he was ill. A huge correspondence was held between him, the Colonel and Colonel Peko [Picot] on the one hand and Llopart, the Commandant, and Colonel Hauser, Chief of the Swiss over [those] interned [Chief Swiss Medical Officer], on the other.

The result was that Campbell Bell was first forbidden to go to the clink, then to visit any of the interned and was finally turned out of the country altogether. From then till Woodward came on March 6th, we were without a C of E Chaplain. We managed to get one for Xmas and on odd occasions after, and now and then the Colonel would read a service. Matheson the Presbyterian offered to hold services but as no one was very keen on him, his offer was declined.

Xmas 1916 was ushered in with an issue of punch at the hotels at 10 p.m. on Xmas eve, this was the centre item, in the Regina, of a concert that lasted till 4 a.m. Next day there was a swell dinner with oxtail soup, turkey and the chef's conception of a plum pudding. The Red Cross had sent some plum puddings which arrived too late. They were kept for Easter and as there were not enough to go round, the hotels drew for them. At 5 p.m. [there] was an Xmas tree in each hotel and the men were given parcels of presents from the Swiss chocolate firms etc.

In October, I had joined the Cork Club at the Bellevue Hotel, the object was to raise funds for a jollification at Xmas. Every member paid a subscription each Swiss pay day and was obliged to carry a certain cork and to show it whenever challenged to do so by a fellow member, also it was incumbent on him to appear at the Bellevue on Sundays between certain hours and also at the club meetings. Any infringement of the rules was punished by fines.

The Eiger [Hotel] also had a cork club and we decided to invite each other. They held theirs on 26th and we had ours on 31st. As we were able to profit by their mistakes ours was I think the most successful. The programme consisted of a concert, dancing and refreshments. Our old friend Billy-born-drunk who belonged to neither club appeared at the Eiger attracted by the free drinks going, we were on the lookout for him at the Bellevue and when he came he was gently but firmly shown the door.'

On the Western Front, 1917 contained a succession of largely Allied offensives which sometimes made tactical gains, such as the seizure of important ground features, but failed to break through the strong enemy positions. In the spring, the Germans consolidated their defence on the formidable Hindenburg Line and the locations remained relatively immobile throughout the year. In Mesopotamia, now Iraq, British forces were advancing northwards through the Turkish Ottoman defences and would eventually reach Baghdad. In Palestine, a large British advance was initiated that led to the capture of Jerusalem by December.

Chapter 7 Switzerland

Also, by the end of the year, British divisions would be serving in Italy to bolster their ally against Austro-Hungarian and German forces.

As an aside, Kenneth's brother Hugh had decided to leave his New Zealand idyll and return home to do his bit. He enlisted in March, was commissioned into the Army Service Corps in May and was then posted to 553 Auxiliary Horse Transport Company, part of the 64th (2nd Highland) Division which remained at home and provided a base for training and home defence. We will find out what 1918 held in store for him in due course.

Back in Switzerland, no doubt Kenneth and his associates heard news of the momentous wartime events as they unfolded, but beset by the need to create worthwhile activities and amusements, they soldiered steadfastly on. Despite the delightful aspect of their mountain fastness, many internees were suffering from boredom, debilitating physical injuries and the draining mental effects of years spent as a prisoner of war; 'barbed-wire disease'. Kenneth continues his catalogue of activities:

'On January 3rd, the cinema started. This was a private venture on the part of Major Charley and some other officers who bought the box, machine and all and used to charge admission. They used at first to show afternoons and evenings on Thursdays or Fridays with a fresh programme each day in the large ballroom of the Des Alpes. The afternoon shows were discontinued in early May. It was run at first by Sergeant Scott whom I have already mentioned and on February 28th, I joined the staff as assistant operator. As I knew nothing of cinemas before, this was one new trade I learnt at Mürren. On 10th May, Scott went to Vevey for a motor course and I carried on with Sergeant Howe who had been an operator in civil life.[178] He gave it up on July 18th and from that time I was the chief operator. The

---

[178] Possibly Sergeant Stanley Howe of the 18th Manchesters. ICRC op. cit.

officer-in-charge was Mr. Russell.[179] He managed the whole thing, money, ordering the films etc. and was an easy man to get on with. I shall refer to the cinema again later.

On February 28th was the first YMCA concert. These were held every Monday during the winter. They were not up to much as both room and talent were limited. The performers stood on a platform some five feet square and the audience crowded round them. On May 14th and the following week, they held what they called an Eisteddfod – a series of competitions singing, reciting limericks, speeches and all sorts of things. But until the new hut was opened they could not rise higher than that.

On March 6th Canon Woodward arrived. Of all conceivable men he was the one, *par excellence*, for the job. He was Canon of Southwark Cathedral and sort of rector of it. He had joined up for 12 months, been wounded and invalided home and finally sent to Mürren to finish his time.[180] It was a thousand pities he could not stop, but he had promised the man who took on his work at Southwark that he would return in a year. He was up to all sorts of fun, an ideal man, immensely popular, there was not an officer or man or civilian in Mürren who had not a good word to say for him. Later when we got up a memorial in the vain hope of getting him back, everyone who heard of it was anxious to sign. He had been, I found, at Marlborough [College] with me, and if ever anyone did the old school credit it was he.

On March 31st, the Debating Society rose to a mock

---

179 Probably Lieutenant John Russell of the 2nd Royal Sussex. ICRC op. cit.
180 Canon Clifford Salisbury Woodward was Precentor of Southwark Cathedral and Rector of St. Saviour and St. Peter. He was an army chaplain in the war, during which time he was wounded and won the MC. He became Bishop of Bristol, then Gloucester.

Chapter 7 Switzerland

trial. Woodward as Counsel was immense. He was so good and it was such a success that we had another on May 12th before he left. We had three more, but they never came up to these first two, no one could equal Woodward. Jebb-Scott was the judge for that first one and bought wigs for judge and counsel, but he worried so over it he would never take part again.

Woodward held a lantern service on Good Friday in the Cinema Hall, and on Easter Day April 8th, I first went to the YMCA Family Tea. This was an excellent institution held every Sunday. One had to put one's name down beforehand for it, and eat as much as one liked for 50 cm. There was a general conspiracy to get Woodward on these as he was heart and soul of the whole thing. They were amusing affairs, Woodward pulling everyone's leg in turn, old Whitwell droning out his incessant, 'By the way', Mrs. Hobday's 'liquid laughter', a sort of cackle, just like a horse neighing, and Hobday being jovial in his inimitable fashion. When the new hut opened they had to stop owing to food shortages etc.'

This is the first mention of the Hobdays. According to Lieutenant Colonel Picot, Mr. J. W. [John] Hobday was appointed Secretary of the YMCA in Switzerland in January 1917 and took over from Mr. Whitwell some time thereafter. Picot lauds the part played by the YMCA and states, 'The Association appears to me more than well served by its staff, and evidently has the happy faculty of choosing the right man for the right place. Nothing could have been better, for instance, than their choice of Mr. Whitwell and Mr. Hobday, the former for his large-heartedness, the latter for his administrative and executive abilities.'[181] It appears that Hobday, who had worked as Secretary of the YMCA

---

181 Picot op. cit., Page 180.

in London, was assisted by his wife, Rose, and at least one of his two teenaged daughters.[182]

Kenneth now describes a new venture:

'About this time, Tyler conceived the idea of mock election and approached the Debates Committee on the subject. Woodward and I were appointed a sub-committee to meet him and arrange it with this result. Mürren was divided into three constituencies as nearly as possible in equal numbers, some two or three hotels in each. There were two parties; Blue and Red. Williams ran the Blue and I the Red. We each had three members for each constituency besides ourselves and an agent; Tyler was mine.

We started on April 21st with a joint meeting, then each party had a meeting to themselves and finally there was another joint meeting. The thing caught on and there was huge excitement over it and on Polling Day April 30th Mürren was bathed in colours and 350 voted. The voting was by ballot, there were three ballot boxes, one for each constituency. The result was that each side won one constituency easily, the Blue won the odd one by eight and the whole thing by five votes. We each had a programme allotted to us, the Blue was woman suffrage, reform of education and nationalisation of drink, the Red was nationalisation of mines and railways, franchise reform (one man one vote, one vote one value) and agricultural reform.

One of my candidates was Private Wright of the 1st Canadian Mounted Rifles who became a great friend of mine.[183] He had only gone to Canada a month or so before the war. Later I christened him 'The Squimp', which

---

182 The National Archives UK, Census Returns of England and Wales, 1911.
183 108646 Private Rawleigh Wright. He was the son of Sydney and Jean Wright, of Crofton Park, London. CWGC op. cit.

Chapter 7 Switzerland

name caught on and he was more often called that than his own name.

About that time, Dr. Garnet arrived from England. He was a most wonderful old man who could talk learnedly on any subject under the sun. He belonged to the London County Council Education Committee and had come to advise and report on Charley's institutes. He was quite a long time in Switzerland.'[184]

We have already noted that wives and mothers were able to visit Mürren, but this policy broadened. Some internees even managed to get married, their fiancées arriving in Switzerland with an appropriate entourage. Considerable efforts were made to make these occasions efficacious and, in the winter, a large sleigh was used to convey the bride to church, decorated with the Union Jack.[185] Kenneth makes his own observations:

'On April 18th was the first of many weddings held in Mürren. On May 23rd, five couples were married at once in the C of E church not to mention one on the same day in the RC. This quintuple wedding was quite an affair and took three-quarters of an hour. The five couples just filled the altar rails. Behind as a rear rank came the bridesmaids and givers-away with the best men behind them as supernumeraries. It was lucky there were not more than five. On May 5th, Bishop Berry held a Confirmation in the C of E church.[186]

When Sergeant Scott left on May 10th, I took on the job of

---

184 Dr. William Garnett MA DCL was a British professor, focussing in physics and mechanics. Amongst many distinctions, he was an educational adviser to the London County Council.

185 Derived from: Douglas op. cit.

186 Berry has not been identified. From the matter-of-fact way Kenneth introduces him, the bishop may have visited on more than one occasion. It is suspected that he was a retired bishop on holiday engaged for this very task or a locum bishop in Europe for the summer.

arranging the electric lights for the 'Gaff' as the concerts in the Des Alpes were called. These had been getting more and more feeble, and another man and I had discussed the idea of getting up a play with the YMCA concert and debating society material. At last I broached the subject in the debates committee and we decided to hold a joint meeting with the entertainments committee and see what could be done. This meeting was held on May 2nd and the result was we started rehearsing the farce 'Face the Music'.[187] As soon as the Gaff party found this out they did their best to stop it. Unfortunately, Mr. Spargo was chairman of both the entertainment committee and the Gaff party and had been put in charge of our play.[188]

We rehearsed in a desultory way and got no further and towards the end of the month it was obvious the whole thing would collapse. The idea had been that the play should be acted at the opening of the new YMCA hut. Wright and I were determined the thing should go through and we interviewed every member of the cast except Spargo with the result that a meeting was called on 30th May in which everyone spoke their minds. We made some changes in the cast and started again this time in earnest.

Finally, the play was acted at the opening of the hut on June 26th and was a huge success. It was so far superior to all

---

187 A farce in three acts by J.H. Darnley. The programme survives. Kenneth played the part of Sergeant Duffell (a detective). Rawleigh Wright played the Reverend John Smith. A number of the Mürren-based ladies that Kenneth has introduced us to also had parts.

188 Seemingly, Lieutenant William Henry Spargo from South Africa, who was wounded and captured on 8th August 1916 whilst serving with the 1st/8th Kings Liverpool during the third attack to take Guillemont on the Somme. He had a fractured elbow, the result of enemy artillery fire, which ultimately resulted in the amputation of his left arm. He was repatriated to the UK in September 1917. Derived from: Records of the Museum of Liverpool and the War Diary of the 1st/8th Battalion King's Liverpool Regiment (The National Archives UK, WO 95/2923/1)

Chapter 7 Switzerland

the Gaffs that it killed them. While they charged admission for rotten shows we had put on a decent one free. After this there was only one more Gaff on August 14th, very few of the men went, I didn't. Scott had returned before that, but a lot of people from the Kurhans [probably Kurhaus] did and I heard it was the worst of all, a really disgraceful show.

On May 14th, there was an outing for those who attended the C of E evening services. We paid part of the cost and Woodward paid the rest from some money he had been given before leaving England. We went down the valley and to the Trummelback Falls. There were 36 of us in all and it was a most successful day. This was Woodward's last appearance as he left on the 18th. Two days before he left, Mr. Bulstrode arrived directly from the firing line. He was a very different man, he was very Low Church, and his one idea seemed to be tracts and prayers. He never got on at all. He spent most of his time going on long walks or collecting flowers and finally resigned as 'he had not enough to do.'

An experienced army chaplain, The Reverend Roger Bulstrode had served in France and Belgium with the 20th Division on the Western Front, including the fighting at Guillemont on the Somme in September 1916. He was then posted as C of E Chaplain to Mürren. In October 1917, he joined the 48th Division in Italy, ending the war as acting Assistant Chaplain General of St. George's Military Church, Rouen.[189]

'On May 28th, the last debate for the season was held. That same night another idea of Tyler's came to a head. I had been let into the secret and had attended a meeting on the subject on April 27th, but it was a close secret. The idea was to name all the roads, lanes, paths and open spaces of Mürren with the names of London thoroughfares. Jebb-

---

189 Private Papers of the Reverend R. Bulstrode. Imperial War Museum Documents, 1276.

Scott had taken the matter in hand, raised the money and a lot of sign boards had been painted and got ready. On the night in question, seven of us who had secretly got passes till 2 a.m. repaired to the Jebb-Scott chalet and when all was quiet planted the sign boards on holes already prepared. We got all done by 11.15. Next morning there was quite an excitement, those from London were quite pleased at the idea but those to whom London names meant nothing rather laughed at the whole thing.'

As these diversions developed in April and May, a substantial offensive, The Battle of Arras, was taking place on the Western Front. Despite making a sizeable advance, British progress slowed, and the attack then became an expensive deadlock. Unaffected by such momentous events, the Mürren internees continued to invent ways to fill their lives. The prisoners' newspaper 'The Wooden City' had been a great success at Göttingen and now the Mürren inmates turned their hands to journalism:

'On May 29th, I attended another meeting over another idea. I am not sure, but I think this also emanated from Tyler's fertile brain. This time it was a paper to be called 'B.I.M. British International Mürren'. Mr. Hubbs,[190] a Canadian officer and a newspaper proprietor in Canada was Editor, I was one of the correspondents. The first number came out about the end of June. For a time, it was most interesting and amusing, and though it changed editors two or three times, it kept quite popular until Major Charley returned from England and got hold of it. Then its name was changed to 'British Interned Magazine' and it was made to represent all Switzerland and got filled with accounts of Charley's classes at Meiringen and Seeburg.

---

190 Lieutenant Frederick Hubbs of the 4th Canadian Mounted Regiment, a printer and publisher from Hastings, Ontario. Derived from: the Canadian Great War Project op. cit.

Chapter 7 Switzerland

At last the Mürren Notes in one number were so scandalous, no other word suits it, that on June 3rd 1918, it was publicly burnt on the football ground at Mürren. We did it in style, one man was dressed as a parson and read a funeral oration, another dressed as an acolyte carried a banner bearing the BIM poster altered from 'Now on Sale' to 'Not on Sale', three volleys were done on gongs and the Last Post sounded.

On Empire Day and the King's Birthday, we had ceremonial parades when the flag was hoisted and saluted. Meanwhile the hut was nearing completion and the question of lighting arose. Knowing that we had got the church lighting cheap by doing the lighting ourselves, the YMCA had asked Scott to do it for them. But when the time came he was still away at Vevey, so they asked me to do it instead. What little I knew about the matter I had learnt in the church lighting, but I took it on, and with Wright and one or two others to help me, made a start. But I soon saw that without more help I should never get done in time. Major Charley wanted the electric wiring class, defunct during Scott's absence, to help, but only one came and he the one who knew the least. Luckily, I got a man to help me who had been a lines man at home and with the electrician doing part of it we got all done including footlights etc. in time.

The hut was opened by Lady Rumbold, [wife of] the British Minister for Switzerland on June 26th.[191] We had got the stage fitted with proscenium curtain etc. and the stage

---

191 Sir Horace George Montagu Rumbold, 9th Baronet GCB, GCMG, KCVO, PC was British Minister for Switzerland from 1916. He was later British Ambassador to Berlin from 1928 to 1933, warning the British Government about the ambitions of Hitler and Nazi Germany. The American ambassador to Belgium, Brand Whitlock, visited Switzerland in 1917 and lauded the attractions of Lady Rumbold, née Etheldred Constantia Fane. Derived from: '*The Letters and Journal of Brand Whitlock'*, edited by Allan Nevins, Appleton-Century, New York, 1936.

Keeping The Old Flag Flying

walls papered. The opening ceremony was in the afternoon and various speeches were made, one of which had far reaching results. Colonel Peko [Picot], after enumerating the horrors of Mürren in winter and the delights of down below, called for a show of hands to decide how many wanted to stay another winter. The vast majority voted to go below. He thereupon promised them to close Mürren before winter. This he had no business to do as the decision did not rest with him and ever after, he did his best to make good his words.

In the evening was our play 'Facing the Music' and after it the cast were entertained to a champagne supper at the Des Alpes. On July 2nd, the Canadians had a Dominion Day outing, (July 1st was a Sunday), to Gunten on Lake Thun. During July 13th and [in the] following days, the Anglo-Swiss Trading Co. sent some men up to film Mürren.[192] The result, long expected, was finally shown in Mürren on July 24th 1918. There were two films, one showing the scenery and the Swiss villagers and the other devoted to the interned. The man had taken them too slowly, they being the first he had ever taken, otherwise they were quite good.

On July 26th, the Regina won a football match. This was a great occasion as they had not won before. I have not, and I am afraid I cannot say much about the cricket and football [sic]. At the beginning of the season, the officers gave up the tennis courts of the Des Alpes, situated on the skating rink, and the hotel authorities allowed the ground to be used for football and cricket. There were a lot of both during the summer, but I don't know much about it. Cricket was generally played in the morning and early afternoon and football began at 4 p.m. For tennis, the Kurhans [Kurhaus]

---

192 Established in 1915, Anglo-Swiss Trading Co. were 'General merchants, manufacturers, and dealers in celluloid, especially for aviation purposes'. Flight Magazine, 30th July 1915, Page 566.

Chapter 7 Switzerland

courts were available and later in the season we men were allowed to use them after 7 p.m. but it was not a satisfactory arrangement. The cinema class started on August 2nd, but as the cinema closed a month later it did not come to much.

Ever since the church outing on May 14th, we had been collecting funds for another. At the end, it became a case of now or never. Bulstrode was away for some time and we had to wait for him, then it had to be put off for the Repatriation Commission and then a good number were going away on working parties so that if we could not have held it on August 24th I don't suppose it would have come off at all. But despite a heavy thunderstorm in the night we had a lovely day. This time we went to Grindelwald, starting early and walking to Zweilutochinen [Zweilütschinen] and taking the train from there and all the way home. We had a glorious day and most of us did all the main Grindelwald sights. There were 40 in the party this time.

Sometime before this, the Lunns had announced that they would close the Palace and Des Alpes hotels at the end of August. I think this was partly bluff to induce the Swiss authorities to come to a decision as to whether Mürren was to remain open or not. If so, it did not succeed and the hotels duly closed. The officers then moved to the Regina and the men in the Palace and Regina were divided among the other hotels. At first, I was down for the Alpenruh but I managed to get it changed to the Jungfrau. The Jungfrau was the then empty hotel on the ground floor of which the YMCA had started. When the new men came through in December, the two top floors had been opened as a hotel. After the hut was opened, the YMCA and institutes still kept on the ground floor for classes etc. In the Jungfrau, I got a room with Wright and was with him for over six months.

The closing of the Des Alpes meant the closing of the cinema. They allowed us to run till September 6th and then the whole thing was packed away until it opened again in the YMCA.'

It appears that the conditions of internment evolved as the war drew on. A few prisoners of war from both sides had been repatriated via Switzerland as early as 1915, but this scheme was limited to individuals suffering from specific injuries or diseases. The ICRC then arranged with the Swiss Government to accept a larger number of prisoners who would remain there as internees and Kenneth had benefited from this agreement.

'The terms under which internment occurred changed over the course of the war, as individual countries made bilateral agreements. Under a May 1917 agreement between France and Germany, internees were automatically repatriated to their home country after being in captivity for more than eighteen months, if over a specified age. An Anglo-German agreement in mid-1917 broadened the terms of eligibility for internment to men who had spent at least 18 months in captivity and who were recognised as suffering from so-called 'barbed-wire disease', meaning the mental strain of being held prisoner. It was also agreed at this time that internees whose recovery was likely to be prolonged would be repatriated.'[193] Kenneth describes the effect of these changes on the ground:

> 'Meanwhile nothing was heard or thought of but repatriation. From the beginning of August everyone seemed to have gone repatriation mad. The commission started on August 18th and all the officers but five, and about half the men passed. They left finally on September 8th in four trains, as far as Lauterbrunnen. After they were gone everything seemed very dull and empty, and to relieve this we got up the third mock trial on September 21st.
>
> During this period, some of us were fighting tooth and nail to keep Mürren open, the alternative, Interlaken, did

---
193 'Switzerland and the First World War' at: www.switzerland1914-1918.net.

Chapter 7 Switzerland

not appeal to us at all. Llopart was on our side and Peko [Picot] was against us. On September 25th, everyone voted on Mürren v. Interlaken and the latter held the large majority. Next day some big Swiss authority came and saw the place and I think it was due to his favourable report that we succeeded. Anyhow it was decided that those who had voted to stay should stay and those who had voted to go should go. They left for Interlaken on October 15th.

On September 26th, the surveying class started. The idea of this class had been mooted in the spring before the snow went. All the summer Major Charley and Dr. Carnet [not identified] had been trying to get an instrument. They succeeded at last in getting one, just as the snow was due once more, and we started. After the move to Interlaken, I used to go down every Thursday to take a class there. It was a deadly job. I had to go to the Swiss office on Wednesday for a pass, it took the whole day Thursday and I had to hump the heavy instrument across the two changes, I never could get supper in time and generally had to run for the train at night, and finally had to go to the Swiss office again on Friday to get my money back. I stuck it out till December 6th when the whole thing was stopped for the winter.

With October 1st, bread cards were started. These were the first numerous cards for all sorts of commodities, but in Mürren we could still get bread for tea at the shops on the sly.

We had a concert in the YMCA on October 1st and put on the sketch 'The Dear Departed'. This was the second YMCA theatrical venture and was a great success.

On October 9th, Mr. McCready came and next day Bulstrode left. At first, we thought he was a second Woodward, but we soon found our mistake. He was even lower church than Bulstrode, but that did not matter, what did matter was that though Bulstrode with all his faults practised what he preached; McCready certainly did not. The things he said and the things he did put everyone against him. He came to be under Tyler's thumb and between them on December 10th they started the Jolly Boys Club. This was supposed to be an offset to the Ramblers and nearly everyone joined. They gave a concert in the YMCA on Xmas day with boxing and other items. But I think the idea was for the Jolly Boys to run Mürren and when they found Mürren would not be run by them, the Jolly Boys died a natural death. After not being heard of for months, it was wound up in the spring and the money given to the sports fund.

Sometime in the new year McCready transferred to his headquarters in Interlaken. Mürren, Interlaken and Meiringen were under him, and [he] only came to Mürren for a service once a fortnight. The news that he was going was received with absolute indifference by all. His last words to his successor were, 'Now you have come I am sure I don't know what you will find to do to fill in your time'. The reply was, 'During the last 18 years I have not found enough time to do all I wanted to'.

Early in October, snow came and the skiing began, and on October 13th, a ski club was formed which took over the skis from Mr. Lunn and let them out to the men, a far better arrangement than the year before. On that same evening, the debates started again. The first was held in the Jungfrau but afterwards they used to be in the hut and Saturday evenings were set aside for them. It was a far more successful season than the one before and we kept it up till May 3rd when we finished with a mock trial.

When the hut was opened, Hobday, then YMCA Secretary, was most anxious to get the cinema there but

Chapter 7 Switzerland

his chance did not come till the Des Alpes closed and the cinema was homeless. Then however, the negotiations over taking it over were protracted to such a length that I began to think nothing would be done. Finally, all was settled and we began to move it into the hut on October 15th.

The first show was on November 9th. At first the box was on the stage and when that was required for theatricals etc. it was put on a moveable platform. This was such an awful job that at last we decided to install it in one of the dressing rooms at the side of the stage. For this purpose, we had to remove the ceiling and front wall of the room and build the box in. We started on this on December 29th and the first show from the new position was on January 4th. From January 9th onwards, we gave two shows weekly on Wednesdays and Fridays, it had been Thursdays before, till July 24th with the exception of the week following June 8th when the lamp was away being repaired. On July 24th owing to the Spanish influenza a Federal Council order closed all cinemas in Switzerland.

We got a 600-candle power lamp of the incandescent type which we used for lantern lectures. This lamp we also used to run through the films beforehand and as it gave no heat we could stop where we pleased. We used to go through the films and translate them, which as they were all in French made them far more easily understood by the men. At first Mrs. Lunn and Private Baillie of the London Scottish used to do this,[194] but later on they both went away and after another man had taken it over and also gone away,

---

194 510083 Private Reginald Baillie of the 14th Londons (London Scottish) arrived in Mürren in mid-1916. ICRC op. cit. Kenneth's sister Ada met him on her visit that October. She wrote that he 'had been on the famous charge', probably a reference to an assault on the advancing Germans at Wytschaete, near Ypres on the 31st October 1915, which was lauded in the British press, and 'he was in a bank in London until the war broke out. He always looked smart and like an officer'.

I did it myself for a month, [from] March 19th to April 19th, with only the young Hobday girl to write it down.

It was an awful job as I had to put it into good English and all. One day, March 29th, it took over four hours to do. At last, Mrs. Lunn returned and though I still helped I did not have it all to myself. But after all it was worthwhile in the Des Alpes except when they could get someone to translate at sight and quickly at that, they were not translated at all and before I joined the staff I used to say I would not have gone if I had not understood French.'

Kenneth does not include it in his memoir, but in October his sister Hilda wrote to inform him that their mother Adelaide had died peacefully on 12th October, aged 74. It was, by all accounts, a blessed relief from suffering after a long illness. Adelaide was laid to rest at Aspley Guise next to her husband and son Harold.

On the Western Front, the British and German Armies were embroiled in the Third Battle of Ypres, more widely known as Passchendaele, fighting each other to a bloody, mud-choked standstill. Kenneth does not mention this offensive, but now tells us how Mürren prepared for the next winter:

'On October 17th, every hotel was closed but the Bellevue and Alpenruh; the best and the worst. The Alpenruh keeping open was pure graft as besides being the worst fed it was right outside Mürren, 'in the next village' as Wright described it. Wright and I went to the Alpenruh. Although the food was so bad we used to make a complaint on an average every other day, I look back at our time there as a very happy one. We had a nice room with Rifleman Grundon of the London Rifle Brigade,[195] generally known as 'Tubby' from his shape. We got on splendidly and had

---

195 Probably 301320 Private Harold Grundon of 1/5th Londons, a railway clerk who hailed from Forest Gate in London. ICRC op. cit. and The National Archives UK, British Army WWI Service Records, 1914-1920.

a lot of fun together and numerous 'rough houses'. Wright was most often the victim and after a noise that attracted general attention, our door would burst open and he would be carried out having offended in some way, or he would fly from the wrath to come, with us after him. But we all of us took our turn at being the butt of the other two.

The problem of heating the YMCA was put off until it was decided whether Mürren was to stay open or whether the hut had to be moved elsewhere. The result was that the cold weather caught them unawares and it was bitterly cold in there. But at last the electric heaters were going on October 23rd and then all was well. The job of installing these was far too complicated for me and it was left to the electricians.

The heating of the church was both inefficient and costly, and McCready had the idea of holding services in the hut and did so from November 11th to December 2nd, when as some people objected they were held in the church once more. Williams was Church Orderly and a very bad one as we suffered from cold smoke which was all the stove could produce under his care. On November 13th, the YMCA achieved its final victory over the old Gaff party when it took over their properties. A room in the Jungfrau was set aside for them and I was put in charge.

On November 28th, 11 officers and 54 men came from Germany and the Edelweiss and Alpina hotels opened. On December 28th, six officers and 94 men arrived and the Eiger and Jungfrau opened.

During the intervening period, we had only three officers in Mürren and those easiest of the lot. Loppy had been Commandant and, as all the bad characters had gone to Interlaken, everything had been remarkably peaceful and

Keeping The Old Flag Flying

quiet. Sometimes after the new men came it was required to put a man in clink but no one knew where that was. The last clink had been in one of the Eiger chalets but as the Eiger was still closed, they did not know what to do. That incident shows how peaceful and law-abiding we had been. The new men did not upset this happy state of things and as such things as orderly officers of the old style were not revived, all remained 'cushy' at Mürren.

At Interlaken, there was a very different state of things. There, a bad SBO and an equally bad sergeant major, the senior one of the Army, made life intolerable and we were glad we had stayed at Mürren.

Our new SBO was Major Barlow,[196] and though a senior, Major Nutt of the Artillery,[197] came with the second party [Barlow] still carried on. There was a brigadier and several colonels who came to Switzerland at this time but Colonel Peko [Picot] arranged that only majors should be SBOs as he did not wish to be told home truths by senior colonels as he had often in the past. I believe both the former, of Mürren and Château-d'Oex, had gone home swearing to break him. Among the new officers was Mr. Warburton who was an actor in civil life and was made YMCA Officer and a splendid one he proved to be.[198]

---

196 Major Nelson Barlow who served in the 1st Hampshires and had been captured whilst commanding C Company in the Forest of Compiègne in August 1914. ICRC op. cit. and The National Archives UK, British Army WWI Service Records, 1914-1920.

197 This was probably Major Arthur Nutt DSO, who commanded 52 Battery Royal Artillery at the Battle of Le Cateau in August 1914, was wounded in the throat and taken prisoner. His wound would have made him a candidate for Switzerland. ICRC op. cit. and The National Archives UK, British Army WWI Service Records, 1914-1920.

198 Lieutenant Ernest Warburton of the 15th Sherwood Foresters who was wounded and captured during a trench raid at Arras in October 1916. ICRC op. cit. and The National Archives UK, British Army WWI Service Records, 1914-1920. It seems that he continued his thespian career after the war. An Ernest

Chapter 7 Switzerland

On November 29th, the men who had been repatriated on appeal left for home. One of these on arrival at the station found he had left his false teeth at the Alpenruh and had to run back the whole length of the village to get them.

About this time Tyler evolved a new scheme which was that a select few should form a club and take a room at the Belmont as a sitting room. Some eight of us joined at first and on December 1st, we took two rooms. Mrs. Lunn lent us some comfortable arm chairs from the Des Alpes and we settled in. Our numbers varied rising I think to 15. Later, finding we did not use the second room we gave it up. It was an excellent idea and we kept the club on till the end of June.

Wright and I had been doing our best to get out of the Alpenruh and as we both worked in the YMCA we got Hobday to pull strings for us. We wanted to get to the Bellevue, but on December 6th, we were suddenly told we were transferred to the Edelweiss. I was very angry and our new room was not a patch on the old one, but after a short time I found I had struck the best hotel I had been in yet. We shared a room with Alger, an Australian.[199] On April 12th, as I objected to the habit he had formed of stopping downstairs talking and coming to bed late, Wright moved in with Southall of the London Rifle Brigade,[200] and on July 3rd, I moved into a single room by myself.

On December 12th, we put on 'Facing the Music' again

Warburton appeared in *'The Three Sisters'* by Chekov at the London Court Theatre in 1920. Wearning, J. P., *'The London Stage 1920-1929'*, Rowman & Littlefield, Lanham, 2014.

199 2634 Private Frederick Alger, a butcher from Perth, Western Australia. He was with the 16th Australian Infantry. Australian War Memorial at: https://www.awm.govau/people/rolls/R1504324.

200 Possibly 300398 Private Allen Southall of the 5th (City of London) London Rifle Brigade. 1914-1918 Prisoners of the First World War, ICRC op. cit. and The National Archives UK, British Army WWI Service Records, 1914-1920.

with some changes in the cast as some of the old lot had left. Opinions seemed divided as to which performance was the best. In our later rehearsals, we had been coached by Mr. Warburton who took charge of all theatricals after this.

Xmas 1917 was chiefly a YMCA affair. The hut was decorated, plum puddings made there and for three nights in succession there were festivities. On Xmas eve there were waxworks, *Pierrots* [pantomime characters] and tableaux, on Xmas day the Jolly Boys concert and on Boxing Day the YMCA social which consisted of games, Xmas tree and dancing, and food including the plum puddings. On Xmas morning every hotel had bacon and eggs for breakfast with a dinner of turkey and in our hotel, quite respectable plum pudding and beer.'

As Kenneth digested his plum pudding, his sister Hilda had arrived in Boulogne for a second stint as a VAD volunteer, working in a convalescent centre. Now Kenneth tells us what he and his cohorts got up to during the first part of 1918:

'With the New Year in, [we] started rehearsing our greatest theatrical effort 'The Speckled Band'[201] which took place on February 19th. During most of this time, Trooper Ormston of the Life Guards and I were busy with the effects.[202] He painted three really splendid sets of scenery and I got the lighting and other effects ready. It was a busy time. On January 22nd, Mr. Warburton produced three dialogues which were very good. On January 26th and February 9th, there were ice carnivals on the rink. Most people were in fancy dress and the band played during the evening.

---

201 Probably Sir Arthur Conan Doyle's own adaptation of his story 'The Adventure of the Speckled Band'; a thrilling Sherlock Holmes mystery.
202 Possibly 2694 Trooper George Ormston of the 1st Life Guards. ICRC op. cit. and The National Archives UK, British Army WWI Service Records, 1914-1920.

Chapter 7 Switzerland

During all this winter besides the cinema twice a week and the debates on Saturdays, there was something on practically every Tuesday in the YMCA, either a whist drive or a lantern lecture or a concert or a play. To show how busy I was at this time I find in my diary for March 21st the following, 'This is the first evening I have had off for over 10 days.'

We had had all the rehearsals for 'The Speckled Band' in an empty room in the Jungfrau and only had the last two on stage. The first of these was on February 16th and I shall not forget that night. I had made a dressing room down the hall in front of the cinema box as I did for all concerts and things of that kind, and the small room on the other side of the stage was reserved for scenery and properties. But there were so many of the latter that there was no room for them and they got into the utmost confusion.

Besides that, everything went wrong. A lot of things got lost, the fireplace fell and broke its lamp and a borrowed bag fell into a pail of glue. The whole thing dragged, we began at 9.30 p.m. and at 12 had still one act to do. Warburton was in despair. Next day, Sunday, we had a rehearsal in the Jungfrau and it went much better. On Monday morning, we went through the last act on the stage and at night had the dress rehearsal. I had built a property room down the other side of the hall and this time all went well. The show itself on Tuesday 19th was a huge success. It was of course due to Warburton as we could not have put on a melodrama like that without him.

Hobday was very keen that we should do it again at Interlaken and we did on March 2nd. Wright and Ormston had gone down some days before to get the scenery etc. ready. It was a great success there too. That night there was a terrific fall of snow and the lights went out in the middle.

Keeping The Old Flag Flying

Luckily it was between two scenes and they came on again in a few minutes. We got two suppers that night, the YMCA gave us one before and Captain Glass of Interlaken stood one after.[203] We were to have returned next day but the snow had isolated Mürren and we did not get back till the 5th.

Meanwhile on February 28th, there had been another Repatriation Commission and Warburton had passed for home. He was an awful loss, if he had stayed we might have risen to ever higher dramatic flights. Williams and Tyler also passed. They left on March 21st. There was nothing like the excitement over this repatriation that there had been over the last. On April 30th, we put on 'The Man of Destiny' and also the 'Dear Departed' over again, they went very well.

On May 6th, Major General Hanbury Williams who had taken over Peko [Picot]'s job came to inspect Mürren. He shook hands and talked to every man in the garrison and was obviously a huge improvement on his predecessor. He had organised the internment camps in Holland.[204] That same day two Irishmen went to Lauterbrunnen, one returned but the other, Private Chapman, was missing for some days. It appeared that the one who returned had done so by train, but Chapman had decided to walk. They had search parties out for him and on May 10th he was found dead having fallen down a gully. Apparently, he had got benighted and lost his way. He was buried at Lauterbrunnen on the 13th. This was the first death actually at Mürren though one or two had died in hospital who came from there.[205]

---

203 Captain Harold Glass of the 4th Middlesex. He was wounded and captured at the start of the war in 1914 at Mons. ICRC op. cit.

204 During World War 1, Major General Sir John Hanbury-Williams GCVO, KCB, CMG had been Head of the British Military Mission to the Russian Army in the Field and was in charge of the British Prisoners of War Department at The Hague from August 1917 to March 1918, and at Berne from April 1918 to December 1918.

205 10170 Private Nicholas Chapman from Dromara in Ireland served with the

Chapter 7 Switzerland

On June 3rd was the King's Birthday Parade, they did not have one on Empire Day. Those repatriated on appeal left on June 11th and on the 13th the surveying class started again. This time they had got an English and not a Swiss instrument, but the class only consisted of two.

The Canadian celebrations for Dominion Day took the form this year of a night's stay at Grindelwald. We could get there by electric [train] and were thus freed from the restrictions that shortage of coal imposed on steam railway traffic. The Australians and New Zealanders came with us. We left Mürren at noon on July 1st and had a big dinner that night and returned to Mürren by the 6 p.m. train the next day.'

In June that year, Kenneth's brother Hugh had deployed to Salonika in Greece where a multi-national coalition, formed by British, French, Italian and Russian forces, was fighting alongside the Serbian Army against the Bulgarian Army on the northern Greek border. He joined the 15th Auxiliary Horse Transport Company (798th Company ASC) that used horses and hundreds of mules to ferry stores along the main routes from Salonika towards the front. This was a vital but unglamorous task and the routes were badly affected by the weather as the year drew to an end. Hugh remained there into 1919, returned to England that July, was swiftly demobilised and returned to New Zealand.

Unbeknownst to the internees, in March 1918 the German Army on the Western Front, reinforced by masses of troops released from duty on the Eastern Front due to Russia's capitulation, had launched a major offensive, aiming to win the war before the arrival of millions of American reinforcements later in the year. This onslaught threatened the viability of the British defences on the Somme, but due to some heroic defensive

---

2nd Royal Irish Rifles. He is interred in Vevey (St. Martin's) Cemetery. CWGC op. cit.

actions and the logistic shortcomings of the Germans, it had failed and the Allies were now on the offensive. The Americans had arrived and, in 100 days of activity, now operating as a modern army with close coordination between infantry, tanks, artillery, engineers, logistics, communications and air forces, the allies breeched the massive German Hindenburg Line and drove east. The war would be over by the end of the year, but at Mürren, as throughout the continent, a deadly infection was about to strike as Kenneth now explains:

> 'In July, the Spanish influenza, or *grippe* as we called it, which was raging all over the world in a regular plague, reached Switzerland.[206] The Federal Council promptly forbade all cinema concerts and in most places church services. So, our cinema had to stop with the rest, our last show being on July 24th. This restriction may have had its uses in other places, but at Mürren it was quite absurd as the men mixed just the same. As a matter of fact, the only case in Mürren at this time was Captain Llopart, who contracted it from a patient in Gimmelwald.
>
> On July 28th, McCready's successor Mr. Todd made his first appearance.[207] He was a very different man, more after the style of Canon Woodward. Later on, he made Mürren his headquarters and we got to know him well and he was universally popular. He was a great 'Scrounger'. It is rather hard to describe what scrounging is, as it is not stealing, though very like it I suppose. Commandeering is more the word. Todd had no conscience when scrounging was concerned as he talked about it quite a lot and told many tales of his feats at the front in that direction, he got known as The Scrounger. He had a dry sarcastic way of talking

---

206 The successive waves of this virulent pandemic illness killed millions of people across the globe.
207 Whilst there are likely contenders, 'Mr. Todd' has not been positively identified. Presumably, he was the new Chaplain.

when he wanted to choke anyone off, and at one debate he successfully downed Lunn to the great joy of everyone. He was what one might call a medium churchman and his sermons were good. He always published the subject beforehand. He was not at all afraid of work and used to go once a month to Grindelwald to give the English ladies there a service, a thing none of his predecessors had ever done.

The YMCA hut although it had only been built 12 months was at this time showing distinct signs of wear. It was disgracefully built, and the snow of the preceding winter had strained the structure and cracked the half-round supports. On July 30th, it was repaired with iron tie rods running from eave to eave. These got terribly in the way of the cinema and when we started again we had to shift the sheet in front of one tie rod, even then the shadow of the next came across the top of the picture.

On August 2nd, Mr. Hobday went to Berne. He was in charge of all the YMCAs in Switzerland and in future he made Berne his headquarters leaving his wife to run the hut at Mürren. From this date troubles began. Mr Hobday, though rather effusive in his manner, was a good sort and got on well with everyone. Mrs. Hobday meant very well but she had a dictatorial manner that used to set people's backs up. She also had a terrible laugh just like a horse neighing and the general result was that she was most unpopular. Just before the end I heard that she had spent a lot of her own private money on the YMCA at Mürren.

Whether it was her temper or simply misunderstanding all round she seemed to be the 'Stormy Petrel' of Mürren Society and was generally at war with someone. In the summer of 1917, she had fought every lady in the place. Then she had gone home for some months and on her return, was much more peaceable though there was a skirmish now and then. Early in 1918, she had started fighting again and she and I had many a scrap. While he was there the 'Old Chum', as we called Mr. Hobday, that being his favourite form of address to other people, generally poured oil on troubled waters, but after he had gone Mrs. H. was left to fight alone.

When Mr. Hobday left, a war was in progress but this time it was one which the majority of those interested sided with her. When Mr. Warburton left, a Captain Ackerley took on the job of running plays etc.[208] He was quite young, only about 20, and rather a fool. He put on a Bernard Shaw sketch on April 30th and after that had done nothing. The only plays he would consider were those that were either blasphemous or immoral and apart from anything else, one could not expect the YMCA to stomach that sort of thing.

The plan had been to have a play once a month or so during the summer, but it had all fallen through. Early in July, Mrs. Jebb-Scott started to get up a couple of sketches but on the 29th, Captain Ackerley told her he was the only person allowed to get up plays and so she had dropped them. With winter coming on the situation was intolerable. We could not see why we should be forbidden by this young ass to have any plays except his undesirable ones. Finally, Mrs. Jebb-Scott and I talked it over and she suggested a small sub-committee of the entertainment committee should choose the plays and the casts and arrange the rehearsals. I saw Mrs. Hobday about this on August 7th and she quite agreed with us.

---

208 Captain Joe Ackerley served in the 8th East Surreys, was wounded twice and taken prisoner at the Battle of Cherisy in 1917. 'A playwright, novelist and editor, Capt Ackerley was well known in literary circles'. Obituary notice for Captain J. R. Ackerley, Queen's Royal Surrey Regimental Association Newsletter, No. 2, November 1967, Page 5 (Surrey History Centre Reference: J552/2). Ackerley wrote the play *'Prisoners of War'* (1925) a 'sombre drama' based on his experiences at Mürren.

Chapter 7 Switzerland

On August 12th, Mr. Hobday was at Mürren and we had a meeting of the committee on the subject. Captain Ackerley who had got wind of the scheme had not intended to come but Mr. Hobday called for him and brought him along. The sub-committee was appointed consisting of Mrs. Hobday, Mrs. Jebb-Scott, Captain Ackerley and myself. Captain Ackerley announced to several people his intention of blocking everything we did and in this he was aided and abetted by Mrs. Lunn who was anxious to get on the sub-committee herself, and we were in for a big fight when Major Nutt, who had just taken over SBO, solved the problem by removing Captain Ackerley from his position of military member of the YMCA and appointing Sergeant Larkins of my battalion in his place.[209] After this there was peace for a while.

On August 4th, General Williams came up to present the 1914 ribbons. It was a wet day as it generally was when he came so the presentation took place in the YMCA. There was a church parade first. Unfortunately, it was the turn for the Presbyterian Chaplain and we had to endure his endless prayers. After the service, we all went to the hut and there the ribbons and chevrons were presented.

During the summer, Southall and I had gone on many long walks. We used to go out for the day on Sundays and had been pretty well everywhere one could go within a day's walk of Mürren. I had always had an ambition to pick some Edelweiss myself but had not so far found any, but on August 18th, we found a lot close to Sefinen Fugga and I managed to get some on quite an accessible spot.'

The Sefinenfurgge is a mountain pass which crosses the col between the peaks of Hundshore and Bütlasse through stunning

---

[209] Probably 16272 Sergeant Lawrence Larkins of the 7th Canadians, who originally came from Bromley in Kent. Pay and Record Office op. cit.

scenery, some five miles west of Mürren, at an elevation of 2,612 metres. That Edelweiss he picked endures to this day; six stems from one plant, neatly pressed in a book. Kenneth continues:

'On September 1st, some 200 men came to Mürren from Germany. These were quarantined for four days on arrival because of the *grippe*. On August 30th, everyone moved into the Edelweiss and Alpina and the new men were put into the other hotels. Supplies of tobacco, cigarettes and biscuits were taken to these hotels for them and during the time they were quarantined they had tea taken to them every day. This lot of new men were quite a different class from those who came to us the winter before, some had only been called up the preceding April and they never mixed well with the old hands. The result of putting them in separate hotels was also bad in this respect and for a long time there was quite a lot of bad feeling between the two sets. When they came out of quarantine they seemed largely to live in the YMCA, where on one afternoon they consumed 650 cups of tea.

On that same evening, there was a welcoming concert and tableaux run by the Ramblers. The interdict on entertainments was by way of being lifted then and on September 11th, the cinema started again. On September 7th, the sports were held.

All this summer, Wright and I had been drifting further and further apart. He had fallen in love with the daughter of the proprietress of the Edelweiss and spent all his spare time with her. At first, he used to come out with Southall and me, then he began excusing himself and finally we never asked him to come. Several people noticed the change in him. At the end of April, he announced that he was going to leave the YMCA at the end of the month, but in May he was still there, and no one knew the reason he had changed his mind. After that he seemed to belong body and soul to

Chapter 7 Switzerland

Mrs. Hobday and used to tell her everything. He and I had a row on September 18th because he refused in a very nasty manner to let me have the key of the hut in the morning when I was in a hurry to get to work and he was late.

On September 20th, Mrs. Hobday made a great fuss because a rehearsal was fixed for half an hour earlier than she thought it ought to be. We had got another professional actor, a Mr. Le Grand, and he was getting up two sketches.[210] She attacked him and we, who did not then know Le Grand, were afraid he would chuck the whole thing. So, I saw Major Nutt who was in the other sketch and asked him to intervene. Wright overheard me and told Mrs. H. When I heard he had done this I was furious, and we had a great row and were never good friends after that. My subsequent interview with Mrs. H was far more amicable than I expected, I found her side of the argument was a strong one, it was as usual simply a misunderstanding. But after this, I had no use for Wright.

These sketches came off on October 1st. Le Grand took a part in one of them and spoilt it by not knowing his part. His general swagger and bad manners set the whole lot against him and his boasting won him the nickname 'Hamlet'.

On October 5th, we played the sketches again at Interlaken. There were some sports on next day and anyone who liked could go down for the occasion. About 100 went including the actors and those going in for the sports. Le Grand made himself extra unpleasant. The Hobdays provided a supper both before and after the play. Le Grand, who sat next to his

---

210 Probably Lieutenant Henry Le Grand of the Intelligence Corps, who was taken prisoner in 1915. The National Archives UK, British Army WWI Service Records, 1914-1920. A Mr. Henry Le Grand is listed as performing in Shakespeare's '*Henry IV Part II*' at the Court Theatre in London in 1921. The Stage, 24th February 1921, Page 16.

hostess, distinguished himself by grumbling about the food and left early 'to get his hair cut'. Next day a party of us hired bicycles and went to Briente [possibly Brienze on Lac Brienzersee]. We left for Mürren that evening.

On October 2nd, I caught my finger in the cinema machine and nearly took the top off. On the 8th, I was playing tennis in the morning, later it came on to snow and I could if I cared have skied in the afternoon. Both Wright and Southall gave me teas on their birthdays and had invited me. So, on the 13th, I gave a tea party and asked them and a few others. We discussed the subject of a club for the winter. The Belmont was now full of troops, but we found another place and would have started the club again but for the Armistice.

Orders had come out from home that everyone must work. This at Mürren included classes and a regular educational scheme was started on October 14th. Every available room was used and classes were held in the YMCA every morning from 9.45 to 12. More snow fell on 16th. Both this fall and that on the 8th looked like the permanent winter's snow, but both times it went away again and the final snow did not come until November 25th.

The war news at this time was most exciting. Mr. Jebb-Scott used to come daily and read out the news in the hut in the afternoon. On the 19th the debating society which had started again and was going strong had a symposium or series of essays on the terms of peace. Some of them were meant to be extreme and bizarre, but the strongest hardly came up to what the Armistice terms actually were less than a month later. On the 22nd, 20 more men came from Germany.

We fixed up an ambitious programme of entertainments up to and including Xmas. One of the first items was a

Chapter 7 Switzerland

concert to be got up by the ladies. The two ladies responsible were Mrs. Jebb-Scott and Mrs. Woods. The concert was well in hand, but they wanted a small sketch to fill it out. They got one and Mrs. Jebb-Scott and one of the men were to take part in it. They wanted to have a rehearsal on the stage before the dress rehearsal and October 20th they sent a note to Wright, who was running the YM in Mrs. Hobday's absence, asking if they could have one for 20 minutes between 12.30 and 1.00, when the hut was always shut. The reply they got was a curt refusal. When the matter was referred to Mrs. H. by phone she backed him up. The ladies were so furious that the concert was cancelled. Mrs. Hobday came back that day and had a free cinema show instead.

On the next day 23rd, she called a meeting of the entertainment committee to consider the matter. She and Wright spent a lot of time and trouble to bring round to her side the Padre, who had been away at the time and was the only member of the committee who had no opinion on the matter. When the committee met she crammed the Padre into the chair without consulting the rest. It was a most foolish thing to do as in that position he was absolutely impartial, and she lost the only friend she might have had. After a stormy meeting, we passed a vote of censure on Mrs. Hobday and the YMCA. She could give no reason for her refusal save that it was a rule and apparently no exception could be made ever.

The matter would not have rested there but the *grippe* came again, and all entertainments were stopped. This happened next day. The *grippe* which had been got down in the summer was now raging again down below and on the 24th, there was a supposed case in Mürren and everything was stopped again. This time it was one of the men. I don't think he had it as he got better later, but others soon did.

On the night of the 25th, the Edelweiss Hotel caught fire. Everyone in the hotel had just had baths. The bathwater was heated by a boiler in the bathroom and the fire in the boiler had been going full blast all day. In the evening, some men noticed smoke about the place but being unable to find anything they thought it was the chimney. About midnight someone heard crackling and, on going to investigate, found the passage full of smoke. He gave the alarm at once. The double wooden wall of the bathroom was blazing inside and in a few moments, the whole hotel would have gone. As it was it soon got out.

I think it was a chill caught from turning out of doors in the middle of the night with very little on that upset Lovis and made him susceptible to the *grippe*.[211] Also, he worked in the Swiss Sergeant's office and the Sergeant went to Berne and came back with the *grippe*. Lovis was taken ill on the 27th but did not report sick till 28th, when he was removed to the Eiger Chalet which was being used as a hospital. Lovis was in my room and I and the other man in the room were quarantined and sent to the chalet.

There were two chalets belonging to the Eiger and they should have put the patients in one and those under observation in the other, but they put everyone in the same. The result was that I got it on 30th and a few days later the other man got it and the orderly who was nursing us got it as well. There were altogether about six cases at this time. No one was at all bad, one man was delirious for one night and that was all. At the same time, it was raging at Interlaken and some six of our men died there. They said there was a lot of bad management there and Captain Llopart went to investigate.[212]

---

211 Probably 4365 Private Frank Lovis of the 16th Londons, who was an internee. ICRC op. cit.
212 Kenneth describes his ailment in his characteristically measured way.

Chapter 7 Switzerland

Meanwhile the YMCA at Mürren was only open at certain hours and the men were supposed to go there in groups according to hotels. On the 7th, I was allowed up and, on that day, Lovis and I and three others moved to the other chalet, where the others joined us where they got better.'

The fighting on the Western Front came to an end on 11th November 1918. Germany was forced to give in by the determined advance made by the Allies, by a lack of resources, and mutiny and conflict at home. The formal agreement, the Armistice, was signed at 5.00 a.m. in a railway carriage at Compiègne. The terms imposed on Germany were severe and required the Germans to evacuate German-occupied territories on the Western Front within two weeks and to retire behind the Rhine. All German-occupied territories elsewhere were to be abandoned, the Germans were to surrender huge amounts of military weapons and equipment, and most of the German fleet was interned. At the Treaty of Versailles in 1919, Germany was made to accept responsibility for the war and to pay reparations to certain countries that had formed the Allied Powers.

At home, in Great Britain and in the Empire, there was national rejoicing. On the front line, there was largely no celebration amongst the exhausted troops, only silence, a numbing bewilderment and nervous exhaustion. For Kenneth and his internee friends, as the fact that they might now be able to go home was dawning on them, some celebrated. But they were still confronting the dreaded influenza which was now to take a disastrous toll. Kenneth describes the scenes:

'We were still quarantined when the Armistice was signed and so missed what celebrations there were. These consisted chiefly of an alcoholic kind. There was some

---

Whether he contracted the milder, initial form of the pandemic or the deadlier second wave is unknown, but it is assumed that having recovered, he was now immune.

ringing of bells and singing but drinking was the main thing and a good many Ramblers fell from grace that night.

I came out of quarantine on the 13th. I found they were rehearsing for 'The Private Secretary' and had reserved a small part for me. But with the *grippe* restrictions and the Armistice I did not think it was likely ever to come off and I gave up my part. I did not think it wise to be out late at night rehearsing. The play was given up on the 21st.

On the 19th, the Padre, another man and I took the church harmonium back to Grindelwald. There was a small one at Mürren but when we came they lent us a better one from Grindelwald. We had a very nice trip and the harmonium gave us much less trouble than we expected.

The *grippe* had quite died down in Mürren, but about this time the station master's wife went to Berne and brought it back. She and her husband went to play cards with the Eiger people and next day both of them, their baby and seven civilians in the Eiger were down with *grippe*. On the evening of the 20th, we were back to the Edelweiss as our chalet was wanted for some of our men who had got it too, and the Eiger was quarantined. This time we got it properly. Civilians and our men fell sick in scores and later began the deaths. On the 23rd, the chalet being full the men in the Eiger were sent to Interlaken and the Eiger was turned into a hospital.

Just before this on the 21st, the General [presumably Hanbury Williams] came to say goodbye. We paraded on the football ground and after distributing some 1914 ribbons that had not been given out before, he shook hands with each man. On the 24th, church services were prohibited. That afternoon Wright had tea with Southall and me for the

Chapter 7 Switzerland

last time as it turned out. Next day they both went to the Eiger with the *grippe*.

On the 25th, the remaining men in the Edelweiss and Alpina from which hotels most of the *grippe* cases were coming were sent to bed. Those of us who had had it were allowed out and had to feed and see to the others. On the same day, I took over Wright's place in charge of the YM. All the staff but one had the *grippe* and there remained Miss Bluitt. Miss Bluitt had been governess to Major Barlow's children, when they went home she came to look after the Hobday's children and help in the hut.

That day the hut was closed to all. We used to sell tobacco, cigarettes etc. through the window and men from each hotel came twice a day to fetch tea etc. to sell in their hotels. The next day [the] 26th, Captain Llopart insisted on Miss Bluitt taking the Hobday children to Interlaken as they were living in the Regina and most of the officers there had got it. She locked up the hut and left, and next day she and two of the children were down with it. Next day, [the] 27th, Mrs. Hobday arrived. She had not got the keys, they came up later, but we broke in and Ingham, the one remaining on the staff, and I carried on till he left on December 4th.[213]

On the 28th, the first man died, his name was Fletcher.[214] They did not keep the pneumonia cases separate and another man who had been in his room died later. They had a most incompetent doctor there then, by name Mamie, who was 'too delicate to be called up in the night'. Later another very

---

213 The only Ingham identified as at Mürren was Company Sergeant Major (Drill Sergeant) David Ingam of the 1st Scots Guards. ICRC op. cit.
214 241862 Lance Corporal John Fletcher from Apperley Bridge, Bradford, who served with the 2nd/6th West Yorkshires. He is interred in Vevey (St. Martin's) Cemetery. CWGC op. cit.

good doctor came and brought a nurse, but he was too late to save many of them.

Then began the most ghastly time, a tragical end of our two years stay. Until this year we had not had a death at Mürren, and I think only one man had died at a hospital who came from Mürren. In the ensuing week, we lost eight; seven at Mürren and one at Interlaken. Civilians were dying too and Captain Llopart was worked to death. He behaved like a hero and got hardly any sleep at all. He chiefly looked after the civilians. He would come to the Eiger, where there were a lot of civilians as well, at 4 a.m. and yet he was up and out again before 8. At last he had a small breakdown in his digestion, but after 24 hours in bed he was up and about again. I think that 24 hours saved him from a regular breakdown.

Several men volunteered to nurse at the Eiger and on the 29th, Major Nutt asked me if I would stop on and run the YM as it was obvious the sick men could not go home with the others. This I agreed to do, and Baillie volunteered to stay and help me.

It was a terrible time. One heard of three or four names of men who were dangerously ill and would ask after them and then say, 'All the rest are alright aren't they?' 'No, so and so, and so and so is very bad', names one had never heard before in that connection, but this happened daily. One is not supposed to take dead bodies down by rail, but as the snow had now come we used to smuggle them down on the 5 a.m. train. They insisted on some of our men going with them and this became an almost daily fatigue.

On December 1st, Shearer died.[215] At this date, there were

---

215 1271 Private James Shearer from Cullen, Banffshire, Scotland, who served with the 1st Gordon Highlanders. He was aged 23 and is interred in Vevey (St.

Chapter 7 Switzerland

only three left in the Regina – Major Nutt, Mr. Woods and a Mr. Green [not identified], an officer who had had it before. On the 2nd, 10 men who had recovered went to the Alpina, among them was Southall. These were now called upon to sit up at nights in the Eiger with the men who were badly ill. Next day, [the] 3rd, Watford and Harding died. Harding had been in Fletcher's room when he died and got worse from that date. On the same day, Hetherington died at Interlaken, he was one of the men who had gone there from the Eiger on November 23rd.[216]

On the 4th, all the men except those who had been ill went home. Those who were nursing them stayed behind and a few others like Baillie and myself. They went in four trains. I had seen so many go that I did not mind it at all, but Major Nutt who was staying with Mr. Woods felt it very much. He had hoped to go home with 400 healthy men. Wright had been very ill indeed. He was in Shearer's room and when in his delirium had got up and started smashing things, Wright got out of bed and rang for the orderlies. They declared after that the chill had then killed him. On the 3rd, we heard he was dying and was in fact dead from the waist downwards. On the 4th, he had made an extraordinary recovery and his limbs were warming up again, but he died. He looked awful and I should not have known him, he was then unconscious.

Baillie and I were the only ones available now to take him down and we did so next morning at 5 a.m. A son of the Eiger, a great strong healthy man who had died the same day was taken down at the same time. The last time I had

---

Martin's) Cemetery. CWGC op. cit.
216 8596 Private James Watford from West Norwood served with the 9th East Surreys. 8844 Private John Harding from Leicester served with 2nd Sherwood Foresters. He was aged 34 and married. 11714 Private Alfred Heatherington served with the 2nd King's Own Scottish Borderers. They are all interred in Vevey (St. Martin's) Cemetery. CWGC op. cit.

Keeping The Old Flag Flying

caught that train was when I went to Grindelwald for the day with Wright about a year before. We had to hang around Lauterbrunnen for some time and then got up for an hour or so to have a clean-up and then went down again for the funeral. Southall, Major Nutt and Mr. Woods came too and the Hobdays met us at Lauterbrunnen. The Padre took the service. A Swiss firing party came from Thun. We buried Watford and Harding at the same time. The Hobdays had brought a Union Jack which we put on Wright's coffin.[217]

Next day [the] 6th, Baillie and I opened the hut to the men who were left. They got free two cups of tea daily from the YMCA, a third of a ¾ lb packet of biscuits from a fund Mr. Woods had and, in the evening and morning, Bengers[218] or Cocoa from the Red Cross. The hut was opened from 11 to 12 and from 1 to 4. They used to come in chiefly in the afternoon, have their tea and biscuits and play billiards, and were generally all gone at 3.30.

Kay died on 6th and Southall and I took him down next day.[219] We overslept and at 5, they sent for us. We kept the train waiting 15 minutes. Luckily there were no other passengers. Watson died on the 8th,[220] and until we left, that was the last.

On the 10th, Mrs. Hobday arrived and we started packing up and selling. An inventory had to be made of all the things belonging to the Jungfrau Hotel and everything else was

---

217 Rawleigh Wright was aged 23. He is interred in Vevey (St. Martin's) Cemetery. CWGC op. cit.
218 A 'food drink' somewhere between baby milk and invalid food.
219 S/3472 Rifleman Daniel Thomas Kay, aged 21, served with the 12th Rifle Brigade. His mother lived in Poplar, London. He is interred in Vevey (St. Martin's) Cemetery. CWGC op. cit.
220 26/1107 John Watson was aged 25. He served with the 4th Battalion the New Zealand Rifle Brigade. He is interred in Vevey (St. Martin's) Cemetery. CWGC op. cit.

Chapter 7 Switzerland

sold that could be. The hut on the ensuing days resembled an auction mart. All sorts of people, hoteliers, shop people and peasants came and bought all sorts of things. Baillie did most of the selling. I kept out of it, I am no good at that job and hate bargaining. They started sending the convalescents to Friburg [Fribourg], about 20 miles south west of Berne] and four men left that day. Captain Llopart got the order rescinded and no more went. They were much better at Mürren.

One of the men who had volunteered to stay was Callander. He worked in the Regina kitchen. Later, he got *grippe* and was rather bad. On the 14th, he was normal for the first time and like a fool got up. The consequence was that he had a bad relapse and was not expected to live when we all went home on the 20th.[221]

On the 12th, all the chairs in the hut had been packed up and sent off to the people they were hired from and after that we had to sit on tables, boxes or borrowed forms. On the 18th, the YMCA gave a final farewell feed and cinema. The sick men were nearly all well by this time. My assistant was one of them and we managed the last cinema show quite well. Next day, we packed up what was left and locked up the hut and left it for good. The Hobdays had come up again and they went back to Interlaken that afternoon.

Towards the end I had been getting rather sick of it and I was not sorry to go. We left at 8 a.m. on the 20th in two trains. I was in the second and thus was on the first funicular of interned to come to Mürren, and on the last to leave.'

---

221 It seems that this was S/7280 Private Alexander Callander who served with the 9th Battalion Black Watch (Royal Highlanders). He died on 21st December 1918 aged 33 and is interred in Vevey (St. Martin's) Cemetery. His father lived in Forfar, Scotland. CWGC op. cit.

Chapter 8
Home

Kenneth and his fellow internees had endured years of captivity in Germany and enforced leisure in Switzerland. Whilst it was infinitely better to be living in relative freedom than suffering a prisoner of war camp regime, the confined environment at Mürren would have been frustrating and claustrophobic, and life must have appeared to some extent aimless and hollow. The onset of influenza must have seemed a very mournful way to end all this, but now, as Christmas 1918 approached, they were on the way home, certainly joyful, but perhaps apprehensive as to what might await them on their return. Kenneth now describes the machinery that got them there:

> 'Our journey through Switzerland was uneventful. Two men had come with us who were stopping in the country, both consumptives.[222] One was on a stretcher and we left him at Interlaken. Some of our party were still in a weak state and went in a separate compartment, these included some of the officers who had been rather bad.
>
> At Interlaken, we got into a train composed of 2nd Class carriages in which we went to Pontarlier [across the French border]. We hung it with flags and some men chalked *Deutschland unter Allies* and *Kaiser Kaput* on the carriages

---

222 Suffering from tuberculosis (TB), a fairly common, incurable illness in those days, of which Kenneth's brother Harold had succumbed before the war.

Chapter 8 Home

to the great indignation of the Interlaken Station Master. We got to Berne at 2 p.m. There we had a feed and our luggage was searched. We left there at 4.30 and got to Pontarlier at 8 p.m. Captain Llopart came as far as Berne and we gave him a great send off when he left. A Red Cross hospital train should have met us at Pontarlier but did not arrive until 2 a.m. So, the majority of us were put in a sort of concert hall for the night. The floor was strewn with mattresses and blankets and we slept on them.

We boarded our hospital train at 11 a.m. next day [December] 21st and it was a great change. The comfortable berths, endless feeding, and beautiful white bread were a huge joy, especially the latter which we ate dry like cake.

We passed Dijon at 6 p.m. and at 9.30 p.m. on the 22nd, we reached Le Havre and went on board the *Grantully Castle*.[223] All through it had been a toss-up whether we should be home by Xmas and I believe we caught the last boat home before Xmas day. The *Grantully Castle* was full, and we slept on mattresses on the floor below. She is a top-heavy old tub and rolled abominably, and hardly anyone ventured out till we got under the lea of the Isle of Wight. She was so slow and though we sailed at 11 a.m. we did not get to Southampton till 1.30 p.m. next day.

There we went on board another hospital train something like the other. We left Southampton at 3 p.m. and reached Waterloo at 5. It was lovely going through the English scenery once more and at express speed, and most of us stood the whole time looking through the window. At Waterloo, we were taken to the King George's Hospital close by in motors. It was a first-class hospital and the sisters were kindness itself. They received us with open arms. The

---

223 *HNT Grantully Castle* was a hospital ship. She had served as a troopship in 1915, landing troops at Gallipoli.

hospital was a clearing house for repatriated prisoners and all but the worst of their patients had gone and they did not want empty wards for Xmas. We however had other ideas as where we wanted to spend Xmas.

Next day Xmas eve at 12, a Board came round. Each man was asked if he wanted an operation and on saying, 'No' was given two months' furlough [leave]. But we Canadians were told we must go to a Canadian hospital first. With great difficulty, I got a pass till 10 a.m. on the 28th, I managed to catch the 11.55 at Euston and got to Staverton at about 7.'

As we have already discovered, Staverton was the home of Kenneth's sister Ada. No doubt a warm and happy reunion took place.

'As I could not get to London by 10 a.m., I left Staverton on the night of the 27th and got to the King George at 9 p.m. where they gave me a supper of chicken meat pie and tea. The other Canadians turned up in the morning and seven of us were sent off by the 2.20 p.m. train for Wokingham and went on by motor to Bear Wood Convalescent hospital.'

Bearwood in Wokingham, Berkshire is one of the great country Victorian houses of England, built in the 19th century by John Walter, the proprietor of the Times newspaper. It became a Canadian Convalescent Hospital during the war, but apparently the grandeur of the past had been replaced by something more functional, as Kenneth now relates:

'It was a great come down from the King George and our 'wards' were more like attics, they had parades twice a day and one had to line up for meals. Also, there were numbers of repatriated prisoners, like ourselves, who had been waiting there for weeks, what sisters they had spent their time finding fault with the way the beds were made. We found a place in Wokingham, where we could get tea

Chapter 8 Home

and sit about, and we went there nearly every afternoon. Wokingham was some two and a half miles off. They had frequent concerts from London and cinemas, and on New Year's Eve, a whist drive and supper.'

For the veterans, entering the New Year, it must have been frustrating to be 'processed' in England rather than whisked back to Canada. Kenneth explains the procedure:

'We went before a Board on the 31st and I passed Category A. Then we waited. On January 3rd 1919, I and two others were told we were on the list to go out on Tuesday. Next day the two others were taken off, but I remained. There were some 30 in the party to go. On the 5th, Cousin Philippa Watson, having heard I was there, got permission for me to go to their place and stop the night. It was a nice change and I enjoyed it very much.'

It seems that Phillipa was Kenneth's first cousin and lived in Finchamstead, Berkshire, only a few miles from Bearwood. Kenneth now had some welcome leave:

'At last on the 7th, after numerous parades and red tape, I got away and after spending the day in London, I got back to Staverton at 9 p.m. on two months' furlough. I spent this furlough in travelling about, visiting friends and relatives. I went to Staverton, Aspley Guise, Pinner, Dumfries, London, Hastings and Godmanchester. On February 17th, on passing through London, I went to see Wright's mother.'

As we found out in the last chapter, Rawleigh Wright had been Kenneth's good friend at Mürren, sadly dying of influenza shortly before the others left there. His mother Jean, a long-term widow, lived in Hazledon Road, Lewisham where presumably Kenneth met her.

Otherwise, Kenneth's itinerary took in his brothers and sisters. Aspley Guise was the family home, but the Foysters' house, Guise

House, had been sold and it is believed that Kenneth was visiting his sister Hilda who was living elsewhere in the village, having curtailed her VAD deployment to France in January 1919 in order to be at home as he passed through England. Kenneth's brother Arthur lived in Pinner with his wife and daughter, and Hastings was the old family home where some cousins still lived. It is assumed that Kenneth also visited his brother Hugh's wife Amy who was in England awaiting his return from service in Salonika. Godmanchester was the family home of the Tillards, Kenneth's mother's relations. Why he went to Dumfries is a mystery.

Leave at an end, Kenneth now was able to travel to Canada:

> 'On March 7th, my furlough being up, I reported at Seaford Camp.[224] On my arrival, I was asked if I would care to go back to Canada with the 7th Battalion. It appeared that the Colonel, Colonel Gilson, had expressed a wish to take any old members of the battalion who cared to come with it. I at once put my name down to go with them.'

Lieutenant Colonel William Forbes Gilson DSO* had led the 7th since October 1916.[225] He had won two DSOs; in October 1917 and November 1918, for gallant leadership of his battalion. Kenneth continues:

> 'I was then placed in E Company of the 1st Reserve Battalion, the BC Reserve, and given my hut etc. Owing to its being too late to draw a mattress, I had to sleep on the bare floor that night. I had done this for months on end in 1914, and had got quite used to it, but I had got soft since that time, and it took my hips days to get over that night. I got a straw mattress next day.
>
> Seaford was not a bad camp, and as returned pioneers[226]

---

224 To the east of Seaford in East Sussex, which was much used by the Canadians. The northern part was known as 'Chyngton Camp'

225 The appellation '*' means that he had won the award on two occasions.

226 Possibly 'prisoners', though the 1st Division might have been referred to as

Chapter 8 Home

we were not expected to do anything, so used to spend the days going for walks, and the evenings at cinemas etc. There were two cinemas in camp and one in the town, where there was also an inferior music hall. We were allowed down the town after 4 p.m. on ordinary days, and after 1 p.m. on Saturdays and Sundays.

The eating arrangements were bad. There were some eating huts and there were two sittings. E Company was on the second sitting, but we often got into the first. They used to march the first sitting by companies down to the mess huts. One company used to go there four abreast, and as they could only go on two at a time through the door there was always a scrum, and we used to get in in the subsequent confusion. Once I and four others got jammed in the doorway for quite half a minute.

The food was not bad but as one had to bring one's knife, fork, spoon and mess tin to eat with, and as mess tins are beastly dirty things, it was not very appetising, and we nearly always had supper down the town, so as to have one civilised meal. They provided troughs of hot water to wash the mess tins etc. in after. The baths were the best I have seen, with plenty of hot water, and there were plenty of washing sheds besides with cold water. The camp was a large one, composed of the usual wooden huts. I have no idea how many men were there.

At Seaford, I met lots of men I had known in the battalion. Some of them I had thought dead, among them Scott[227] of our platoon, who came back with the 7th with us, and White who used to muck in with me in Germany. The vast majority of these men I met had been prisoners.

'pioneers', being the first to deploy.
227 Possibly 16933 Private Leslie Scott who had also been captured at St. Julien. Pay and Record Office op. cit.

Keeping The Old Flag Flying

On March 14th, those who were going back with the 7th were transferred to the Demobilisation Company and put in a hut to ourselves. Our time was now fully occupied by parades. These consisted in passing doctors, dentists, filling in forms, drawing 'last pays', handing in equipment, and all sorts of formalities. They had a quick way with people who were absent from these parades, they simply transferred them back to the company they came from, which made them far more amenable next time they got into the Demob Company.

Everyone was keen to get away, as it was dull at Seaford and leave was unobtainable. A certain number of companies were full of the more recently joined men or 'Umpties', as we called them, who had to wait till all the old timers were gone. The Umpties were mostly conscripts, and had regimental numbers, ranging up to four million and more. The Canadian Corps were numbered right through with large gaps at intervals, and one's service could be told from one's number.

At last on March 31st, we left Seaford to join the 7th Battalion at Witley. There were some 20 of us, and we went via Lewis, Brighton and Havant. We bribed a tradesman to carry our kits to the station at Seaford in his cart, but at Witley we had to carry them ourselves, we were not sorry to get to the camp. Here again we had a hut to ourselves and managed to get mattresses the first night. It was a rather dilapidated hut, and the camp was not as good in many ways as Seaford. The eating arrangements were better. There was room for all, and they supplied cups and plates. The baths were not nearly so good. There was a long row of shops and canteens called 'Tin Town', which has since been burnt down, and which included a theatre which put on some rather good shows.'

Chapter 8 Home

Witley Military Camp was set up on Witley Common, Surrey. Nearly 20,000 Canadian soldiers occupied the camp in 1919, waiting to return home. But '... on the night of 14-15 June, a small group of dissidents started trouble by trying to free some soldiers arrested for persisting in playing Crown and Anchor [a dice game of chance] in defiance of previous regulations curbing widespread gambling in the camp. The disturbance spread to canteens and the civilian area. On the following night, the Garrison Theatre was burned and nearly all the civilian shops in the area were destroyed.'[228]

After four years of warfare, the 7th Canadian Battalion that Kenneth now re-joined was much changed from the one that he had left in 1915. The 1st Canadian Division was followed on the Western Front by a 2nd Division in September that year, a 3rd followed in December and a 4th Division in August 1916. These divisions formed a Canadian Corps and in June 1917, this formation was led by Lieutenant General Sir Arthur Currie, Kenneth's old brigade commander.

The Canadian Corps fought consistently and effectively throughout the war. It captured Vimy Ridge in April 1917, took part in the Allied defence against the German Spring Offensive in 1918 and in early August that year, led the offensive at the Battle of Amiens, before ending the war at the Belgian city of Mons. About 424,000 Canadians served overseas during the war. Of these, 59,544 died and some 172,000 were wounded[229]. The men of the 7th Battalion would have been comprehensively reinforced many times during the intervening three years, and it seems unlikely that Kenneth would meet any soldiers he had served with in 1915. But this proved erroneous as he now had some happy reunions:

> 'Here I also met a lot of old friends. One of these was our old F Company Colour Sergeant Keeley[230] who had left us

---

228 Nicholson, G.W.L. op. cit. Page 505.
229 Derived from The Canadian War Museum at: www.warmuseum.ca.
230 Possibly 16841 Colour Sergeant Harold Keighley, originally from London.

on the Plains to get a commission in the Imperials. He had returned to the 7th and was now Company Sergeant Major of No. 3 Company. He got Scott and me into his company. The rest were attached to No. 2. Among those who had survived the war and who were still on the strength were our two boy buglers of 1914; Parkinson[231] and McVie.[232] The latter came of an extraordinarily lucky family. He and one his brothers were in the 7th, another brother was in the 16th, another in the Navy and the father, whom I afterwards met in Victoria, had also been at the front, and all had survived. The eldest brother had been wounded five times.

Another survivor was our mascot, Nicolls. As a boy of fifteen he had boarded our train when we left Devonport in 1915, and finding that his father was in the Navy, and his mother dead, Major Rigby had adopted him and he had been with the battalion ever since. He came on to Victoria with us, which was his first visit to Canada. I did not know him again, as he had grown into a great stalwart youth of over six feet.

During our stay at Witley, I and Keith, a chap I had made friends with at Seaford, made many excursions to neighbouring towns. We visited Guildford, Godalming and Aldershot. We went to the last named on April 5th, and missed by half an hour a weekend pass, which I otherwise could have availed myself of.

The 7th Battalion has always moved by night. The first instance was, I believe, a punishment for the semi-mutiny in Devonport Harbour, but it seems to have become a tradition, and midnight is the 7th's marching hour. True to that, we left Witley at midnight on April 9th. We had supper first and

---

Pay and Record Office op. cit.

231 Possibly 16807 Bugler Leonard Parkinson from Victoria. Ibid.

232 Possibly 16924 Bugler James McVie from Victoria. Ibid.

Chapter 8 Home

then marched to the station and entrained. There were only some four hundred of us all told, so we got easily into one train. It took two trains to take us to Salisbury Plain. All the officers had passed through the ranks. Colonel Gilson had been a company sergeant major in 1914.[233] Before the war he was a policeman in Kamloops. The Senior Major was the Regimental Sergeant Major of 1914.'[234]

At last the Canadians were on the way home. Kenneth's matter of fact description of the process must cloak the sheer relief and jubilation of those Canadian soldiers who had endured, in their separate ways, the horrors and privations of war:

'We arrived at Liverpool at midday and went on board the *S.S. Carmania*.[235] I did not think our accommodation on the *Virginia* very grand, but this was worse. The ship was fitted up to carry the largest possible numbers, and the lowest deck was made into a large hold with wooden berths packed tight into it and here we were placed. Even those cabins that were left had extra berths put in between others, so that one had to enter them end on and crawl into place. Besides the 7th, there were on board the 5th, 10th, 13th and 14th, and the crush was great. We only had the third-class deck, and when the weather was bad it was better to stay below than go up on the crowded decks.

We sailed on the afternoon of the 10th and did not have a bad voyage on the whole. Every day at 7.30 there was a parade, the [ship's] Captain, a horrid bumptious little man,

---

233 As 16957 Colour Sergeant William Gilson of G Company, 7th Canadians. Ibid.
234 Possibly 16201 Sergeant Major David Philpot. Ibid.
235 *R.M.S. Carmania* was an interesting ship. A Cunard liner, she was requisitioned by the Royal Navy in 1914 as an armed merchant cruiser and in September 1914 fought a duel with the German AMC *Cap Trafalgar* in the South Atlantic. Incongruously, the two ships had disguised themselves to look like the other. *Carmania* sank the German ship. She later took part in the Gallipoli campaign, then was used to transport Canadians home after the war.

inspected the ship, preceded by a bugler, and followed by a dozen or more officers. We were not allowed down till this ceremony was over. The men used to make fun of this by marching round the steerage in single file, headed by a man blowing a tin whistle or mouth organ.

Smoking was forbidden below and the Captain was death on it, but no one has ever been able to prevent soldiers smoking when and where they want to, and he was just as unable to stop it as the Germans were. They used to put sentries on the water tight doors, though how anyone could open them without tools was a mystery. We were not sorry when on April 17th, we finally reached Halifax.

Having the furthest to go, the 7th were to have landed first, but the 13th and 14th were due for a reception at Montreal, where they belonged, so they went before us. As it was we got there first. After waiting a long time, we at last got on shore, when we were given refreshments and then went on board the train.

Most of the troops were being sent by the Canadian Government Railways, and the Canadian Pacific Railway (CPR) only got those left over and above what the others could manage. We fell to the lot of the CPR, and to advertise the fact they treated us uncommonly well and rushed us across in almost record time.

There was one civilian orderly to each car, who cleaned the car, washed the dishes, etc., and all we were asked to do was to provide five men per car to bring the food from the kitchen. They fed us well too, far better than we were fed on the boat. We were three to a division, so that two slept below and one in the upper berth. I was with Scott and a man called Phillips [not identified], and we took it in turns to have the upper berth. We left Halifax late that night and

Chapter 8 Home

passed Montreal Junction on Easter Day, April 20th, well ahead of the 13th and 14th. We had gone via St. John and got on the CPR's own line there.

We reached Winnipeg on the morning of the 22nd. We were to have spent some time there, but orders came to move on. They gave us a good reception, with a band and refreshments in the station. The same took place at Brandon. At Calgary next day, we came in for the reception of the 10th, which belong there, and were following some 10 minutes behind us, and a very good reception it was.

We were late getting to Calgary, as we had been held up a lot. The Connaught Tunnel[236] in the mountains had fallen in, and blocked traffic. The eastbound traffic, much congested after the block, met us, and we had to continually side-track to let a train go by. The consequence of this was that we could only reach Vancouver late in the evening of the 24th. As the Vancouver people wanted us to arrive in the morning, we got our orders to hang up at North Bend for 12 hours. Great was the grumbling in consequence, especially as North Bend is only a very 'one-horse' place. They took the opportunity of getting the Battalion Colours dedicated, and all North Bend turned out to see the ceremony.'

The Daily Province newspaper reported the dedication which was conducted by Major (Father) Madden MC.[237] Under the title of 'Famous Unit of Famous Division Welcomed Home', the paper then describes the exploits of some of the 7th's returnees, including Sergeant W. L.

---

[236] A railway tunnel under the Selkirk Mountains in south eastern British Columbia, near the city of Revelstoke.
[237] Presumed to be Father Ambrose Madden who was Chaplain to the 2nd Canadian Brigade from 1915. He won both a MC and a DSO in 1917. Derived from: Crerar, Duff. *'Soldiers: The Service in the Field'*, in Padres in No Man's Land, Second Edition, 118, Montreal: MQUP, 2014.

Rayfield VC,[238] and noted that none of the returning officers had been commissioned when they left Canada for the war. It mentions that the soldiers had decorated the train coaches with 'great green bushes showing from scores of windows. On one coach, great green letters of moss bore the name of the unit. On the sides of other coaches some clever artist had drawn the coat of arms of British Columbia and other descriptions.'[239]

On almost every coach were chalked signs indicative of the pride of these men in their regiment. Some of these signs read:

'First in, last to leave'.
'Oh, well, here we are'.
'First line telephone girls'.
'The Fighting 7th'.
'From the Rhine across the Rockies to God's country'.
'Smile, damn you, smile'.[240]

Eventually the happy Canadians found themselves approaching home and Kenneth describes the consequent merriments:

'We arrived at Vancouver at 9 a.m. on the 25th. We left our kit on the platform and went up on the wharf where the crowd was. Here we got refreshments and met our friends. I did not expect to meet anyone I knew, but I found some, including Byng-Hall [Major Percy Byng-Hall DSO, Kenneth's Company Commander in 1915], also several men shook hands with me because my blue shoulder straps announced my being of the First Contingent.

---

238 2204279 Walter Rayfield, then a private, won the VC for 'For most conspicuous bravery, devotion to duty, and initiative during the operations east of Arras from 2nd to 4th September, 1918'. He made two valiant assaults on enemy positions and carried a wounded colleague to safety under fire. Recorded in The Gazette (London Gazette), Issue 31067, Second Supplement, 14th December 1918, Page 14779.
239 The Daily Province, currently a division of Postmedia Network Incorporated, Vancouver BC, 25th April 1919, Page 4.
240 Ibid.

Chapter 8 Home

After some half hour there, we fell in, and led by a rather feeble band marched through Vancouver. The place was a mass of flags, and crowded, but Canadian crowds can't cheer, and though they tried once or twice it was a feeble attempt. We marched for some distance, and then the Colours were paraded for the last time, and we got into motor cars and were taken to Hastings Park to be demobilised. It was an exciting ride, as each car raced the rest, and it looked like a horse race.'

Kenneth's restrained description of this noteworthy parade is not echoed in The Daily Colonist, which declared, 'Famous 7th Warmly Greeted', described the impressive march of the 400-strong 'army of heroes' and reported the mixed emotions of Colonel Gilson; pride in his battalion and sadness at its demise.[241]

'Arrived at the Park, after speeches by the Lieutenant-Governor[242] and others, we got our kits which had arrived before us, and then passed through the Discharge Depot. I was lucky in finding my kit and got done one of the first. It was a well-arranged affair. One passed along from one desk to another, handing in equipment, signing papers, giving particulars, getting documents, and all the time one carried a paper which each desk initialled. At last this was taken, and all the initials being correct one passed through a door fully armed with Discharge Certificate, button and pay cheque, shook hands with Colonel Gilson, and was a civilian once more. I got a lift back to the town in a motor, and went to the Knights of Columbus Hut,[243] where they put you up for 24 hours free. I spent the afternoon at a show, and on return found Phillips, and spent the evening at a show with him.

The Victoria bunch had agreed to go to Victoria together

---

241 The Daily Colonist, Victoria BC, 26th April 1919, Page 3.
242 The Lieutenant Governor of British Columbia was The Honourable Sir Francis Stillman Barnard KCMG.
243 The Knights of Columbus is a large RC fraternal service organization.

Keeping The Old Flag Flying

by the 10.30 a.m. boat next day [the 26th]. We had a grand meal on board, also free, and with us went a lot of Victoria people who had come to meet us at Vancouver. Among them was Byng-Hall, and I had a long talk with him on board. We got to Victoria at 3 p.m. We did not have as good a reception as we had had a send-off, but there was a large crowd to greet us, and a band. We marched to the steps of the Parliament Buildings, where the Mayor[244] made a speech, then we marched back to the wharf and dismissed.[245]

I hunted up my boxes, and after some search found a suit of clothes not too badly moth eaten, most of them were. I changed, and by supper time was in civilians once more.

On May 2nd, there was a reunion of the 7th Battalion, which consisted of dancing, supper, etc., where I met and talked to many old friends, and once more had a long talk with Byng-Hall.

Thus end my adventures during the Great War. They were trying at times, but I would not have missed them for the world. I used to wish often in the old days that I had been born to more exciting times, but I think now that I have lived through one of, if not <u>the</u> most exciting times in the world's history.

I don't suppose I shall see another war. I hope not. After this we can do with a century of peace, but when the next war comes I hope our descendants will do as we did, and that they will be as successful as we of this generation have been in keeping the old flag flying.'

---

244 Robert J. Porter, who became Mayor in January 1919. The Daily Colonist, 21st January 1919, Page 7.

245 Kenneth's arrival home, along with others who had also returned, was noted in The Daily Colonist, 27th April 1919, Page 4.

Chapter 9
After the War

The Great War was over, and Kenneth and his five remaining siblings returned to their peacetime lives. The war had taken its toll on them and their family, as it had for most people in the British Empire, however Kenneth's brother Arthur found that he had been awarded an MBE for his munitions inspection and electrical construction activities during the war.

Kenneth arrived back in British Colombia to find that Canada had been transformed by its participation in the hostilities. 'Canada emerged from the First World War a proud, victorious nation with new-found standing in the world. It also emerged grieving and divided, forever changed by the war's unprecedented exertions and horrific costs.'[246] The national effort required to launch and sustain its contribution to the war, coupled with the considerable involvement of the government in people's lives nearly tore Canada apart. Promises to suppliers had been broken, increased voting rights were limited, and social and linguistic divisions remained. 'A massive and unprecedented voluntary effort had supported the troops overseas and loaned Ottawa the money it needed to fight the war. The resulting post-war debt of some $2 billion was owed mostly to other Canadians, a fact which fundamentally altered the nature of the post-war economy.'[247]

---

246 *'Legacy - The War's Impact on Canada'*, The Canadian War Museum at: www.warmuseum.ca.
247 Ibid.

'Despite the social and political challenges of the post-war, most Canadians also emerged from the struggle believing they had done important and difficult things together. Their primary fighting force at the front, the Canadian Corps, had achieved a first-class reputation as one of the most effective formations on the Western Front. Their generals and politicians had played an obvious role in victory, and the country itself enjoyed an international standing that few observers in 1914 could have predicted.'[248]

In this emerging, somewhat challenging new world Kenneth had to re-establish himself. It is quite clear that he remained utterly proud of the part he had played in the war and of his battalion. On 19th July 1919, he attended a Peace Celebrations Grand Parade that was held in Victoria, which included the 7th Battalion in the order of march, and on 24th September, he was invited to a ball at the Empress Hotel, Victoria in honour of the Prince of Wales, who was visiting the city.

On 6th October, Kenneth went to a British Campaigners Association Reception and Dinner held at The Drill Hall, Victoria to honour General Sir Arthur Currie GCMG KCG, the Association's Honorary President. In 1915, Currie had commanded the 2nd Brigade in which the 7th Battalion served, he later led the Canadian 1st Division and finally commanded the whole Canadian Corps. It was a most distinguished career: 'The most able of the Canadian commanders and one of the best in the British Army. Had it been politically feasible, Lloyd George[249] may very well have called on him when he was contemplating replacing Haig [as Commander-in-Chief BEF].'[250]

As we have already learned, Kenneth's cousin Ross and his wife Betty were living in Saanich, a suburb of Victoria, and Betty's sister, Edith Maud Sadleir, was also living in the city. Edith seems

---

248 Ibid.

249 The British Prime Minister from December 1916.

250 Cassar op. cit., Page 60.

Chapter 9 After the War

to have been universally, and inexplicably, nicknamed 'Totum'. She had been born in Balsall Heath, Birmingham in 1874, a shoe-manufacturer's daughter and one of seven children, had emigrated to Canada in 1911 and was working as a stenographer, possibly at the Victoria Parliament buildings.

It is clear that Kenneth took up courting Totum soon after his homecoming as on 1st October 1919, the couple married at Christ Church Cathedral, Victoria. The relative rapidity of these nuptials may indicate that the couple had met before the war when she was living with Ross and Betty, though Kenneth does not mention her in his wartime memoir. In 1919, Kenneth was aged 39 and Totum was 46. By 1920 the newly-weds had taken rooms in Government Street, Victoria.

Now Kenneth needed a job. He clearly had strong views about the employment rights of ex-servicemen, perhaps reflecting his own hunt for a viable occupation. A communication from Kenneth in The Daily Colonist in 1920 takes to task a 'newcomer' letter writer, who had not served in the war, for bemoaning the lack of jobs. Kenneth proposes that veterans should be given priority.[251] His outpouring did not meet universal approbation.

On 25th April 1920, Kenneth attended a special service at the Cathedral, 'In Memory of those Members of the CEF who fell gloriously in action at the Second Battle of Ypres on April 22nd, 1915 AD'. In addition, he had himself photographed wearing the full kilted regalia of The Canadian Scottish Regiment, which was formed from the 50th Regiment (Gordon Highlanders of Canada) and the 88th Regiment (Victoria Fusiliers) during the reorganisation of the Canadian militia in 1920.

Now Kenneth's career took a new turn, into the building business. After the war, the Canadian Soldier Settlement Scheme provided some returning veterans with land on which they were able to build farmhouses and Kenneth joined a self-

---

251 The Daily Colonist, Victoria, Vancouver Island, BC, 13th January 1920, Page 15.

styled architect, Frederick Wood, in forming the Wood-Foyster Construction Company in Victoria. Kenneth titled himself as a director, also styling himself as 'Late 7th Batt CEF' on the company notepaper. Newspapers carried advertisements for the firm and it seems, at the outset, that it would be successful and profitable.

In 1920, Kenneth's sister Hilda commenced a year-long round the world tour accompanied by Mabel Barber, an old VAD friend, who had also attended Philip Foyster's funeral in 1916. They journeyed to Canada, first staying with Hilda's brother Lionel in New Brunswick where he was still ministering, then in July, they travelled to Victoria to visit Kenneth and Totum, staying for about three months. Hilda reports favourably on Kenneth's new spouse, confiding, 'They seem very happy indeed and I think he is uncommonly lucky.' She found Kenneth in good spirits, but a little fatter than of old and had 'still not cured himself of shouting!'

Whilst it seemed destined for some sort of success, Kenneth left the Wood-Foyster Company a few years after it was formed, for unexplained reasons. By 1925, he had become an assistant teacher at the Selkirk School , a boarding and day school for boys located in Selkirk Avenue. This appears to have inspired a new career direction and he moved from Victoria to Vancouver in the mid-1920s, joining another school first and thereafter opening a new establishment at his new home, in West 29th Street, titled the Bilton House School, which seems to have endured until 1935. From then onwards, now aged 55, he lived in rooms with Totum in a house located in Pendrell Street in Vancouver.

Kenneth and Totum continued to live in Vancouver but they had no children. It appears that Kenneth continued to teach until 1950 when he was aged 70, but where has not been discovered. That year Totum, aged 76, was taken to the Vancouver Hospital following a fall in which she suffered a head injury. This

Chapter 9 After the War

and a background of heart problems caused her death on 14th August 1950.

In 1951, Kenneth visited England to see his remaining family. His sister Ada and brother Lionel, who had returned to England, had passed away in the 1940s, but he met Arthur who had retired as a company director, Hugh who had returned from New Zealand with his wife to live in Wiltshire, and Hilda who was living with her husband, Selby Hanbury, in Sussex. He also revisited Hastings and Aspley Guise. It seems to have been a happy reunion, but Kenneth stated that on account of his age, he would never be able to return.

Back in Canada, he became Treasurer of St. Paul's Church, Pendrell Avenue in Vancouver near his home, and took great pride in the vigour and efficiency he brought to the role. He remained in touch with his family and in one letter to a niece he confided, 'My wounded arm is now after 40 years as good as the other. That hand is liable to get cold easier than the other and Totum used to say that side would twitch in my sleep. The thumb that side is leaner than the other but not as noticeable as it used to be.'

Kenneth lived on for another decade and at some stage moved into rooms in a boarding house in Barclay Street, West Vancouver. He died on 30th May 1963, aged 82, and was cremated in Vancouver.

Kenneth Basil Foyster lived a varied and colourful life. On the face of it, he was positive and straightforward, had practical, versatile abilities and a cheerful demeanour. Indeed, one of his young nieces was reported as looking forward to the return of her 'favourite uncle' from the war, and it is hoped that he eventually found his metier in teaching. He married late and well, but had no children and lived distant from his other family members in the far west of Canada which became his home.

Perhaps his wartime service, notwithstanding its threats and privations, was a high point in his life. He was a brave and loyal soldier, he fiercely believed in his country's cause and the need to contribute to it and was abidingly and justifiably proud of the part he had played. In his words, he had 'kept the old flag flying'.

And that is as good an epitaph as any.

List of Sources:

Published Books

Addison, H. R., *'Who's Who'*, 1907.

Aitken, Sir Max M. P., *'The Official Story of the Canadian Expeditionary Force (Volume I)'*, Hodder and Stoughton, 1916.

Baumgarten-Crusius, Artur, *'Sachsen in Großer Zeit'*, Leipzig, Akademische Buchhandlung R. Max Lippold, 1919.

Beck A. M. De, *'In Honour of the Canadian Contingent 1914'*, published online by the Brantford Library at: https://brantford.library.on.ca/files/pdfs/localhistory/1stcontingent.pdf.

Bosher, J. F., *'Imperial Vancouver Island - Who Was Who 1850-1950'*, Bloomington, XLibris Corporation.

Cassar, George H, '*Hell in Flanders Fields - Canadians at the Second Battle of Ypres'*, Toronto, Dundern Press, 2010.

Crawford, T. S., *'The Canadian Army on Salisbury Plain'*, Halsgrove, Wellington, 2012.

Crawford, T. S., *'Wiltshire and the Great War: Training the Empire's Soldiers'*, Marlborough, Crowood Press Ltd., 2012.

Crerar, Duff, 'Soldiers: The Service in the Field', in *'Padres in No Man's Land'*, Second Edition, 118 Montreal: MQUP, 2014.

Dominik, Hugo, *'Das Matrosen-Regiment Nr. 5'*, Oldenburg, Stalling, 1929.

Douglas, John Harvey, *'Captured'*, George H. Doran Co., New York, 1918.

Gerard, James W., *'My Four Years in Germany'*, New York, Grosset and Dunlap, 1917.

Harker, Douglas E., *'The Dukes'*, Victoria, British Columbia Regiment, 1974.

Iarocci, Andrew, *'Shoestring Soldiers: The 1st Canadian Division at War, 1914-1915'*, University of Toronto Press, 2008.

Kipling, Rudyard, 'Young British Soldier' in *'Barrack-Room Ballads'*, Methuen, London, 1892.

Lewis-Stempel, John, *'The War Behind the Wire: The Life, Death and Glory of British Prisoners of War, 1914-18'*, Hachette UK, 30th January 2014.

Lord Northcliffe, *'At The War'*, London, Hodder and Stoughton, 1918.

Macdonald, Lyn, *'1915 - The Death of Innocence'*, London, Penguin, 1993.

McClung, Nellie L., *'Three Times and Out'* told by Private Simmons, Boston and New York, Houghton Mifflin Company, 1918.

Morris, Jeremy, *'Ingram, Arthur Foley Winnington (1858-1946)'*, Oxford Dictionary of National Biography, Oxford University Press 2004; online edition, January 2011.

Morton, Desmond, *'Silent Battle - Canadian Prisoners of War in Germany 1914-1919'*, Toronto, Lester Publishing Ltd., 1992.

Nicholson, G.W.L., *'Outside the Corps'*, Canadian Expeditionary Force, 1914-1919, Montreal: MQUP, 2017. Print.

Picot, Lieutenant Colonel H. P., *'The British Interned in Switzerland'*, Edward Arnold, London, 1919.

Pope-Hennessy, Mrs., *'Map of the Main Prison Camps in Germany and Austria'*, London, Nisbet and Co. Ltd., 1920.

Royle, Trevor, '*The Gordon Highlanders: A Concise History'*, Edinburgh, Mainstream Publishing, 2007.

Scudamore, Major T. V., *'A Short History of the 7th Battalion C. E. F.'*, Anderson and Odlum Ltd., Vancouver, 1930.

Stange, Carl, *'Das Gefangenenlager in Göttingen'*, Louis Hofer, Göttingen, 1915.

Thorne, Major J. C., *'Three Years a Prisoner in Germany'*, Cowan and Brookhouse, Vancouver, 1919, digitised by The

List of Sources:

Internet Archive at: threeyearsprison00thorrich.pdf.

Wearning, J. P., *'The London Stage 1920-1929'*, Rowman & Littlefield, Lanham, 2014.

'The Letters and Journal of Brand Whitlock', edited by Allan Nevins, Appleton-Century, New York, 1936, published on-line at: http://www.ourstory.info/library/2-ww1/Whitlock/bw09.html.

'List of Officers and Men Serving in The First Canadian Contingent of The British Expeditionary Force, 1914', Pay and Record Office, Canadian Contingent, London.

'Armorial families: A Directory of Gentlemen of Coat-Armour (Volume 2)', published online at: https://archive.org.

Newspapers, Magazines, Records, Articles and Regimental Histories

The Gazette (London Gazette), various editions at: www.thegazette.co.uk.

The Encyclopaedia Britannica Online at: www.britannica.com.

'Rt. Rev. Dr. C. S. Woodward – A well-remembered bishop', The Times, 15th April 1959.

'British Empire', The Columbia Encyclopedia, 6th Edition, 13th January 2015 published online at: www.encyclopedia.com.

The Times, 13th August 1900.

Hastings Observer, Saturday 23rd August 1919.

The Daily Colonist, Victoria, Vancouver Island, BC, various editions.

The Daily Province, Victoria BC, currently a division of Postmedia Network Incorporated, various editions.

Vancouver Sun, 8th November 2014.

The Stage, 24th February 1921 and 13th February 1930, kindly researched by The Stage Media Company Limited.

The Catholic Standard, 29th January 1954.

Yorkshire Post and Leeds Intelligencer, 29th September 1920.

Bowen, Lynne, *'Vancouver Island Coal Strike'*, The Canadian Encyclopedia, Historica Foundation, 1st September 2007.

Cotter, Cédric, *'The 1918 Bern Agreements: repatriating prisoners in a total war'*, 29th March 1918, contained in ICRC's Law & Policy at: http://blogs.icrc.org/law-and-policy/2018/03/29/1918-bern-agreements-repatriating-prisoners-of-war.

Fisk, Robert, *'In 1914, Britain feared civil war in Ireland more than it feared war in Europe'*, The Independent, 19th January 2014.

Hume, Stephen, *'Remembrance: When war came close to home'*, The Flight Magazine, 30th July 1915.

'Legacy - The War's Impact on Canada', Canadian War Museum

Polauke, Marina, *'Die Siedlung im Ebertal'* at: https://goettingensozial.wordpress.com.

'The Story of The Royal Leicestershire Regiment' on the website of the Regiment at: https://www.royalleicestershireregiment.org.uk/history-of-the-regiment-2.

Queen's Royal Surrey Regimental Association Newsletter, No. 2, November 1967, Page 5 (Surrey History Centre Reference: J552/2).

'Living Heritage - Parliament and Ireland, The Third Home Rule Bill', published online at: www.parliament.uk.

'The Wooden City - A Journal for British Prisoners of War', various editions, Library of The University of Pennsylvania, The Penn Libraries at: www.library.upenn.edu.

The Niagara Historical Society Museum, *'A Brief History of the CEF - The First Canadian Contingent 1914-1915'*, published online at: www.niagarahistorical.museum.

Sergeant John McIlree and Private Fredrick Arnold, CBC Interviews, 1967, CBC Licensing.

List of Sources:

Private Papers of the Reverend R. Bulstrode. Imperial War Museum Documents 1276.

'Sir Sam Hughes 1853-1921', Historic Sites and Monuments Board of Canada published online at: www.ontarioplaques.com/Plaques/Plaque_Kawartha15.html.

Marlborough College Records, kindly researched by the College.

Records of the Museum of Liverpool.

Records of The North Saskatchewan Regiment, kindly researched by the Regiment.

Records of The British Columbia Regiment (Duke of Connaught's Own), including the diary of Private A.D. Corker 16874, 7th Battalion prisoner of war, from 24th April 1915 to 24th June 1918, kindly researched by the Regiment.

Vancouver Crematorium Records, kindly researched by the Vancouver Crematorium staff.

Other Websites

The National Archives UK (Contains public sector information licensed under the Open Government Licence v3.0):

War Diary of the 7th Canadian Infantry Battalion: 16/10/1914-30/11/1916, WO 95/3768.

War Diary of the 8th Canadian Infantry Battalion: 01/02/1915-28/02/1918, WO95/3769.

War Diary of the 2nd Battalion The Bedfordshire Regiment: 01/10/1914-31/12/1915, WO 95/1658/2.

War Diary of the 1st/8th Battalion The King's Liverpool Regiment: 01/01/1916-31/01/1918, WO 95/2923/1.

Records Created or Inherited by the Foreign Office.

British Army WWI Service Records, 1914-1920.

Census Returns of England and Wales 1911.

Commonwealth War Graves Commission (CWCG) at: www.cwgc.org.

Canada at War at: www.canadaatwar.ca.

1914-1918 Prisoners of the First World War, International Committee of the Red Cross (ICRC) WW1 Archives at: https://grandeguerre.icrc.org/en.

The Canadian War Museum at: www.warmuseum.ca.

The Canadian Great War Project at: www.canadiangreatwarproject.com.

Göttingen Sozial at: goettingensozial.wordpress.com.

Historic UK at: www.historic-uk.com.

The History Learning Site at: www.historylearningsite.co.uk.

Information Technology Associates at: www.theodora.com.

Catholicism.org at: catholicism.org.

UCL School of Slavonic and East European Studies at: www.ssees.ucl.ac.uk.

Young Men's Christian Association at: www.ymca.org.uk.

The Long, Long Trail - The British Army in the Great War 1914-1918 at: www. longlongtrail.co.uk.

The Great War Forum at: https://www.greatwarforum.org.

The Imperial War Museum at: www.iwm.org.uk.

Switzerland and the First World War at: www.switzerland1914-1918.net.

Australian War Memorial at: https://www.awm.govau.

The Red Duster at: www.red-duster.co.uk.

World Naval Ships Forums at: www.worldnavalships.com.

All Hallows' Church, Leeds at: http://allhallowsleeds.org.

St. Peter's Anglican Church (Château-d'Oex) at: https://stpeters.ch/british-soldiers-interned-switzerland.